THE FUTURE OF THE WILD

THE FUTURE
OF THE WILD

Radical Conservation for a Crowded World

JONATHAN S. ADAMS

BEACON PRESS, BOSTON

BEACON PRESS
25 Beacon Street
Boston, Massachusetts 02108-2892
www.beacon.org

Beacon Press books
are published under the auspices of
the Unitarian Universalist Association of Congregations.

09 08 07 06   8 7 6 5 4 3 2 1

This book is printed on acid-free paper that meets the uncoated paper
ANSI/NISO specifications for permanence as revised in 1992.

Text design by Patricia Duque Campos
Composition by Wilsted & Taylor Publishing Services

Library of Congress Cataloging-in-Publication Data

Adams, Jonathan S.
  The future of the wild : radical conservation for a crowded world / Jonathan S. Adams.
    p. cm.
  Includes bibliographical references.
  ISBN 0-8070-8510-3 (cloth : alk. paper)
  1. Conservation biology.   2. Ecosystem management—Citizen participation.   3. Nature
conservation—North America.   I. Title.

  QH75.A345 2006
  333.95′16—dc22   2005007688

For Susan, Madeleine, and Joseph

For Mom

CONTENTS

INTRODUCTION IX

PART I
THINKING BIG

CHAPTER 1
A PARLIAMENT OF OWLS 3

CHAPTER 2
DO BIG THINGS RUN THE WORLD? 23

CHAPTER 3
SAVE SOME OF EVERYTHING 46

PART II
SCIENCE AND COMMUNITY

CHAPTER 4
CONSERVATION IN EXURBIA:
FLORIDA AND CALIFORNIA 71

CHAPTER 5
APPOINTMENT IN SONORA 88

CHAPTER 6
THE NATIVE HOME OF HOPE 108

CHAPTER 7
SAVE ENOUGH TO LAST:
FLORIDA AND THE EVERGLADES 141

PART III
YELLOWSTONE AND THE BEST HOPE OF EARTH

CHAPTER 8
BLIND MEN AND ELEPHANTS 175

CHAPTER 9
GUARDING THE GOLDEN GOOSE 207

CONCLUSION 229

ACKNOWLEDGMENTS 234

NOTES 236

INDEX 257

But ask now the beasts, and they shall teach thee;
and the fowls of the air, and they shall tell thee:
Or speak to the earth, and it shall teach thee:
and the fishes of the sea shall declare unto thee.
JOB 12:7

Imagine the North American wilderness as the explorers Lewis and Clark saw it: forests thick with chestnut trees in the East, prairies teeming with bison and rivers overflowing with salmon in the West. Now picture the continent today: superhighways link colossal cities, suburbs stretch farther and farther into the countryside, industrial farmland goes on for miles, and a few patches of greenery and a national park or two break up the monotony.

Those two images don't fit together: the frontier closed, the wilderness disappeared, and there is no going back. Yet, across North America and indeed around the world, conservation scientists, activists, and communities have begun crafting visions for conserving and restoring wild creatures and wildlands over larger areas than ever before, raising the hope for a far bolder and more lasting kind of conservation than we have ever seen.

Such visions smack of particularly naive optimism. Several centuries of farming, logging, mining, dam building, and rapid population growth smashed the wilderness into thousands of shards, a few of them large but most of them tiny and increasingly isolated. Even with national and global commitments to putting the pieces back together (although no such consensus exists today and none seems near), the task would seem impossible. Not only would we need to halt the current march of humanity across the landscape, we would need to reverse it.

That may not be as far-fetched as it sounds. The young science of conservation biology has matured to the point that it now helps us understand how nature works across miles and miles of land and water. That understanding can guide efforts to save wild species across their native habitats rather than as doomed and decaying museum pieces, and enable human communities to become again part of the landscape rather than simply abusers of it. Beginning in the early 1980s, biologists, ecologists, and pioneers in conservation biology started redrawing the boundaries of their ideas about how the world works. They moved up the scale from individual animals to populations to natural communities to broad landscapes to regions to continents. Government agencies, scientists, activists, and human communities around the world increasingly recognize that the environment does not end at the last traffic signal in town, or at the county line, or even at the border post. Effective conservation demands a far broader perspective.

The stories in this book together form the outlines of a new narrative for conservation. The usual narratives revolve around heroic individual efforts to protect special places, or around communities coming together to defend a treasured lifestyle and in the process conserving their environment. The first narrative is older, but in its current form often involves scientists in leading roles. The second narrative usually leaves science out altogether, or involves it only at the margins. The new conservation, as seen in this book, brings those two narrative threads together.

A new vision for conservation means deciding where to put new parks and other protected areas, worrying about the habitat in between those reserves—for humans and nonhumans alike—and wrestling with the ideas emerging from conservation biology, with mouth-filling terms like population viability, landscape connectivity, and disturbance regimes. This is heady stuff for scientists and land managers alike, as it suggests new ways to think about and carry out conservation.

Thinking more broadly about conservation also requires addressing head-on a fundamental issue facing science and society: What is the proper scale for conservation, and is there only one? The glib answer is conservationists need to be concerned with all of the countless scales in nature. True enough, and an indication of the scope of the problem, but in reality that is no answer at all. The very notion of scale leads to confusion, even among ecologists, and has spawned countless books and articles. For now, suffice it to say that scale refers to the physical dimensions of things or processes; it is something you can measure. So talk of the scale of a leaf or a landscape makes no sense. How big is a leaf? Some leaves are as big as your thumbnail; others are as long as your arm. The landscape for a bear covers many square miles; for a beetle it may extend just a few square feet. Scale also refers to the scale of observation: Over what area and what time period do we observe, say, wildfires or changes in a population of animals?[1]

Scientists understand just the outlines of how nature functions across just a handful of scales, to say nothing of all possible scales. In order to simplify enormously complex problems, for decades ecologists focused on scales they could reproduce in the laboratory or study easily in the field. Most studies have had a physical dimension of less than about ten yards, convenient for experimental manipulation but hardly relevant to species even as small as a mouse.[2]

Ecologists are not alone in their discomfort in dealing with questions of scale. Economists are far worse: the vast majority of economists never even bother to ask the question of the proper scale of the economy relative to the environment. In standard economic theory the economy can simply grow forever, the second law of thermodynamics be damned. As economist Kenneth Boulding once said, "Anyone who believes exponential growth can go on forever in a finite world is either a madman or an economist."[3]

Determining the proper scale for conservation requires that we rethink some of the fundamental notions of ecology. The most pervasive traces its roots to the ancient idea of nature as balanced and self-regulating, changing in an orderly progression, grasslands becoming forests in an inexorable process known as ecological succession. Trust in such order and stability allows us to carry out conservation in small, predictable places, and lies at the heart of most natural resource laws and the very notion of private property.[4]

To the detriment of many a well-laid conservation plan, however, nature provides only the illusion of stability. Ecologists three decades ago began to see natural disturbances like fires, floods, and hurricanes as essential to the persistence of life, rather than simply instruments of ecological ruin. This led to the understanding that nature reserves must be large enough to accommodate such disturbances. Of the countless examples, none paints a clearer picture than an effort to protect and restore old-growth forest in the eastern United States. The Cathedral Pines preserve in Connecticut contained about twenty-five acres of old-growth pine, one of the last examples of that type of forest in the region. In 1989, tornadoes wiped out nearly the entire stand. Had the tornadoes hit an old-growth forest measuring hundreds of thousands of acres, they would have opened up small sections of forest to new growth. Instead, they brought havoc.

In ecology, quite literally the only constant is change.[5] Before people began farming or otherwise transforming huge areas of land, human-scale landscapes consisted of patches of forests, meadows, flood plains, grasslands, and so on. The patches would slide about in response to floods and fires like a kaleidoscope, or what ecologists call a shifting mosaic, but over a large area and a long period of time the amount of each type of habitat would remain more or less the same.

Parks and reserves need to be large enough to absorb the blows from a once-in-a-century fire or flood, or at least be part of a landscape that would allow them to recover from such an event. Parks that are simply tiny refuges tucked into a landscape otherwise completely converted to intensive human use will not long survive.

The constancy of change carries enormous implications for both conservation and the laws that support it. You cannot just draw lines around relatively small areas you deem important for ecological or any other reasons and assume all is well. The fundamental unpredictability of nature also means that no technocratic elite can lay claim to perfect knowledge. Science must inform decisions about how we should, or should not, use Earth's lands and waters, but those decisions will rest not on science but on the values of individuals and their communities. That opens the door, for good and ill, to broad and diverse human communities and all the fallible institutions we have created to govern ourselves.

THINKING BIG

The first section of this book, "Thinking Big," provides a historical and conceptual context for conservation and introduces some of the language of conservation science. The examples here and in the rest of the book, from the desert southwest to the Maine woods, from the Everglades to Yellowstone, illustrate how a broader perspective on conservation can shape the future. The examples do not form a comprehensive picture or a scientifically drawn sample. They come largely from the United States, not because Americans have a corner on the best conservation science or practice but because the efforts here have matured enough to offer some tangible lessons. The issues these examples raise, however, have implications far beyond the boundaries of the United States.

We are in the midst of a dramatic shift in conservation. With few exceptions, science has played only a minor role in the conservation drama, usually yielding the stage to politics, aesthetics, and economics. Governments and individuals have set aside grand or symbolic lands, like Yellowstone or the Grand Canyon, or lands that had little economic use, like the parks of the Mountain West, brimming with rocks and snow. Scientific considerations remained secondary in these decisions because scientists had not yet formulated the central questions: How much land does a puma or a spotted owl really need? How do natural processes like fires and floods determine the kinds of plants and animals that live on a certain piece of land?

By formulating such questions, scientists essentially began to draw a few tentative lines on a blueprint; finding and applying the answers has proven to be like building the house without all the tools and with no clear end in mind. Ecologists generally thought too small and conservationists looked in the wrong places—inside the parks rather than beyond their borders as well, to the broader landscapes in which the parks are embedded. The answers to key questions thus remain elusive. Traditional conservation skills, like wildlife management, and even the more recent scientific specialties, like landscape ecology, will not suffice by themselves. Conservation must come to grips with the human communities that surround parks as well as the more distant communities that value parks and wildlands as refuges or simply as visions of wilderness that they may never see. Conservation has traditionally overlooked, intentionally or otherwise, the needs and values of those communities. Hence a protected area becomes a line in the sand, a challenge and an invitation to conflict.

Creating parks and other sorts of reserves is an essential but desperate action, based on the idea that we can by force of law ensure that what happens on one side of that line in the sand differs fundamentally from what happens on the other. In almost all cases, however, the line reflects human convenience rather than ecological necessity, and the boundary will be wholly illusory for every creature except humans, though often for humans as well. The line remains a necessity, because for now we have no choice but to draw it and make a stand. But conservation does not have the troops to defend the parks if people decide not to value them. The sooner we reach the point where we no longer need to draw bright lines, or need to draw them only as a matter of administrative convenience, the more of Earth's diversity we will be able to save.

Conservation cannot succeed if it remains largely a war against humanity. Conservation need not take on the challenge of solving all the world's ills, from poverty to injustice, but it cannot be ignorant of those ills nor be seen as an obstacle to their resolution. The ecological wounds that humans have inflicted, particularly but not exclusively the loss of species and their habitats, are all too evident and familiar. Yet reciting the litany of losses and decrying people as the cause—justifiable as that may often be—will no longer suffice. Conservation cannot just be the art of saying no, not here.

Conservation must offer a sense of the possible, and a reason for hope. Hope comes, paradoxically, from thinking big. We cannot save the earth one species at a time, if for no other reason than we know nothing about the vast majority of species with which we share our planet. The idea that we can save the northern spotted owl—in the early 1990s, among the most symbolically loaded creatures on Earth—or any other species by focusing exclusively on that species has no basis in science. Even proceeding one park at a time won't work in the long run, as nearly every park is simply too small by itself to maintain all of its plants and animals. We need to consider both the park and its surroundings; as Jora Young, a senior scientist with The Nature Conservancy, puts it, "Our job is to stand on the borders of our parks and look out."[6]

Once you take this perspective, the size of the challenge becomes clear. The following chapters explore some of the work that organizations such as World Wildlife Fund, the Wildlife Conservation Society, The Wildlands Project, and particularly The Nature Conservancy are doing to ensure the survival of wild species. While this is not a book about The Nature Conservancy, my employer, that organization—one of the richest, least controversial, and for many years the most complacent in the United States—now finds itself at the center of a promising but highly uncertain movement, one that melds a commitment to the people who husband their land with the best thinking in conservation science. The outcome of that fraught process may be the last best hope for the earth and all its creatures.

Each of those organizations, and conservation more generally, often focuses on the traditional and still vital conservation task of setting aside land. Many current efforts, however, break new ground, combining increasingly sophisticated science with a deeper appreciation of the rights and responsibilities of the communities that live and work near the areas deemed crucial for conservation. These and other organizations and in-dividuals demonstrate that while we need to do more, success lies within reach. We certainly do not know everything about how the world works and never will, but we know enough to make a start, if we are wise enough to learn from our mistakes. Neither the amount of land necessary nor the costs of managing it are out of the question; we just need to make a choice about what we value most.

Many conservationists would rather let science and reason determine the outcome of such a choice, and leave values and emotion out. That is not possible. Fundamentally, conservation is about choosing: How much land and water will we relinquish for other species? How much is enough? We have set aside a little more than one-tenth of the earth's surface in rel-atively strictly protected areas for nature. What will happen if we do no more? Conservation science can reveal the consequences of those choices, but science cannot determine the right choice. That determination reflects what we hold dear, and what we decide we can live without. The only way to choose between various outcomes will be on the basis of values, on deci-sions about what we want to conserve. No group of experts can make that choice for us; we must make it ourselves.

Few of us question our right to dominate nature, so conservationists need to educate the public about the consequences of such actions, about hubris, about what scientist and author David Ehrenfeld calls "the arro-gance of humanism."[7] The alternative to that arrogance is acceptance, a welcoming of the wild and an understanding of our place in it. This does not require ushering wolves in the front door; acceptance instead recog-nizes that we do not need to draw hard lines between ourselves and the rest of creation. Such acceptance stems from any number of sources—morals, ethics, aesthetics—transformed in the prism of politics. Conservation sci-ence increasingly sees the need to think at broader scales more than ever before, but the political organizations that will act on these newfound sci-entific principles will not be global or even national, but local.

The central role of values in conservation also offers hope for the future, though this too may seem a paradox. After all, history provides ample, in-deed overwhelming, evidence of the propensity for human beings to favor definitive gain for themselves over speculative benefits to their grandchil-dren or, even worse, their neighbors.

That appears to be changing, albeit haltingly. The idea of community, long in decline but never quite extinguished, has begun to reemerge as a viable alternative to a homogenizing global culture. As communities reassert themselves as political entities with the capacity and desire to share responsibility for their land, the possibilities for conservation grow. Conservation has long suffered from being a largely urban movement with little to offer rural communities except rules and regulations those communities, rightly or wrongly, see as unfair at best, outright theft at worst. If conservationists and communities can develop a shared vision for what a given landscape should be, as is happening in more and more places, and if those communities are held accountable for their actions, that vision becomes enormously more powerful.

Groups of people living near each other need more than just proximity to form the kind of communities that can take on the roles and responsibilities necessary for big conservation to succeed. They must have what sociologists call social capital, a deep sense of trust and obligation to their neighbors. The appreciation of the connection between strong communities and the ability to manage land well is not at all new. John Wesley Powell, the one-armed Civil War hero who explored the Grand Canyon, saw it in the 1870s among Mormon settlers in Utah and Spanish farmers in New Mexico. If people were to survive in the arid lands west of the 100th meridian, then best to leave control of pasture in a community's common range and water in the hands of *acequias*—a system of communal management of water by associations of farmers in New Mexico that to this day cooperatively maintain irrigation ditches and distribute water. Powell's proposal, wrote Wallace Stegner, "embodied official encouragement of a social organization so revolutionary in 1878 that it seems like the product of another land and another people."[8]

Communities that have strong bonds among their members and clear ethics about their relationship to the land draw on deep wells of social capital in the form of trust, civic and religious organizations, and traditions. Where such capital exists, communities become tangible, not the figment of a sociologist's imagination. People long at loggerheads over how to use, or not use, the land around them may be able to build shared visions for the future, if they can listen to what science has to say. This can work. There is hope.

All the cooperative habits of rural America—barn raising, haying, corn husking, cattle branding—provided Powell the evidence he needed to challenge the individualism already rampant in the late nineteenth century. It would only grow in influence. The elevation of individual liberty above all other values has brought us to a point where even suggesting a role for a revived community seems quaint, if not a sneak attack on the sacred right to unfettered private property.

In the American West, rural communities have long clamored for more control over the land they use, usually public land leased from one or another of the federal land management agencies. Conservationists harbor the legitimate fear that relinquishing government control over this land offers no guarantee that the communities would use the land well, and that narrow, parochial interests would not dominate. That concern remains as valid as ever, but now conservation science provides the essential context for community action. For the first time, communities and governments can see the consequences of their choices not only for themselves but for an entire region. Just as important, we can now see glimmerings of collaborative efforts that respond not only to local but to national and even global interests. *Community* means not just a particular place, but communities of interest as well; a deep, abiding, and vitally relevant concern for the future of Yellowstone, for example, is shared by far more people than the fortunate few who live on its borders.

Creating the institutions to promote such collaboration poses a fundamental challenge for conservation at a scale that encompasses, for example, Yellowstone National Park and all of its surrounding forests, ranches, rivers, and towns. *Institutions* means not simply land trusts or philanthropies or schools or synagogues, important as those are, but more fundamentally the institution of the law, or reciprocity, or perhaps a due respect for the land and the future generations who will depend on it. Neither scientists nor any other group can create those institutions single-handed, but science must inform them all. Science provides the rigor by which we can learn about the world around us and how our actions will change it. Combine that discipline with communities committed to the places in which they live, and none of the profound environmental challenges we will face will be insurmountable.

SCIENCE, COMMUNITY, AND CONSERVATION

The science best suited to informing conservation in a meaningful way, a specialty called conservation planning, began to mature in the early 1990s.[9] The broad perspective it provides allows people to see, for example, how their watershed fits in with those around it, or how nature—and the threats to nature—lies across the arbitrary boundaries of public and private land. The second section of the book, "Science and Community," explores how science and community together support a new kind of conservation.

Conservation planning provides the picture on the cover of the jigsaw puzzle box. Once we dump out all the pieces, we need something to show us where we are going, though we still have to pick up each piece, examine it, and try to determine where it might fit. Conservation planning helps us envision how the world might look—where parks and towns and farms might be—if conservation is successful. It also helps identify, for each place, the important species and the threats they face.

When some conservation planners and other scientists began to step back from the urgent work of protecting this park or that and saw the entire landscape, they had another revelation: conservation lands would never stem the tide of extinction by themselves. Governments will create new parks and reserves, but not quickly enough, and conservationists cannot possibly buy anything but a tiny fraction of the land necessary to protect nature into the next millennia. Much of the land important to conservation belongs now, and probably always will belong, to people who may or may not share an abiding concern for or even a passing interest in the untamed. Conservation has to be as relevant to those landowners as it is to the managers of public land.

Communities must play a greater role in conservation because conserving both private and public land is essential; either one alone will not suffice. Imagine you had a map of your hometown, its watershed, and the surrounding land, and on it you could lay out all the areas that were important from a purely biological perspective: habitats rich in species, locations of endangered species or natural communities, undammed rivers, unusual geological or ecological formations and phenomena, and so on. Now imagine taking that same map and putting atop it an overlay showing the various types of ownership—in the United States, primarily federal, state, and private land. You would find that the important biological areas

cross all ownerships, not conveniently limiting themselves to the public estate. Public land certainly deserves nothing less than our best possible care,
but public land alone would offer but a pale reflection of Earth's infinite variety. Mark Shaffer, a conservation biologist who runs the environmental
program at the Doris Duke Foundation in New York, puts it this way: an
exclusive focus on the public land means "we are defending the wrong
perimeters."

Over the past decade, the philosophy and practice of conservation has
been transformed to include both species and broad landscapes, both protected areas and the places where people live and work. For a time in the
late 1980s and early 1990s, conservationists and others hoped that helping
people improve their economic condition would lead, as if by magic, to
more conservation as well. Parks could do it all—protect nature and raise
the standard of living among the rural poor. That hope has gone largely
unfulfilled, and grinding poverty side-by-side with glorious wilderness remains a cruel taunt and the inescapable fact of modern conservation.[10]

Working across all the relevant scales will require spending more
money to set aside key land, working with governments and communities
to change the way they manage land, and restoring land that has been degraded, like Florida's Everglades. None of this will be cheap or easy. The
United States is enormously fortunate to have both large areas of wildlands
as well as the economic resources to conserve them and to help individuals
and communities that might be affected by conservation. Dozens of communities in the United States have passed bond measures to preserve open
space, essentially taxing themselves in the interests of the environment.
Even so, the worldwide conservation community often settles for table
scraps, relying on meager budgets from governments and the generosity of
individuals. We always seem able to find the money for new roads and new
dams. I'm convinced that we can find the money for conservation, if we
choose to look for it.

The goals of big conservation are within reach if communities place
a high value on wildlands and willingly forego things they now take for
granted, like driving wherever and whenever they want, living wherever
they want, and basically paying no heed to the amount of the earth's resources that they consume. Lasting conservation means dramatic changes
in our relationship to the land.

Among the changes must be democracy revitalized by communities that have a greater say in their environmental affairs, and have the tools to help them make responsible decisions and assess their progress. In the United States, states and local communities cannot have complete say over valuable national wildlands because many of them occur on public land, and that belongs to everyone. Yet without communities willing and able to take on some of the responsibilities, the odds of carrying out conservation on a broad scale grow long indeed.

Communities strong enough to play such a role often derive their strength from a shared love of the land. The attachment to the land exists in traditional agrarian communities, like the Amish, and among some ranchers, most of whom focus on the relatively small areas in which they actually work.

As an example of how things have already changed, consider the idea called the Buffalo Commons. In late 1987, two academic land-use planners at Rutgers University, Frank and Deborah Popper, proposed that the Great Plains was in the midst of yet another downturn in a recurring boom-and-bust cycle of population growth and decline. The Poppers foresaw a depopulated landscape in which the return of the bison could be the foundation for the rural economy as well as the linchpin for the ecology of the plains.

In the late 1980s and early 1990s, most residents on the Great Plains saw the Buffalo Commons as insanity, communism, or worse. In true pioneer fashion, they vowed to stick it out, regardless of what some pointy-heads from New Jersey—New Jersey!—had to say. But by the late 1990s, things had changed. The economic trends that the Poppers had seen brewing indeed became overwhelming, and people on the plains began looking for alternatives, including the same bison herds they had sneered at. In the summer of 2000, the Poppers rode in a centennial parade down the main street of Gwinner, North Dakota. In a reflection of some lingering animosity expressed with dry Great Plains wit, the Poppers rode atop a manure spreader.

Still, the Poppers had claimed a seat of honor in at least one town on the plains. Others would follow, as would new variations on the original idea of the Buffalo Commons. A group of sixteen organizations, including World Wildlife Fund, are now working together to conserve millions of acres across the Dakotas, Nebraska, Wyoming, Montana, Alberta, and Saskatchewan.[11] The time for thinking big has clearly arrived.

The final section of the book, "Yellowstone and the Best Hope of Earth," describes how big conservation might look in a specific place, Yellowstone National Park and the surrounding lands. In order to work at such a scale, conservationists must now be as comfortable in a rancher's living room as they are in a courtroom, a government office, or a field station. That will entail a significant shift from the way conservation organizations work, in order to accompany the even broader changes in science, law, and policy necessary to create a new kind of conservation. While a bigger vision for conservation begins with science, as a practical matter such a vision forces partnerships with people whom conservationists have often avoided. The conservation community has usually communicated mainly with itself and its closest supporters, facing the rest of the world with lawsuits and confrontation. But conservation at a scale sufficient to offer the hope of lasting success demands partnerships among a spectrum of people and organizations, and broad if not universal consensus.

One promising approach, called ecoregional conservation, has emerged over the past ten years. A central focus of this book, ecoregional conservation provides the loom on which we can weave varied human and nonhuman communities together into an ecologically and socially functioning whole. The emerging understanding about how the natural world functions at scales from a few square feet to a thousand square miles offers the promise, at long last, of an alternative to the despairing minimalism of the past thirty-five years of conservation. We should no longer debate the changes we can make at the margins of human behavior so we can destroy the earth more slowly, but together, in a million places across the globe, build on the shared values that will enable us to bequeath a thriving Earth to our great-grandchildren's great-grandchildren.

Some of the changes in conservation will be revolutionary, others evolutionary. All will require new appreciation for where science, community, and values intersect. They intersect when communities make value judgments about what to conserve and what to develop, with science as a guide to the consequences of their choices. Engaging communities in decisions about the future of the land around them makes such evident sense that the power of the idea led some conservationists to get a bit overzealous in the early 1990s, deciding that community-based conservation was actually the only hope. The promise of the approach has not been realized, largely because simultaneously protecting animals and their habitats from some kinds of human intrusion while allowing for others has proven far more difficult than anyone imagined. The idea will not go away, however, because the people living on the edges of protected areas will not go away; in fact, there will be more of them. In some places, they form cohesive communities, and these communities can and should be more involved in conservation. In other places, community is far more elusive, and staking the future of conservation in those places on the hope that some common ground exists is simply wishful thinking.

The greatest hope lies in combining conservation science with the power of community and a reinvigorated democracy that is responsive to both local and national concerns. The Jeffersonian ideal that government should rest on civic dialogue at the level closest to those who will be affected by government decisions has enormous power.[12] Local decisions, however, too often build on a purely local view of ecology. Decades of pitched battles pitting environmentalists against loggers, miners, ranchers, and developers have left deep scars that will make dialogue difficult, to say the least. Until now, however, the opposing sides had no way of seeing how their landscape fit into the broader ecological puzzle, or how to judge its importance relative to the larger whole.[13]

Far more than ever before, conservationists and rural communities can find common ground, and they can develop shared visions for the future that reflect not simply local interests but global ones—visions that form the foundation for making decisions about how the land, both public and private, is to be both protected and used. No one, not even the most hardcore city dweller, wants to live in a paved-over world with no wild creatures. A shared vision will include places for wilderness, for city parks, and for working farms and ranches. If science informs those visions, then perhaps humanity can find a way to a lasting coexistence with nature.

The term "common good," however, seems naive and old-fashioned, and the notion of civic virtue even more so. In the standard economic model, the miracle of free markets means that everyone can look out for themselves and still everyone should benefit. Perhaps, but for the past several centuries environmental trends have been running in entirely the wrong direction. Markets and the triumph of the individual need tempering with broader concerns for communities and for things that have, for now, no value in the marketplace, such as spotted owls and wolves.

The American psyche of the twenty-first century will resist such tempering. As legal scholar Eric Freyfogle points out, the American love of individualism and liberty has grown to the point that it constrains our ability to even talk about the common good.[14] People must see themselves as part of something larger, something defined not by the boundaries of their property but by their mutual obligations to and dependencies on their neighbors and the land around them.

Freyfogle also echoes the agrarian spirit of Kentucky farmer and writer Wendell Berry in arguing that to own land is to accept lasting responsibilities to the land itself, to the local community, and to the generations before and after.[15] This is a truly conservative position, though in contemporary politics people who call themselves conservatives see fit to impoverish their grandchildren—economically, ecologically, and otherwise—to gratify their immediate need for wealth and power.

Berry, and before him Aldo Leopold, the forester and wildlife manager who became the most influential conservation thinker of the twentieth century, emphasizes that using land well is not simply an issue of economics but of ethics. For both writers, the obligation for the individual to contribute to the common good is paramount. Communities of people committed to husbanding land so that it sustains life—cultivated and wild—for generations form the foundation of lasting conservation.

PART I

THINKING BIG

CHAPTER I

A PARLIAMENT OF OWLS

Without enough wilderness America will change. Democracy, with its
myriad personalities and increasing sophistication, must be fibred and
vitalized by regular contact with outdoor growths—animals, trees,
sun warmth and free skies—or it will dwindle and pale.
WALT WHITMAN

A breeding pair of northern spotted owls requires roughly five thousand acres of old-growth forest. Protecting several hundred pairs—a bare minimum if the owls are to survive more than a century or two—means protecting a million acres. Beginning in the late 1980s, conserving a creature that needs so much room forced the federal government, and by extension the general public, to confront for the first time the realities of conservation across an entire region of the country, including public and private land, old and new protected areas, and all the places where people live and work.

The task came with a steep price and high political stakes. Read in sequence, the plans for protecting the spotted owl capture the slow dawning of a new idea. The first generation of plans protected thousands of acres, the next protected hundreds of thousands, and the last plans proposed protecting millions of acres of forest. The plans focused initially on individual pairs of owls, and gradually widened their scope to include the landscapes of which owls are merely the most famous representatives. Other species, particularly a small seabird called a marbled murrelet and five species of salmon, entered the fray.

At this time, few policymakers or land managers saw the ideas of conservation biology as important to their work, if they paid them any heed at all. The science was then just a few years old, though it had been evolving for two decades. No one incorporated the emerging scientific principles into any management plan for a national park, forest, or wildlife refuge, or in any plan to bring endangered species back from the brink.[1]

The consequence of that oversight became clear once the northern spot-ted owl took the stage as one of the most famous species in the country, if not the world. This owl makes an unlikely revolutionary: an attractive but far from imposing bird, it stands about a foot and a half tall, weighs around two pounds, and has dark brown feathers and white markings. Scientists know it as *Strix occidentalis caurina,* one of three subspecies of spotted owls, with close relatives in the Sierra Nevada Mountains of California and in the desert Southwest, extending into Mexico along the Sierra Madre.

But enough description. None of that begins to explain why anyone outside of a handful of specialists and the dedicated and occasionally ob-sessive community of birdwatchers has ever heard of this rather non-descript bird. The spotted owl traces its enormous fame not to beauty but rather to rarity and to choosiness over where to build a nest: almost exclusively in the oldest forests in the Pacific Northwest. Those two char-acteristics brought science, law, politics, and economics together and transformed the spotted owl into a fulcrum on which modern conservation has turned.

The spotted owl embodies not only changes in the way scientists answer questions about how to protect endangered species, but also changes in the way communities confront the challenges to their lifestyles and traditional economies. The ripples from the spotted owl controversy continue to spread more than a decade after the owl itself left the front pages. Today, conservation requires us to think about individual species like spotted owls, but also to think far bigger, big enough to conserve huge stretches of land, only parts of which will fall into the national parks and other pro-tected areas that have long been the foundation of conservation efforts.

IN ACCORDANCE WITH THE LAW

In 1988, the Forest Service adopted a management plan for the spotted owl within its jurisdiction. Environmental and industry groups read the plan and immediately sued, claiming it violated a number of federal laws. In March 1989, a federal district court judge, William L. Dwyer, who would become the judicial equivalent of sugar in the gas tank for the timber in-dustry, issued a temporary injunction halting 135 timber sales in spotted owl habitat. A month later, the Fish and Wildlife Service announced its intent to list the spotted owl as threatened under the Endangered Species Act.[2]

In response to the growing controversy, the four major land management agencies of the federal government—the Bureau of Land Management, the Fish and Wildlife Service, the Forest Service, and the National Park Service—created a committee of scientists under the direction of Jack Ward Thomas, then chief research biologist at the Forest Service, to develop a scientifically credible strategy for the conservation of the spotted owl. This panel, called the Interagency Scientific Committee, and another federal effort that followed from it a few years later, called the Federal Ecosystem Management Assessment Team, made conservation biology part of the debate over how to manage public land, and made clear to the general public that if we were serious about conserving species like the spotted owl, then we had to start working on far broader scales than ever before.

In May 1990, the interagency committee proposed a plan for spotted owl management that would protect 5.3 million acres in large habitat conservation areas across seventeen national forests. The plan represented the most extensive application to date of the concepts of conservation biology to a real endangered species problem across a wide area.[3] The committee report, widely known as the Thomas Report, put an important stamp of approval on a scientific approach to designing a system of conservation areas. The plan took another key step beyond simply protecting the woodland reserves. The land in between the reserves would have to be safe for the owls as well, and that meant no clear-cutting. No clear-cutting meant timber sales from the public forests would have to fall. Here science ran smack up against bred-in-the-bone traditions of the Forest Service, which saw providing trees for the sawmills—"getting out the cut" in agency lingo —as far and away its most important responsibility. The committee also broke with the common wisdom of the day by arguing that the preservation of the spotted owl was actually the wrong question; if we wanted to save the owl, Thomas and his colleagues said, we would have to expand our field of vision to include the old-growth forests that provided a home to the owls and thousands of other species, known and unknown.

In 1990, that amounted to a revelation, at least outside the still small community of conservation biologists. The timber industry, in stark contrast, envisioned a bizarre form of spotted owl conservation in which teams of biologists would capture pairs of owls and shuffle the birds around between patches of forest as the chain saws and bulldozers moved in behind them. Thus would spotted owls have become conservation refugees, adrift and homeless.

Science took a back seat to politics in the struggle over land use even after the Thomas Report, with all of its cutting-edge ideas. Report in hand, the Forest Service and its political bosses demonstrated the power of willful ignorance. The agency announced that some timber sales in spotted owl habitat fit the panel's guidelines and would proceed. Judge Dwyer thought otherwise. His ruling in a suit filed against the agency rang with tightly controlled judicial fury: "More is involved here than a simple failure by an agency to comply with its governing statute. The most recent violation of [the National Forest Management Act] exemplifies a deliberate and systematic refusal by the Forest Service and the Fish and Wildlife Service to comply with the laws protecting wildlife." The tongue-lashing continued: "The problem here has not been any shortcomings in the laws, but a simple refusal of administrative agencies to comply with them. . . . This invokes a public interest of the highest order: the interest in having government officials act in accordance with the law."[4]

Congress and the land management agencies chose not to meet Judge Dwyer's challenge head on, but instead searched for creative ways around his ruling. They invoked the God Squad and the Gang of Four—the former a committee of agency heads, authorized under the Endangered Species Act, that can short-circuit protection of listed species if vital economic interests are at stake; the latter neither a cadre of Chinese communists nor a late 1970s punk band, but a group of scientists (including Thomas again) brought together for an independent assessment of federal forests in the Pacific Northwest. The Gang of Four (so named by a petulant timber industry spokesman likely hoping for a more malleable bunch) found that things were even worse than the original Thomas committee had surmised. Looking at more species than just the spotted owl, the scientists found that timber harvests would have to drop even further. The administration of the first President Bush simply ignored this inconvenient finding.

The Forest Service kept going before Judge Dwyer with new ploys to continue cutting as many trees as they wanted in spotted owl habitat, and His Honor kept tossing the agency out of his courtroom on its ear. The Forest Service's repeated forays into court became almost comical, despite serious issues of policy and science. "Boneheaded," pronounced the editorial page of the *Seattle Post Intelligencer*. "For bureaucratic intransigence and administrative ineptitude, it's hard to beat the U.S. Forest Service's record in handling the spotted-owl issue."[5]

Finally, in the summer of 1992, Judge Dwyer issued a permanent injunction. He prohibited any timber sales in spotted owl habitat until the Forest Service fully complied with federal environmental law and developed a suitable plan to protect the owls. Loggers fumed about the injustice of it all, but the fundamental fact remained: the Forest Service could not cut a tree in spotted owl habitat until Judge Dwyer gave his approval, and he would not be easily swayed.

Just a few months after Judge Dwyer issued his injunction, some residents of the Applegate Valley in southwest Oregon saw the ruling as an opportunity. Environmental activist Jack Shipley reasoned that no one could fight over timber sales anymore, since there wouldn't be any more timber sales. So he invited some of his environmentalist friends to a potluck dinner. No smug victory celebration, the guest list also included the owners of local sawmills, as well as federal land managers. Shipley wanted them all to start thinking together about the whole watershed in which they lived. Not many people had considered things at this scale before.

A new organization called the Applegate Partnership emerged from the dinner at Shipley's house. The partnership adopted as an operating principle the slogan "Practice Trust—Them Is Us." Members even sported buttons with the word *they* with a red slash through it. Hokey, perhaps, but with a message: sawyers, activists, and agencies were in this together. The Applegate Partnership did not change the world, but it opened the door to collaboration between often conflicting segments of the valley's community and the federal government. Shipley and the others discovered they could work together, and they could begin to change the way government agencies made decisions.[6]

* * *

Even where there are many diverse interests, as in the Applegate Valley, communities that have maintained or revitalized their social capital can still find common ground. In the United States, unfortunately, political trends can obscure the very existence of that common ground. Politicians have narrowed their perspectives at the same time that scientists have expanded theirs, with a single-minded focus on local control over land. This approach, usually associated with notions of states' rights or the county-supremacy movement—which makes the absurd claim that the federal government cannot enforce federal laws on federal land—represents the latest attempt to circumvent the major environmental laws. Opponents have been unable to weaken those laws substantially despite years of legal attacks and endless, overheated rhetoric, so they try an end run by turning decisions over to the states. Conservationists rightly worry that the end run might actually work, and thus usually oppose most efforts to shift control of natural resources to rural communities.

The conservationists' fear has deep roots in politics and passion; efforts to wrest control over the land from government have long reflected nothing other than a desire to exploit public resources for private gain. In the United States, this chutzpah goes back to 1872 and the creation of Yellowstone National Park, the point at which the federal government stopped trying to give all public land to the states (by and large, the states didn't want what was left in public hands by the mid–nineteenth century, because it was too dry and difficult to farm) and decided to keep some instead. The battle over who gets to use public land and for what purpose was joined and it has raged ever since, though more passionately at some times than others. In 1947, for example, the public land question became a national debate, largely thanks to the journalist and historian Bernard DeVoto. From his seat in the "Easy Chair" column in *Harper's Magazine,* DeVoto led a public campaign against the effort by ranchers and other private interests to seize control of western public land in the United States. The cry from the West, DeVoto said, was "get out and give us more money."[7]

That cry has had remarkable staying power. Federal control over public land is as settled as a constitutional principle can be, but that did not prevent the outbreak of the Sagebrush Rebellion of the early 1980s. The rebels, who at one time counted President Ronald Reagan among their number, said they wanted to transfer federal land to the states. But the rebellion—really more of a fad—faded away quickly when it became clear that not even the rebels themselves truly believed their slogans. They did not want the government to hand over the land, they wanted the government to give them control of the land but not responsibility for it, and they wanted an increase in the fat subsidies they enjoyed for grazing their sheep and cows on the public range. Get out and give us more money.

The Sagebrush Rebellion gradually morphed into a more sinister form, the Wise Use movement. It is neither wise nor a movement. *Movement* suggests progress, but the Wise Users want at the very least to freeze the status quo, and preferably to move law and policy back to the early twentieth century, when private property and the interests of industry ruled the day. The groups at the forefront of the campaign, with warm and fuzzy names like the National Wetlands Coalition and the Marine Preservation Association, claim to be grassroots organizations, but for the most part they are wholly owned subsidiaries of mining companies and agribusinesses. Still, their message about returning power to the powerless certainly resonates with rural communities, a fact that conservationists ignore at their peril.[8]

With these foes, no wonder the conservation movement clings to an adversarial approach that has indeed won many battles and will remain a vital tool for ensuring compliance with the law. But confronting industry and the Wise Use movement is not nearly sufficient, and, worse, it may blind conservationists to the real opportunities. In the United States, few rural economies still rely exclusively on logging, mining, and agriculture. Instead, their economic future depends on attracting diverse businesses and skilled workers. More and more often, that attraction rests on an intact environment, a basic component of creating communities where people want to live and raise their families. This fundamental shift, combined with the fresh insights of conservation science, offers an opportunity to heal the rift between rural communities and conservation.

ECOSYSTEM DECAY

The spotted owl controversy marked a turning point in how people thought of conservation, but it truly embodied gradual rather than sudden changes in science. Though few realized it at the time, scientists had been laying the groundwork for a new approach to conservation for two decades.

That new approach began, as so often in science, with an attempt to do something else altogether. In the early 1960s, two scientists, Robert MacArthur of Princeton University and E. O. Wilson of Harvard University, did not set out to save the world. They sought answers to two straightforward questions, neither of which, on the surface at least, had a direct bearing on conservation. First, why do larger islands contain more species than smaller ones? Second, why do remote islands support fewer species than less remote ones?

The focus on islands formed a special case of the science of biogeography—the study of where animals and plants are, where they are not, and why.[9] MacArthur and Wilson argued that the number of species on an island resulted from a balance between the two competing forces of extinction and immigration. As some species on an island become extinct, others colonize the island from elsewhere. They argued that each island has an equilibrium point between extinction and immigration, with the size of the population at that equilibrium determined by the island's size and degree of isolation. Large islands, for example, have sizable populations of species and, with more individuals, those populations are less likely to go extinct than small populations. New immigrants are also more likely to find their way to larger islands than small ones. On the other hand, large, remote islands will tend to receive fewer colonists than less isolated islands, but the extinction rates will be the same. They should thus tend to support fewer species than a more accessible island of similar size.

MacArthur and Wilson had developed a theory applicable not only to islands but to virtually any isolated habitat. Equilibrium theory can apply to mountain tops, caves, tide pools, lakes, areas of tundra within forests, and areas of forest within tundras. Scientists would eventually come to recognize the importance of understanding the dynamics of extinction and recolonization; if you took a broad expanse of forest and began cutting down trees until you were left with many fragments separated by clearcuts, a process called habitat fragmentation, then the smallest, most isolated fragments would lose species faster than the larger, less isolated remnants.

The iron law of island biogeography states that the number of species an area can support is directly proportional to its size. As isolated remnants shrink in area, they will lose species "the way a mass of uranium sheds electrons," writes David Quammen. Tom Lovejoy, one of the founders of conservation biology, who now heads the Heinz Center, a Washington, DC–based environmental policy think tank, calls this "ecosystem decay." Lovejoy even took the dramatic step of chopping up a stretch of Amazonian rainforest to determine what would happen to pieces of various sizes.[10]

MacArthur and Wilson at first drew no broad conclusions about the possible application of their work. Their first scholarly paper on the subject, in 1963, received little notice.[11] One of their sources, however, at least hinted at what the future would hold. Frank Preston, an optical engineer who dabbled, but to great effect, in theoretical ecology, had also been puzzling over the relationship between area and number of species, and the related question of the distribution of rare and common species. In 1962, Preston published a long two-part paper in back-to-back issues of the journal *Ecology*.[12] Toward the end of the second paper, Preston looked up from his mathematical formulations long enough to speculate on their implications: "If what we have said is correct, it is not possible to preserve in a State or National Park, a complete replica on a small scale of the flora and fauna of a much larger area." You cannot make a Xerox reduction of nature and stash it away in some remote corner of the world that no one wants to farm or develop. Scientists would not appreciate the full meaning of that insight for years.

In 1967, MacArthur and Wilson offered the most complete version of their ideas in a book, *The Theory of Island Biogeography*. In it, they too, like Preston, nodded in the direction of the conservation implications of their work. Any natural area could become an island, they wrote, so the principles of island biogeography would apply "and will apply to an accelerating extent in the future, to formerly continuous natural habitats now being broken up by the encroachment of civilization. . . ."[13] Unlike the original paper, the book became one of the most influential ecological treatises ever written. Island biogeography led to some of the most important advances in conservation science, particularly the idea that conservationists should pay close attention to the scale of their efforts and the landscape context within which they are working. The theory of island biogeography got many scientists and conservationists thinking seriously about the effects of habitat area and isolation on population persistence.

✳ ✳ ✳

Other scientists began to apply the theory of island biogeography to various situations, including how to design nature reserves. In 1975, Mark Shaffer (now at the Doris Duke Charitable Foundation) was a graduate student at Duke University. Shaffer and his major professor, Arthur L. Sullivan, wrote a paper in which they noted that chance, not science, largely determines the location of a park. A more systematic approach to preservation, based on island biogeography, would be a strategy for locating reserves based on a consideration of location, number, size, and linkage of the parks. Existing reserves in the United States, they said, are inadequate in size and number, and nearly all the large reserves are clustered in the West. A planned network might have several layers of reserves, starting with areas large enough to support large carnivores.[14]

Sullivan and Shaffer had identified some of the central questions of conservation: How long will a population of animals survive? How should we plan networks of parks to protect those populations? Those questions remain vital and too often unanswered, though nearly everyone agrees that, given a choice, reserves should be large and there should be many of them. The desirability of large reserves comes as close to a universal principle as you will find in conservation biology.[15] Even further, scientists now generally agree on the core principles for reserves, principles that the Thomas committee endorsed with the weight of the U.S. government regarding the spotted owl: reserves should be large and multiple, species that are well distributed across their range are less susceptible to extinction than species confined to small portions of their range, large blocks of habitat containing large populations are better than small blocks with small populations, placing reserves close together is better than placing them far apart, contiguous habitat is better than fragmented habitat, and interconnected habitat is better than isolated habitat.[16]

Even with this general agreement, the answer to any question about setting aside land depends on what you are trying to protect, for how long, and where. Sometimes a small reserve will do the job just fine, so conservation planners need to consider wildlands on many scales, from the bog on the outskirts of town to a ten-thousand-square-mile reserve straddling the U.S.-Canada border that would be roomy enough for a population of grizzly bears to thrive for centuries. This means conservation that transcends the normal human life span and extends beyond traditional political boundaries.[17]

✤ ✤ ✤

An even more fundamental question remains: Why had the creation of hundreds of parks throughout the world not done more to slow the loss of species and habitats? Why were we still fighting battles over creatures like the spotted owl?

Many scientists found such questions troubling, but for one in particular, finding the answers became a mission. Michael Soulé was a graduate student in ecology at Stanford University when he first read MacArthur and Wilson's work. Inspired, he began to think about the implications for conservation. "I think it was the most important contribution to ecology in the twentieth century," Soulé says now. Soulé did not leap immediately into the conservation fray, wielding a well-thumbed copy of *The Theory of Island Biogeography*, but he saw the significance sooner than nearly all other ecologists. In 1978, by-then Professor Soulé and one of his graduate students at University of California, San Diego, Bruce Wilcox, convened the First International Conference on Conservation Biology. Two years later they edited the papers from the conference into a book entitled *Conservation Biology: An Evolutionary-Ecological Perspective*. Other textbooks had covered similar ground, but this one marked a milestone, the birth of a new science. "Conservation biology is a mission-oriented discipline," Soulé and Wilcox wrote, and they issued a call to arms:

> The green mantle of the Earth is now being ravaged and pillaged in a frenzy of exploitation by a mushrooming mass of humans and bulldozers.... Perhaps even more shocking than the unprecedented wave of extinction is the cessation of significant evolution of new species of large plants and animals. Death is one thing—an end to birth is something else, and nature reserves are too small (not to mention, impermanent) to gestate new species of vertebrates.... This is the challenge of the millennium. For centuries to come, our descendants will damn us or eulogize us, depending on our integrity and the integrity of the green mantle they inherit.[18]

Soulé and a handful of others, including Tom Lovejoy and Mark Shaffer, created conservation biology in response to that and other questions, in an attempt to focus scientific inquiry on tangible problems. Like medicine, conservation biology is science with a mission; "the relationship of conservation biology to biology, particularly ecology, is analogous to that of surgery to physiology and war to political science," Soulé wrote in 1985. Also like medicine, conservation biology requires more than just a well-turned equation or an elegant theory. Inevitably, conservation biology applies scientific principles to questions that demand at least as much intuition and faith to answer. Conservation biologists can no more prove to a hardened skeptic the importance of any particular species or wilderness in general than preachers can prove the existence of God to an atheist.

The choice to conserve—a species, a piece of open space downtown, or a vast landscape—rests ultimately on personal and social value judgments, not science. The plain-as-day benefits of ecosystem services like clean water and flood control or the hope of new drugs from the rainforests may tip the balance, but in the end people will either value nature and work to conserve it, or they will choose otherwise. Massive destruction of habitat and the extinctions that follow do not just happen. People choose that path, sometimes because their survival depends on it, but more often they plunge on, heedless or simply greedy.

Conservation biologists thus often find themselves at the uncomfortable intersection of science and advocacy. By no means do all conservation biologists turn the same way when they reach that crossroads. Many academic conservation biologists believe that their influence in public debate rests on their impartial presentation of scientific facts; let others interpret those facts. Scientists in conservation organizations, government agencies, and elsewhere argue that we face the crucial decade for conservation; ecological systems across the globe are poised either to vanish or, with proper stewardship, to remain intact or even recover. At such a moment, refusing to enter the political fray in the interest of maintaining an idealized vision of scientific impartiality strikes many conservation biologists as foolhardy.

This dilemma has no easy solution. Conservation biologists will always have to keep two hats at hand, the scientist and the advocate. The science must be as rigorous and objective as possible, but it will not speak for itself in public debate. Scientists must be willing to take a position on what their results mean without bending them to fit desired outcomes, and distinguish clearly between statements that are based on science and those that are based on personal values.[19]

Neither side in the academic/activist debate doubts that the strength of conservation biology lies in its mission to conserve nature. Yet the inescapable facts of academic life—publications, tenure, science department politics that dismiss anything vaguely "applied"—threaten to erase that mission and transform conservation biology into yet another subspecialty with a few technical journals and tenured professorships. That would be a huge loss for conservation. The excitement of this science comes not from the laboratory bench but from the field, where conservation practitioners attempt to apply theory to a real landscape.

The urgency of that sort of application became much clearer in 1987. That year, William Newmark, a newly minted Ph.D. from the University of Michigan (where Michael Soulé had been on his doctoral committee), published a paper in the prestigious journal *Nature*. Newmark had toured the parks of the western United States and Canada, tabulating observations of animal species. He sought data not on which species the parks harbored, but which species had once been present and now had disappeared. He was looking, in short, for evidence of Tom Lovejoy's ecosystem decay.

Newmark found the evidence, all right. His data showed that the western parks were losing species. The smaller parks lost species faster, but even the largest ones, like Banff in Canada and Glacier in the United States, were not immune. Newmark documented exactly the sort of decay that Frank Preston and then MacArthur and Wilson had predicted years earlier: as nature reserves become isolated from the surrounding landscape, they become like oceanic islands, and they begin to lose species. If no new species colonize the parks, then the total diversity will gradually diminish. Parks and reserves are, by themselves, incomplete.[20]

Newmark's paper highlighted the need to integrate the principles of island biogeography into conservation planning and practice. Some scientists have questioned Newmark's methods—perhaps the species he thought had disappeared from the parks had never really been there in the first place—but the point had been made, and other work by other scientists in other places has confirmed it: small, isolated parks will not suffice to conserve species, their habitats, and the varied processes that support both. It is not complicated: large animals need large landscapes. Those landscapes do not necessarily need to be designated as parks as we now know them, but they need to allow animals to move between areas that are secure.

MANAGING ECOSYSTEMS

A perspective that encompasses both public and private land—both protected areas and working landscapes—emerges, at least in part, from the federal court's ruling that the Forest Service must abide by the law in the Pacific Northwest. This seems at least slightly paradoxical, given that none of the laws in question actually dictate a broader view, and in fact a failed argument set the stage for thinking about conservation that encompassed private as well as public land. But when we look at the ruling, this perspective makes perfect sense. In a case before Judge Dwyer, the Forest Service contended that once a species was listed as threatened, the requirements of the Endangered Species Act negated regulations under another federal law, the National Forest Management Act, which required the Forest Service to protect all native and desired non-native vertebrate species. Judge Dwyer rejected this argument and said both laws applied. The injunction against logging remained in place, and it would not be lifted until the Forest Service took a broader look at the species that live in the ancient forests of the Pacific Northwest.

In response, the Forest Service convened yet another panel, and yet again asked Jack Ward Thomas to find a way out of the mess. This latest group, composed of scientists and technical experts from the Forest Service and the Fish and Wildlife Service, evaluated all species (excluding the microscopic ones) that may be associated with the spotted owl's preferred habitat—late-successional and old-growth forests—and suggested ways to ensure the survival of those species. The group's report listed some 667 species, from fungi to grizzly bears.[21] Suddenly, the forest seemed far more crowded, and conservation even more complicated. Accounting for all those species, or as many of them as possible, would require a broad, ecological understanding of the forests, a far cry from the narrow focus on tree farming that the Forest Service higher-ups usually demanded.

All of the studies, commissions, legal haggling, and attendant publicity created enormous political pressure. The spotted owl became an issue in the presidential campaign between George H. W. Bush and Bill Clinton, with "owls vs. jobs" the misleading shorthand. In fact, far more loggers lost their jobs because of global changes in the timber industry than because of anything environmentalists had done or said. These changes, among them the shift in the economy of the Pacific Northwest away from extractive industries, increased competition in timber markets. Periodic fluctuations in the economy that weaken demand for wood products act quite slowly— they had been brewing for years, if not decades—and remain largely hidden from public view. The withdrawal of land to protect an endangered species, on the other hand, can happen almost overnight, and provides a ready target for the anger and frustration of struggling rural communities, as well as a winning political platform for those long opposed to environmental regulations. Owls and their environmentalist defenders from the East Coast made convenient villains.

Bill Clinton promised during the campaign to bring the warring sides to a peace conference. In the spring of 1993, the new president convened a Forest Summit in Portland, Oregon, to craft a solution acceptable to both industry and environmentalists. The meeting led to the creation of the Federal Ecosystem Management Assessment Team, or FEMAT, led, oh yes, by Jack Ward Thomas. As always, Thomas ran a tight ship with impeccable science; the shortcomings of forest management in the Pacific Northwest cannot be laid on him, but on the intransigence of some within the Forest Service and their industry backers.

FEMAT had a daunting mandate: create a management plan for the forests within the range of the northern spotted owl that would meet the legal requirements of the Endangered Species Act, while also recognizing the needs of communities economically dependent on the timber industry—and do it in three months. Recognizing that that was hardly enough time to devise a comprehensive strategy even for just the federal land in the Pacific Northwest, FEMAT developed ten options for the administration to consider that allowed for varying levels of protection and use. The panel eventually recommended Option 9, which, in their view, struck a balance between preserving late-successional and old-growth forests and allowing at least some timber harvesting to continue.

The Forest Service formally adopted Option 9 (also called the Northwest Forest Plan) in April 1994. Later that year, Judge Dwyer gave his seal of approval: "The question is not whether the court would write the same plan but whether the agencies have acted within the bounds of the law."[22] In that lukewarm endorsement, Judge Dwyer captured the attitude of both environmentalists and the timber industry. Option 9 represented a compromise, and it pleased neither side: not enough logging for the industry, not enough strict protection for conservationists. Still, it garnered support from those not passionately involved in the debate.

✦ ✦ ✦

In its very title, the Federal Ecosystem Management Assessment Team put a new idea squarely on the table for public debate: ecosystem management. The idea of using ecosystems as the basis for making public policy had been around since the 1970s, and ecosystem management became an important part of the conservation lexicon in the late 1980s, at about the same time that the spotted owl made the evening news. But FEMAT institutionalized it within the federal government. When Judge Dwyer approved the Northwest Forest Plan, he put the weight of the federal courts behind ecosystem management for the first time. The courts found a legal basis for ecosystem management not in any single statute but in a myriad of laws, including the Endangered Species Act, the National Environmental Policy Act, the National Forest Management Act, and others. In the case of the spotted owl, the court cited those laws and then said that "given the condition of the forests there is no way the agencies could comply with the environmental laws without planning on an ecosystem basis."[23]

While the term "ecosystem management" began appearing ever more frequently in scientific journals and government reports, it seemed that no two people could agree on what it meant, as definitions of ecosystem management and practitioners or advocates of its use occurred in roughly equal numbers.[24] So it seems strange that nearly everyone agreed that ecosystem management was a good thing. When ecosystem management became part of the process of deciding how to use public land, both the environmental community and those concerned with maintaining resource flows took a keen interest in defining ecosystem management in their own terms. Indeed, one observer suggested that when environmental groups heard the term "ecosystem management" they mainly heard "ecosystem," while industry groups heard "management."[25] This led to the unsettling phenomenon of resource management agencies, conservationists, and industry representatives, who generally couldn't agree on what time it was, singing in unison the praises of ecosystem management at congressional hearings in the early 1990s.[26]

The two sides can each find something they like about ecosystem management because it is actually a spectrum of approaches, from utilitarian to protective.[27] Land management agencies usually stand at the utilitarian end of the spectrum; for them, human use of resources is natural and not necessarily harmful. Many conservationists, on the other end of the spectrum, suspect that the agencies use ecosystem management as window dressing for business as usual. They doubt, for example, that the Forest Service learned from past mistakes like the spotted owl debates and can now manage the forests for both timber cutting and wild species, or even have the political support to do so. Most ecosystem management projects allocate little to reserves, and the entire concept casts into doubt the possibility of excluding people from wild and remote areas. That makes some conservationists nervous.[28] On the other hand, while traditional management values resources primarily in human terms (whether for economic or aesthetic reasons), ecosystem management recognizes the intrinsic value of all components of the ecosystem.

✦ ✦ ✦

One of the problems with ecosystem management lies in defining the word *ecosystem*. That debate has lost little intensity since British ecologist Arthur Tansley coined the word in 1935, giving an old concept a new name. In Tansley's definition, ecosystems include organisms and their non-living environment and are the basic units of ecology, forming parts of a hierarchy of physical systems that runs from atoms all the way up to the universe.[29] The idea eventually sparked the growth of a new specialty called ecosystem ecology. Most non-scientists generally assume that ecosystems are things, and that they are big. So, to the limited extent that the term "ecosystem management" is part of common parlance, it means managing some big chunks of land. Unfortunately, neither of these assumptions about ecosystems is correct. In fact, ecosystem management is not about managing ecosystems at all.

First of all, ecosystems are not things. You can't hold one in your hand. An ecosystem is a way of describing how the living and non-living elements in a given area relate to one another. As such, an ecosystem can be any size, from a rotting log to a watershed to a continent.[30] Now you may say, "I can pick up that rotting log, so why can't I hold an ecosystem in my hand?" You can hold the log and the ants and the termites and the fungi and the bacteria, but you can hardly hold the relationships among all those creatures, or the process of decomposition itself, or the flow of energy from the wood to the soil.

Defining an ecosystem in terms of what goes on within it rather than how big it is means that the boundaries of an ecosystem, while not arbitrary, certainly are flexible. Take the area around Yellowstone National Park, for example. Depending on the factors you consider, Greater Yellowstone ranges in size from 5 million acres, which includes Yellowstone and Grand Teton National Parks and an equal amount of federal, state, and private land outside them, all the way to 26.5 million acres, an area about half the size of Oregon.[31] Drawing a single ecosystem boundary, wherever the line falls on a map, belies the enormous complexity of the issue. Ecosystems span multiple scales of space and time, thus precluding any meaningful, single-dimension definition, and their dynamic, evolutionary character makes it difficult to draw lasting, definitive ecological boundaries.[32] Scientists could spend decades teasing out all the threads that bind an ecosystem together across all these scales and still not have a complete understanding.

Even when boundaries are set, they are rarely if ever impermeable or even distinct to the untrained eye. This leads opponents of ecosystem management, which includes the resource-extraction industries and their ideological surrogates in the Wise Use and states' rights movements, to claim the whole idea is fatally flawed. "Aha!" they cry, like smug lawyers pulling a supposedly damning piece of evidence from their bag and waving it before the jury. "How can you manage something whose boundaries are indistinct and that only exists as a concept and not as a thing?"

This objection, not nearly as clever as its promoters would like us to believe, vanishes once you recognize that ecosystem management is not a set of rules for manipulating, say, an entire national forest by closing roads or opening them, or by extinguishing fires or letting them burn. Rather, it is about understanding how all the pieces of the ecological puzzle—including people—fit together, and using that understanding as the basis for solving whatever problems may arise. Some problems may indeed cover vast areas, but others may be quite local. An ecosystem approach works in both instances.[33]

Conservation must also deal effectively with the things people do, which means working at human scales but also at scales broad enough to encompass large animals and ecological processes that operate over huge areas and hundreds of years. So think of ecosystems as a hierarchy, from a meadow to a continent, and then divide the larger ones into smaller ones on the basis of climate and vegetation, with the smaller nesting comfortably into the larger. In the middle of that hierarchy would be relatively large areas of land and water that share common species and dynamics. In the late 1970s, a geographer at the U.S. Department of Agriculture named Robert Bailey coined the term "ecoregion" to describe these ecosystems that extend over whole regions. Since then, organizations like World Wildlife Fund, The Nature Conservancy, and others have adopted ecoregions (though not always the precise boundaries that Bailey defined) as the foundation of their conservation efforts.

In North America, examples of ecoregions include the New England–Acadian forests, which stretch from Connecticut to New Brunswick; the Sonoran Desert, in Arizona and California; and the central tall grasslands, which once covered parts of Iowa, Minnesota, South Dakota, Nebraska, and Kansas. Ecoregions range in size from the Everglades, which at eight thousand square miles is a mere dot on the tip of Florida, to the Canadian boreal forests along Hudson Bay, which at nearly three hundred thousand square miles are bigger than Texas. Most ecoregions fit comfortably in western states like Montana, New Mexico, or Arizona.[34]

Ecoregions provide a framework for developing conservation solutions at the same scale as conservation problems. Conservation has generally proceeded park by park, or, at best, as in the Applegate Valley, watershed by watershed. Even a large park like Yellowstone occupies only a small fraction of its ecoregion, which World Wildlife Fund calls the South Central Rockies forests. The threats that the park faces, however, extend well beyond its boundaries. Ecoregions account for those broader threats but are not so vast as to swamp the ability of people to build institutions capable of working within them. Many studies have demonstrated that habitat fragmentation poses grave threats to all manner of species, all the more so because it is usually irreversible. But the problem is as much social and cultural fragmentation as biological or ecological fragmentation.

Thinking at the scale of an ecoregion enables us to begin knitting the landscape back together, to understand how human communities fit into the warp and woof of nature, and to overcome ecological, social, and intellectual fragmentation. Blurring the boundaries that separate human jurisdictions but make no ecological sense—those that separate professional disciplines; those that separate one group in society (say, ranchers) from another, like environmentalists; and those that have long separated humanity from nature—reveals countless possibilities for saving life on Earth.

The challenge for ecoregional conservation is to think big and think small; big enough to provide room for spotted owls, grizzly bears, and elephants, but small enough that human communities can play meaningful roles. That requires a deeper understanding of the ecological role that big animals like bears, elephants, and whales play. Do big things run the world? Science offers no simple answer, but even asking the question moves us toward big conservation. Even if big things don't really run the world, we still need to make the world safe for big things.

CHAPTER 2

DO BIG THINGS RUN THE WORLD?

The moot point is, whether Leviathan can endure so wide a chase,
and so remorseless a havoc; whether he must be exterminated from
the water, and the last whale, like the last man, smoke his last pipe,
and then himself evaporate in the final puff.
HERMAN MELVILLE, Moby Dick

The Kenai Peninsula lies roughly two hundred miles southeast of Anchorage on the Gulf of Alaska, just north of Kodiak Island. To the west, across the narrow Cook Inlet, the long, spidery arm of the Aleutian Peninsula juts into the Bering Sea, trailing off after twelve hundred miles into the badly misnamed Near Islands. Residents of towns on the peninsula like Homer and Seward benefit from rich fisheries and boatloads of summer tourists. It rains quite a bit, but never gets too cold, so as the hucksters might say, Move to Alaska! But hurry, because land is going fast. No, people are not flocking to southeast Alaska seeking their fortune or the good life; rather, bit by bit, the ocean is reclaiming the coast, five feet per year in places. At that rate, houses will soon start falling into the sea.

Global climate change may be to blame, or perhaps overzealous developers, but other villains lurk nearby, unexpected, unlikely, and intriguing. Some long-retired Japanese and Russian whalers stand first in line, followed by greedy fishing fleets, hungry orcas, and, finally, fecund sea urchins. The possibility that killing too many great whales in the years following World War II led to beach erosion half a century later contains important lessons about how ecological systems work, and about the scale, in both time and space, at which humans must work to conserve them. Ecoregions provide one way to think about conservation, and some scientists and activists working on an ambitious and controversial effort called The Wildlands Project are thinking even bigger than that, as they envision conservation at a continental scale.

❋ ❋ ❋

The story in Alaska begins with the great whales. Two scientists, Jim Estes and Alan Springer, lead the effort to piece the narrative together. In the 1970s, sea otters—among the most charismatic of all megafauna, and star attractions on the conservation fundraising circuit—had recovered from near-extinction caused by the fur trade in the eighteenth and nineteenth centuries, and returned to historic densities in some parts of their range. In the 1990s, however, some otter populations in the Aleutian Islands and western Alaska plunged again, this time without any meddlesome fur trappers around to foul the ecological works. Estes, a research scientist with the U.S. Geological Survey and adjunct professor at the University of California, Santa Cruz, wanted to know why.

He found, to his surprise, that killer whales were to blame. Before the early 1990s, Estes rarely saw orcas in the coastal waters around the Aleutian Islands. When he did see orcas and otters together, they always coexisted peacefully—a killer whale can make a full meal out of seals and sea lions, while otters are just appetizers. Starting in the early 1990s, however, Estes saw orcas near shore more often, and they began to eat otters in large numbers. The only thriving otter populations found refuge in lagoons too shallow for orcas to enter. On further investigation, Estes and his colleagues learned that orcas had apparently turned to eating otters because the populations of seals and sea lions had collapsed. Again the question was why.

Estes had studied a huge stretch of ocean for more than three decades, but answering this question would require an even longer and broader perspective. For this task, Estes teamed with Springer, an oceanographer at the University of Alaska Fairbanks, and others to explore the possibility that the declines might also be linked to the historical decline of great whales, once major prey for orcas.

The research team looked at whaling records dating back more than fifty years, the nutritional requirements of killer whales, the nutritional value of sea lions and otters, and the number of sea lions and otters that orcas would have to eat in order to cause the observed declines of the prey species in the Aleutian Islands. They discovered that the disappearance of great whales forced some killer whales to find other, smaller prey, a phenomenon known in ecological jargon as a "trophic cascade," or, more heartily, "fishing down the food web." As big whales grew scarce, orcas targeted populations of smaller and smaller coastal marine mammals. Populations of harbor seals began to collapse in the early 1970s, followed by fur seals in the mid-1970s to mid-1980s, then sea lions in the late 1970s to 1990s, and finally sea otters.

The sea lions didn't just have orcas to worry about, either. At about the same time that orcas ran out of other things to eat, commercial fishing and a shift in climate and ocean currents caused declines in the sea lion's favorite foods, herring and sand lance, forcing them to turn to pollock, a much less nutritious fish. The combination of hunting by orcas and a shift in the food supply caused sea lion populations—particularly the Aleutian population of Steller's sea lion, the largest of all sea lion species—to drop by half by the mid-1980s.

As killer whales brought down the numbers of sea otters, the population of sea urchins, one of the otter's favorite foods, exploded. The urchins, which love to eat kelp, in turn have stripped out the kelp forests, creating "urchin barrens," long stretches of bare, rocky sea floor.[1] The kelp forest ecosystem in southwestern Alaska went from robust to nonexistent in just a few years. Intact kelp forests would help reduce beach erosion, as they absorb and dissipate the energy of incoming waves. And so along the Aleutian Islands, and perhaps all the way to Homer, people wait nervously for each new storm.

This simplified description portrays an intricate food web as a row of dominoes, and the story of the orcas and the otters all makes sense once the dominoes begin to fall. Yet the whole scenario is counterintuitive in many ways, with important implications for conservation. The first surprise is the close connection between changes in open ocean populations and changes in coastal environments. Saving a species like the sea otter means thinking big in both space and time, as we may not know the effects of today's fishing practices for fifty years or more, and those practices may have an impact thousands of miles from where the fishing fleets drop their nets.

Even more profoundly, understanding the links between the orcas and the otters forms an important piece in an emerging picture of how ecological systems function. More and more scientists now appreciate the importance of seeing the world through the eyes of an orca, or a wolf, or a tiger.

The scientist Michael Soulé and the environmental activist Dave Foreman, among others, have taken this notion to heart. The unlikely partnership between Soulé and Foreman in The Wildlands Project serves as a telling illustration of the new thinking in the science and practice of conservation.

TAKE IT FROM THE TOP

The big animals at the top of the food chain are the fewest in number, so the predominant view in ecology has long been that those animals have relatively little impact on their environment. Ecologists traditionally focused on how the availability of food limits animal populations, an idea known as "bottom-up" regulation. By this way of thinking, the amount of solar energy that plants can capture determines how many herbivores a system can support, which in turn limits the number of carnivores. Generations of ecologists learned the "10 percent rule" as gospel truth: the biomass of plant-eating animals is 10 percent of the biomass of the plants themselves, and the biomass of carnivores is 10 percent of the biomass of herbivores. It is actually somewhere between 5 and 20 percent, and not in every case, but you get the point.

"The 10 percent rule is true and it is very important, but it is not the whole picture," says Michael Soulé. "The actual structure and composition of the ecosystems can be strongly affected by a few species, whether they are present or absent, such as wolves or jaguars."

Soulé is now professor emeritus at the University of California, Santa Cruz, a reflection more on the state of California's budget than on any slowing in Soulé's restless intellect. He continues an active research and travel schedule from his home base in western Colorado, with particular interest in the role of large carnivores. Soulé, along with Jim Estes and other scientists, has long argued that large carnivores have an enormous influence on how an ecosystem functions and how many other creatures it can support. Large carnivores stabilize prey and smaller predator populations and help maintain ecological diversity in many ecosystems. Remove the top predators, the controversial theory goes, and the entire edifice may collapse.[2]

Soulé, Estes, and their colleagues do not claim they discovered the notion of "top-down" regulation; Aldo Leopold, for one, recognized the importance of predators in the 1940s. Most biologists, however, thought top predators did not have much influence on the ecological system. In the 1960s, scientists devised a conceptual model for top-down regulation, but experimental proof remained elusive.[3] That began to change in 1966, when University of Washington ecologist Robert Paine published a study on predatory starfish and mussels on the rocky, intertidal shores of the Pacific Northwest.[4] Paine found that if he removed a predatory starfish called *Pisaster ochraceus* from test plots, then the overall diversity of mussels, barnacles, and other organisms in the plot declined. Paine discovered that this starfish prefers to eat a particular type of mussel called *Mytilus californianus*, which in the absence of predation outcompetes the other organisms for available space on the rocks. The other species thrive, even though they, too, sometimes become starfish food, as long as the starfish keeps the numbers of the space-hogging mussel in check. Paine drew an indisputable conclusion: in this system, at least, predators have an enormous influence on the kinds of species that will thrive.

Other scientists would also find clear cases for top-down regulation in the oceans and in lakes.[5] The sea otter–sea urchin system off Alaska that Jim Estes and his colleagues have described provides the classic illustration. On land, a complicated question gets downright mind-boggling. Studying large carnivores in the wild requires rare patience and a large stubborn streak, as the effects of their absence may not appear for decades. Still, the evidence mounts: in the absence of wolves and mountain lions, white-tailed deer in eastern forests overbrowse acorns, alter the pattern of tree regeneration, and hence threaten some endangered plants and reduce wild flowers; without coyotes in the canyons of coastal California, the populations of smaller predators such as foxes and house cats has expanded and can decimate the song birds. On Isle Royale, in Lake Michigan, when wolves are rare and moose abundant, the growth rate of firs is depressed. In and around Yellowstone National Park, after the extermination of wolves, elk loafed in large herds in river meadows and overbrowsed streamside vegetation, such as cottonwood, aspen, and willow, which beavers require. So beavers abandoned the large valleys, and cottonwood trees have not reproduced in seventy years, or since the last wolf was shot.[6]

If the loss of top predators shows their importance, so does their return. When wildlife biologists trapped wolves from Canada and relocated them to Yellowstone in the mid-1990s, the elk woke up and started looking over their shoulders. Elk no longer linger in riparian areas, and the streamside vegetation is starting to come back. Thus the return of wolves may have also brought back the beaver, even though beavers are themselves wolf prey.[7]

Experimental proof of the top-down idea, beyond Robert Paine's small plots, will be slow in coming. For now, at least, the best evidence comes from experiences like reintroducing wolves to Yellowstone and comparing relatively intact areas with those degraded by human activity. For example, John Terborgh, one of the world's leading tropical ecologists, has been studying an enormous hydroelectric impoundment called Lago Guri in Venezuela. As the huge reservoir filled in the mid-1980s, hundreds of hilltops became isolated islands. Between 1986 and 1994, 75 to 90 percent of the vertebrates disappeared from the new islands that were less than fifteen acres in area. Without top predators, populations of their former prey exploded: a majority of the species that remain have increased by at least an order of magnitude over mainland levels. The absence of many species and the overabundance of others have created animal communities unlike any that would ever occur naturally. Many of the overabundant species are small rodents that feed on seeds, or leaf-eaters, such as howler monkeys, iguanas, and leaf-cutter ants. So the loss of predators has also caused a reduction in the number of canopy trees in the forest.[8]

Top-down and bottom-up effects interact, and can operate concurrently in the same system, either at the same time or in cycles. Wolves can control the moose population on Isle Royale, but at times vegetation regrows so thickly that the moose can escape, and then the control is bottom-up. Assuming that top-down regulation is important in many ecosystems, conservation scientists are attempting to define the conditions that can support robust populations of large carnivores. Big and secure wilderness areas are clearly important, but so are more subtle processes such as population dynamics, genetic interchange, migrations, and historical patterns of disturbances like floods and fires.

The top-down hypothesis suggests that some species are more equal than others, at least from an ecological perspective. Ecologists have long recognized that some species influence ecosystem function and diversity to a far greater degree than would be expected, given their abundance. Ecologists call these keystone species; Robert Paine's starfish are the most famous, along with beavers, and, perhaps, large carnivores as well. The validity of the argument for any species as a keystone depends on the ecological context—beavers in mountain-meadow streams have far greater importance than beavers living in the banks of large rivers, and carnivores are unlikely to be keystone species where their numbers and the numbers of their prey are low, or where they persist in only a small area.[9]

The abstract notion of keystone species simplifies complex ecosystems, and protecting species that keep a given ecosystem in working order obviously helps all the species in that ecosystem. The concept also focuses on the mechanisms that drive ecosystem structure and function and may bridge the gap between efforts to conserve individual species and to conserve whole ecosystems. In reality, however, the world does not divide neatly into keystone species on the one hand and all the rest on the other. All species interact, but the interactions of some species and some ecological processes are more lasting, significant, and far reaching than others, such that their elimination from an ecosystem often triggers cascades of direct and indirect changes that may eventually lead to losses of habitats and extirpation of other species in the food web.[10] A few wolves and bears restricted to remote corners of Yellowstone National Park and shot when they set foot outside it, or fires that can burn only so far before the smoke jumpers arrive, become ecological specters, appearing on the landscape but leaving no lasting mark.

For some scientists, keystone species and top-down regulation provide pillars for the new conservation. Until the mid-1980s, the justification for big wilderness was anything but rigorously scientific—moral, aesthetic, nationalistic, even health-related, but not scientific. The science of saving wilderness relied on three bodies of evidence that support but do not fully justify large, connected systems of reserves: the species-area relationship that Frank Preston, E. O. Wilson, and Robert MacArthur, among others, had examined; the need for large areas that can withstand disturbances like fires or hurricanes; and the simple fact that large populations are more secure than small ones.

Michael Soulé, Jim Estes, John Terborgh, and others argue that the ecological role of large predators provides the firmest foundation for broad-scale conservation. Focusing on terrestrial conservation, Soulé has teamed with Terborgh and Reed Noss, another founder of conservation biology, to make large predators the foundation of an effort to restore big, connected wilderness areas. They call their approach "rewilding"—an approach in which successful conservation means wilderness areas big enough to support wolves, grizzlies, and their brethren.

❦ ❦ ❦

Rewilding offers a ready-made and intuitive way to measure conservation success, an often challenging problem and the focus of a growing movement among conservation organizations and scientists.[11] For the general public, sophisticated models or measures may be superfluous. The equation is quite simple, at least for people who envision wilderness from far away, rather than live in it or make a career of studying its intricacies: more grizzly bears, wolves, and the like equals successful conservation. Ecological realities will intrude and complicate matters—in Yellowstone, for example, what about fire, and aspen, and beavers?—but for the great majority of people it all comes down to large and dangerous things with teeth.[12]

Rewilding is one part of a far-flung effort to provide a solid scientific rationale for broad-scale conservation. If successful, and of course some scientists dispute the theory while supporting the goal, that would be just half the battle. A consensus among scientists could dramatically reshape the debates about conservation in government and with the general public, but the need for broad-scale conservation will fade in the face of other public priorities without a vision for the future that both inspires and offers practical results.[13]

Not all places need rewilding. Vast wilderness areas that support large carnivores still cover parts of the Russian Far East and Central Africa, for example. The American West, on the other hand, lost most of its large animals thousands of years ago. A dozen species of large mammalian herbivores, including bison with ten-foot horns and herds of huge camels, once roamed North America. The eastern part of the continent featured elephants, tapirs, and bear-sized beavers, among other large herbivores, but today only white-tailed deer and moose remain. Prior to the disappearance of the large herbivores, the role of top predators may not have been as important as it is today, because even fearsome predators such as dire wolves, saber-toothed cats, and short-faced bears could not take on such large creatures as bison, camels, and the others. The herbivores dominated many ecosystems, and probably controlled the distribution of many plant species and habitat types, as elephants still do in Africa. Neither megaherbivores nor large herds of migratory ungulates are common today, and those that remain are little more than leftovers from the last ice age.[14]

For its advocates, rewilding is both an end and a means: an end because of our moral obligation to repair past mistakes—a form of ecological restitution—and a means of maintaining the ecological structure, diversity, and resilience of the fabric of living nature by restoring large carnivores. Rewilding, therefore, requires a network of protected areas bound together by landscape connectors, many of which function as both habitat and migration-dispersal corridors (see Chapter 4). Ecoregions provide a framework for planning such networks, and linking ecoregional networks together could lead to conservation even at the scale of entire continents. For Soulé and Terborgh, rewilding would restore a balance between human society and the rest of creation.[15]

Just as not all places need rewilding, so restoring carnivores will not solve all conservation problems. In some places, natural systems have been so altered that not even as dramatic a change as reintroducing wolves will put them right. In the eastern United States, for example, the populations of white-tailed deer have grown so large that wolves alone would not be enough to control them. Still, rewilding places in stark relief the shortcomings of relying exclusively on isolated, island-like reserves. Even as environmental crises have become more apparent, the scale of conservation efforts has not changed. The implicit premise is that isolated reserves will suffice to conserve all manner of species and habitats. Heavy reliance on isolated preserves assumes that land in between reserves, from woodlots to subdivisions, can sustain the full range of ecological processes and human services, including animal migration, dispersal, and pollination.

Soulé, Terborgh, Foreman, and others have been working for twenty-five years to demonstrate the ecological necessity for big and connected protected areas. For them, these two elements form the foundation of any meaningful program of conservation on a regional or continental scale. Until recently, however, the inadequate scientific theory for conservation hindered efforts to guide conservation across such huge areas.[16]

As the science of conservation biology has matured, more and more conservation organizations have turned to it to guide their actions. By the 1980s, the need for a solid, scientific understanding of how ecosystems function and the fate of the species they contain was inescapable. Universities began creating programs in conservation biology, and the graduates of those programs began finding jobs with organizations like The Nature Conservancy, World Wildlife Fund, the Wildlife Conservation Society, and eventually with a newcomer called The Wildlands Project.

Many of the conservation scientists who came of age in the 1980s and 1990s saw in science the cure for a host of ills, including the destruction of habitats and the extinction of species. Talented and driven by a commitment to a conservation mission, these scientists brought revolutionary ideas, like the effects of habitat fragmentation, to a movement that had changed relatively little in several generations. They would learn, however, that sometimes even revolutionary science falls short. When the survival of something precious is at stake, scientific aloofness may serve a lesser good than engagement, say Soulé and Terborgh. For nuclear physicists that time came during World War II, as many went to work on the Manhattan Project and helped build the atomic bomb. For biologists, that time may be now.[17]

NEW MAPS FOR A NEW VISION

Dave Foreman approaches wilderness conservation with the same passion and single-mindedness as those physicists in the 1940s. He also once voted for Barry Goldwater, and later advocated blowing up the Glen Canyon Dam. Or so he said. A firebrand but neither a fool nor a murderer, Foreman—along with the author Edward Abbey—settled instead for carrying out one of the great pieces of American guerrilla theater, by draping a three-hundred-yard-long black plastic "crack" across the face of the dam.

Long before the world at large came to see Foreman as a dangerous man with pocketfuls of explosives and tree spikes, he labored in relative anonymity to preserve unbroken areas of wilderness as refuges for North America's big, fierce animals, like wolves, cougars, grizzly bears, and wolverines. Now the charismatic symbols of the conservation movement, for decades ranchers shot these creatures as vermin. Foreman lacked Michael Soulé's scientific expertise, but he shared the same passion. He and a few other dedicated western conservationists fought back, driven by a powerful sense that losing wolves meant losing part of themselves. They invaded places usually reserved for well-heeled lobbyists, like the back corridors of Congress, wearing cowboy boots smeared with mule shit, trying to find the votes to protect huge areas of forest and prairie from the logger's saw and the rancher's cattle. They usually lost.

The defeats pushed Foreman to the edge of the political spectrum, but while his tactics changed, Foreman never lost his vision of a vast network of wilderness areas stretching across North America. While with The Wilderness Society, Foreman says, he was always working toward big wilderness, always looking at both big and connected landscapes.[18]

Foreman left The Wilderness Society in 1980. Shortly thereafter, a trip into the desert in northern Mexico marked the birth of Earth First! The founders—if one can "found" an anti-organization with no officers, no by-laws, no constitution, and no tax status—wanted to give the environmental movement a kick in the ass. Mainstream conservation organizations like The Wilderness Society and the Sierra Club had become far too complacent, far too willing to compromise, Foreman and the others thought. Those organizations seemed to have forgotten why they were in business in the first place. Earth First!, on the other hand, put the value of wilderness for the sake of wilderness front and center and made it nonnegotiable. Foreman and his compatriots also chose the route of strategic radicalism: by staking out as radical a position as possible, they hoped to seize the environmental debate from the clutches of James Watt and the Sagebrush Rebels, redefine the spectrum of that debate, and make the rest of the environmental movement look moderate by comparison.

The monkeywrenching tactics of Earth First! remain on the fringes of most environmental debates, and for good reason: "Ideas, creativity, and energy spring up on the fringe and later spread into the middle," Foreman wrote in 1981, in an article for *The Progressive* magazine that amounts to the Earth First! manifesto.[19] That may indeed be the most lasting but least known legacy of Earth First! Long after the tree-sitters have come down from their perches, scientists and government officials will be arguing about and implementing the ideas that Foreman and the other Earth First! founders took from academic discourse and transformed into practical guidelines for conservation: preserve one major wilderness area in every ecosystem in the United States; expand the national parks; recreate wilderness; close roads; remove developments, and reintroduce extirpated wildlife. The Earth First!ers did not invent any of these notions, but they used them as the foundation of a coherent conservation philosophy. For that, and for reemphasizing the centrality of values in conservation, Earth First! deserves great credit.

Such contributions often get lost amid valid and troubling questions about the ethics of monkeywrenching, and Foreman may be partly to blame for that. "Let our actions set the finer points of our philosophy," he wrote in the 1981 article. Sadly, that is exactly what happened, and actions like spiking trees and cutting down power lines overwhelmed the idea of preserving big wilderness in the public mind. That is the far less productive legacy of Earth First!

At about the time that Dave Foreman was dreaming up Earth First! in the Pinacate Desert, in a far less mystical landscape a young scientist named Reed Noss was working for the Ohio Department of Natural Resources and thinking about how to put together regional networks of reserves. Noss was a perfect fit for the still-brand-new science of conservation biology: a passionate advocate for conservation, as well as a scientist with a scholarly bent in a hands-on job.

Noss soon left southern Ohio to pursue his doctorate at the University of Florida, where he worked with Larry Harris. Harris had just written a book called *The Fragmented Forest*, one of the first books to explore the effects of fragmentation on habitats and species, and had been thinking about the idea of the regional Everglades since the 1970s. Noss and Harris began to assess the context in which natural areas are embedded, asking, what does the land around a park look like?

With his experience in Ohio as a guide, Noss recognized that the managers of many parks or forests assumed that achieving maximum local habitat diversity favored diversity of wildlife. That actually works at a fine scale; if you take a uniform stand of trees and intentionally create some clearings, you will likely attract more species, in part because of what is called the edge effect. At the edge of a habitat, say where a forest meets a meadow, you will find both forest and meadow specialists, various species that thrive in either habitat, and still others that literally specialize in living on the edge. So edges often teem with wildlife, at least relative to other areas nearby; one textbook from the early 1970s in wildlife management even encouraged managers to "develop as much edge as possible,"[20] on the crude yet attractive theory that two habitats are better than one.

But creating edge means chopping up intact habitats, and if many land managers do the same thing across a wide area, then the overall effect will be to reduce diversity, not increase it. Trends in species composition in fragmented landscapes, Noss suggested, highlighted the need instead for a broader perspective. Noss called for a regional network of preserves, with sensitive habitat insulated from human disturbance. Only that way, he argued, would ecosystems and the species and ecological processes within them last far into the future.[21]

Noss and Harris developed a preliminary design for a regional reserve network in Florida in 1985, focused on yet another top carnivore: the Florida panther. The initial plan called for the protection of 60 percent of the state. People in the fastest-growing state in the nation would not hear of such things, so Noss started the Florida chapter of Earth First! to promote the idea, and also worked with far more mainstream, low-profile groups, like the Florida Native Plant Society.

Reed Noss's vision of conservation in Florida was not the first attempt to plot out a connected network of protected areas on such a broad scale, but it was among the most influential. Dave Foreman calls Noss's Florida proposal a turning point, the first coherent attempt to plan for conservation across an entire state. The Wildlands Project would build on that foundation, as would the state of Florida itself. In its initial form, however, Noss's map of the state offered a more conceptual than pragmatic vision, as it lacked the specificity that state or local officials would need to put the plan into action.

❖ ❖ ❖

Noss's map, like all maps, began to reveal patterns. Searching for patterns in nature is the most human of activities, a universal urge expressed in ancient and modern cultures. The natural world is a palimpsest, a parchment written on countless times by the movement of the earth's crust, by the evolution of new species and the extinction of old, and, to a distressing degree, by destructive human actions. These varied processes create enormous complexity, yet patterns still emerge. Kent Redford, a conservation biologist with the Wildlife Conservation Society at New York's Bronx Zoo, points out that humans have been attempting to capture and depict these patterns for as long as they have been human. The effort may even define some piece of what it means to be human. Redford finds a thread linking aborigines in Australia tracing the sacred songlines of creation, Algonquins in North America placing the scapula of caribou in their fires and reading the cracks to guide their hunts, and modern scientists mapping the earth. All those methods help humans make sense of the world. The modern approach builds less on faith than the others, but, unexpectedly, without faith—in others, in our communities—it may offer no guidance.

Recognizing the importance of ecological patterns, some scientists and activists began an effort to define the world along ecological rather than political lines, a practice they called bioregionalism. The term, popularized in the early 1960s by ecologist Ray Dasmann and the writer Peter Berg but of otherwise obscure etymology, describes a way of thinking about land and life within a regional framework.

Bioregionalists share an ongoing fascination with using maps as key tools for what they call reinhabiting place. Thinkers like Dasmann and Berg recognized the power of maps before most conservationists.[22] The willingness of bioregionalists, the geographer Robert Bailey, and others to think at the scale of a hundred thousand square miles eventually translated into news ways of thinking about the distribution and persistence of life on Earth, and eventually into the idea of ecoregional conservation.

Maps that guide land-use decisions rarely identify important natural areas, largely because promoters of economic growth have a corner on the production of those maps, and use them to make promises to deliver social or economic benefits. Economic development traditionally trumps nature protection, and opponents of conservation often claim that conservationists and others who point out the impossibility of unending growth and development in fact oppose any form of human progress.[23]

So conservationists have joined the mapping fray in earnest. They face a daunting task. "Conservation is trying to remap centuries of political mapping," says Kent Redford. John Wesley Powell was far ahead of his time when he took on that challenge in the late 1880s. Powell argued for dividing the new state of Montana into counties bounded by the divisions between watersheds rather than arbitrary political lines. The government should then cede the land within each basin to the people who live there, who could then organize themselves into grazing and irrigation cooperatives.[24]

The West refused to hear of its limitations, so settlers and their political patrons thoroughly ignored Powell's warnings. Many people still believed that rain would follow the plow—start planting the dry land of the West, and the new vegetation would bring rain. In 1893, Powell explained to a meeting of irrigators that only a small fraction of the land remaining in public hands could be irrigated: "I tell you gentlemen, you are piling up a heritage of conflict and litigation over water rights for there is not sufficient water to supply the land." The audience booed.[25]

Powell was onto something, but several generations passed before the bioregionalists took up the cause. "Bioregionalism has to exist for ecoregion-based conservation to succeed," says Kent Redford. "We have to have a sense of belonging to something that is not defined politically."

THE MOST IMPORTANT TASK OF OUR GENERATION

John Wesley Powell learned the consequences of challenging the powerful interests in the West, and he ended his career in obscurity. Dave Foreman took on those interests even more directly, and he too paid a steep price. In 1989, the FBI arrested him and four other Earth First! activists on charges that they planned to blow up power lines that carried electricity to the Central Arizona Project, a massive effort to pump water from the Colorado River over a twelve-hundred-foot mountain pass and into Arizona. Foreman eventually pleaded guilty to a felony conspiracy charge and agreed to stop advocating monkeywrenching.[26]

Foreman soon parted company with Earth First! Younger activists in the organization staged a coup, declaring science and technology the enemies of wilderness. This left little room for people like Foreman and Noss. Without them, Earth First! focused far more on social issues and direct action, and stopped thinking about how science could inform the effort to save the big and the wild.

During the long process of hearings and testimony that followed his arrest, Foreman accepted an invitation to speak at the University of Michigan from Barbara Dugelby, a former Earth First! activist from Texas who had gone to Ann Arbor to study conservation biology with Michael Soulé. Dugelby had also invited Soulé and David Brower, who had led the Sierra Club in 1950s and 1960s, and went on to found Friends of the Earth and the League of Conservation Voters. Foreman, Soulé, and Brower had never met, so Dugelby arranged a breakfast. Over pots of coffee at an Ann Arbor diner, three of the patriarchs of modern conservation (a title that Foreman and Soulé would likely reject) talked about the need for a broader, science-based vision for conservation. Science, said Soulé, could demonstrate the need for a system of large-scale, interconnected nature reserves.

Like Foreman, Soulé had become convinced that conservation had withered, bereft of vision, unable to free itself from outdated methods, and blind to new scientific ideas. Soulé saw that conservation needed an over-haul if it was to be anything more than a rear-guard action. Conservation of wilderness needed to occur on the same scales as the threats to that wilderness, over thousands of acres and hundred of years. The Wildlands Project began to take shape in Soulé's mind during a conversation with the Norwegian philosopher Arne Naess, a colleague and close friend, some months after the meeting with Foreman. "I don't know how we got onto it, but one morning we were talking about the fate of nature in North America, and during that conversation it dawned on me that we know what the problems are, primarily habitat loss and habitat fragmentation, so once you identify the disease you can sometimes think of the therapy. The therapy was obvious, it was restoring the connectivity, which was an outrageous idea," says Soulé.[27]

Soulé, who is brilliant and passionate but with an academic's reserve, lacked Foreman's political skills and charisma. Both men's strengths would be necessary to turn abstract concepts into practical action. So Soulé wrote to Foreman for help. "He was the only conservationist, as opposed to conservation scientist, I knew who thought on a scale like that. So I wrote to Dave, who I had only met once, and said, 'we know what the problem is, here is the solution, why don't we do something about it?'" Foreman showed Soulé's letter to a colleague. "Look, somebody *agrees* with us," he crowed.[28]

In 1991, Foreman and Soulé organized a meeting in San Francisco at the house of Doug Thompkins, who had made a fortune after founding the

North Face and Esprit clothing companies, but who was also a moun-
taineer and conservationist. That meeting marked the birth of The Wildlands Project. About a dozen people attended, mostly activists and a few
scientists, including Reed Noss. Harkening back to the initial Earth First!
manifesto, they envisioned a network of grassroots groups dedicated to
saving entire ecosystems. The Wildlands Project built on the fundamental
concepts of conservation biology that Soulé had helped develop, which
taught that many different species, not just the big and the fierce, depend
on large wilderness areas for their survival. Even more, Soulé and Foreman
shared an emotional connection to the symbols of wilderness, but both
also knew—Soulé empirically and Foreman more intuitively—that
wolves and the like actually shape the land; without wolves, places like Yellowstone are both ecologically and spiritually incomplete.

Like the founders of Earth First!, the group that gathered in San Francisco sought to escape what Soulé and John Terborgh call "the defensive
tactics, pleading, appealing, dealing, and suing" methods of mainstream
conservation with a bold and honest accounting, based on rigorous science, of what is necessary to save living nature in North America, and an
alternative land-use agenda to reach that goal. "Our job is not to operate
within the bounds of political reality," Foreman told the writer David
Quammen in 1993. "Our job is to change political reality."[29]

That goal transcends any single organization, no matter how compelling its mission. Yet the unlikely pairing of Dave Foreman and Michael
Soulé—the former a grassroots activist and self-proclaimed redneck eco-
radical, the latter a big-thinking scientist, ecologist, scholar, philosopher,
and Zen Buddhist—pointed toward how a new conservation could begin
to bring about that change in political reality. Foreman and Soulé share
the belief that without a new vision, the last wild places on Earth and
the countless species they support will slowly disappear amid the flotsam
and jetsam of a growing human population and the attendant economic
development.

Foreman is gentle and self-effacing in person. Put him in front of a
crowd, however, and he becomes the stem-winding preacher he always
wanted to be growing up. Foreman got himself thrown out of the Marine
Corps Officer Candidate School: "I was only good at command voice. I
failed everything else," he says. That command voice serves him well, as

conservation's finest orator. "Dream big in space and time," he told a meeting of conservation scientists, activists, and ranchers in Tucson in 2002. "We need to be big to tie the landscape together. Think big in terms of the community and who will be involved. Think big in terms of hope. Without hope we are lost."

The Wildlands Project begins with the attitude that current campaigns to protect wild species and wild places are too timid, that conservation as usual simply isn't working. Even Yellowstone National Park is not big enough to support large carnivores and needs to be connected to the rest of the Rockies, running all the way up to the Yukon. The Wildlands Project rests on the fundamental belief that we can accommodate migratory species in vast protected areas, as well as smaller ones that are linked together in a wildlands network like "jewels in a necklace."[30]

Soulé, Foreman, and the others formed The Wildlands Project to coordinate conservation-area design throughout North America. Noting the failure of small, isolated wilderness areas, parks, and wildlife refuges, Foreman, Noss, and the others proposed a master plan for protecting and restoring the ecological richness and native species and habitats of the continent: a connected system of reserves that would allow for the recovery of whole ecosystems and landscapes in every region. Drawing on Noss's designs for Florida, the plan blended traditional wilderness values of beauty, inspiration, and recreation with other ecological values. "Wilderness recovery, I firmly believe, is the most important task of our generation," wrote Noss.[31]

The Wildlands Project unveiled its audacious plan for the recovery and survival of the environment of North America in a special issue of a new journal called *Wild Earth*, with contributions from Foreman, Soulé, and Noss, along with wilderness recovery plans from grassroots groups in Scotland, the southern Appalachians, Central America, and the northern Rockies. The issue opens with bold strokes:

> Our vision is simple: we live for the day when Grizzlies in Chihuahua have an unbroken connection to Grizzlies in Alaska; when Gray Wolf populations are continuous from New Mexico to Greenland; when vast unbroken forests and flowing plains again thrive and support pre-Columbian populations of plants and animals; when

humans dwell with respect, harmony, and affection for the land; when we come to live no longer as strangers and aliens on this continent.[32]

Taken as a single, continental effort, The Wildlands Project seems absurd, as it would require reclaiming land now used for farming, housing, or industry; tearing out roads; prohibiting new development in areas where conservation biologists see wildlife habitat, but investors see houses, golf courses, and malls; and perhaps, its opponents fear, relocating entire towns. E. O. Wilson wrote that when he first heard of The Wildlands Project, he thought of it as "an admirable whimsy of noble souls."[33]

The Wildlands Project, however, is not a single thing, but rather a loose federation of dozens of local projects. Conservation challenges become more manageable at the scale of stopping a single new housing development or restoring a single wetland. It embodies a simple vision, but Foreman, Soulé, and the other founders of the effort are anything but politically naive about its prospects. Should it succeed, The Wildlands Project will bring about a transformation far more dramatic than retrieving Glen Canyon from the deep waters of Lake Powell. This is conservation on a grand scale, not only working across North America and looking several centuries into the future, but also seeking to overturn an economic model that demands constant growth.

The Wildlands Project and the grassroots efforts it supports use maps aggressively as both planning and marketing tools. They quickly learned that two can play that game. Opponents have created a map that purports to show The Wildlands Project's plan for the United States. If this paranoid fantasy of environmental totalitarianism weren't so sinister, it would be laughable; on the bogus map, half the country, and most of the West, lies within core reserves (in lurid red), with buffer zones covering the rest. The map labels areas around major cities (in green, a nice touch) as "normal use," but they seem feeble blips against the sea of red, symbolic somehow of ravenous wolves and grizzlies overrunning the landscape. Such propaganda seeks not to foster dialogue but to instill fear, and to discredit anyone who would speak up for wilderness.

To its most extreme opponents, all of whom seem to have their own websites, The Wildlands Project assaults everything America stands for, just as other extremists believe that the minions of the United Nations make plans to steal our sovereignty and force people off their land. Anti-conservation journalists labeled reserve proposals "hands off" or "human exclusion" zones. These caricatures attempt to discredit conservation biology and arouse distrust of conservation planning among those who favor both intensive resource use and recreation on public land. That strategy worked all too well; staff of The Wildlands Project in Tucson received death threats. Conservation organizations like The Nature Conservancy and World Wildlife Fund, even if they share a good deal of The Wildlands Project's perspective, now shy away from being publicly associated with the group.

Part of the desire on the part of mainstream conservation organizations to keep The Wildlands Project at arm's length goes back to Dave Foreman, who will always be a lightning rod, even though most of what people know about him is caricature. "We are not proposing kicking people off their land," says Reed Noss. "These are places of conservation significance that we have to work to protect through various means. I still think there is way too much compromise—ideally you compromise with people who share similar values but see different ways of getting there, so you work out an agreement that you can live with. That is why Dave can get along with many ranchers. They share enough values, a love of the land, even if they disagree about cows they can agree about how ranching can be done in a friendlier way."[34]

＊ ＊ ＊

If ranchers and Earth First!ers can break bread together, anything is possible. The changes in land-use policy necessary to reach the goals of The Wildlands Project or any broad-scale conservation effort require changing public values, a process made possible by inspiring people with a positive vision of the future. Big conservation, and indeed democracy itself, depend utterly on both hope and broad participation from all sectors of society. Participatory, grassroots processes are essential because governments make decisions about land-use planning and regulation at the local level for both public and private land. But that local-scale planning needs the regional and continental-scale context; communities need to see the cover of the jigsaw puzzle box in order to see where their particular piece fits.

For Michael Soulé, the decentralized approach of The Wildlands Project offers a way past the ritualized battles between industry lobbyists and conservation activists in the centers of government. He is not naive about how hard this will be. "It will require thousands of meetings, workshops, conversations, and cups of coffee in thousands of cities, towns, and farm houses," Soulé writes. The payoff, however, could be profound: "To the degree that the project invigorates bioregional consciousness and a sense of community, it is one trail back from social alienation."[35]

Yet, the outcomes of community-based consensus processes are not always good for nature; unless everyone can be heard, the process is less like democracy in action and more like the traditional process whereby local economic interests capture the federal land management agencies and push decisions toward resource extraction and away from conservation. Legal scholar Robert Keiter points out that to avoid the "tyranny of the local," local decisions must be both legally and scientifically accountable. Keiter also notes that some issues, such as endangered species and wilderness, are not amenable to locally negotiated solutions, so we will always need strong environmental laws like the Endangered Species Act, and the ability to create national monuments or ban logging in some areas.[36]

For some conservation practitioners, The Wildlands Project's emphasis on making maps and designing networks of reserves can harden into dogma. Not all conservation problems can be solved with a better, more scientific set of protected areas. But the maps are tangible and the process of making them is attractive, so many grassroots groups adopt it almost without question, regardless of the physical or social context. As some critics put it, in the Wildlands approach, there is one prescription, and that is the reserve-design prescription.

Translating the broad vision of The Wildlands Project into something concrete has been difficult. "The challenge we commissioned ourselves to deal with was beyond that of any other conservation organization because of our emphasis on large carnivores, large processes, and connectivity," says Michael Soulé. "We didn't know how to do it. We knew what had to be done, but translating that into product, into plans, blueprints, alternative land-use maps and to strategies to implement them was a real challenge, and it took us seven or eight years to figure it out."

One of the first tasks is to break the problem down into more manageable pieces, both spatially and conceptually. The Wildlands Project has identified what it calls four "megalinkages" in North America, enormous stretches of land that need to be stitched together: the arctic/boreal mega-linkage, from Alaska to Newfoundland; the Atlantic, from Maine to Florida; the spine of the continent, from Alaska, down the Rockies, and all the way to Panama; and the Pacific, from British Columbia to Baja. Within each of these are wildlands networks, and within each network are a handful of critical connections.

The most surprising of the megalinkages may be in the Northeast. Most of The Wildlands Project's planning efforts are in the West, with its vast tracts of public land and widely scattered population. The east has little federal land, and lots of small landowners. The exception is the northern forests that stretch from western New York into northern Maine. Conservationists have proposed a new national park for these woods, Maine North Woods National Park, which would be larger than Yellowstone and Yosemite combined. Timber companies currently own most of the land, but many are looking to sell, and millions of acres have already changed hands.

Some analyses by The Wildlands Project suggest that Vermont is going to be key in terms of connectivity from Maine to the Adirondacks and back up into Canada. Still, there are those who argue that you cannot do landscape-scale conservation in Vermont, because the largest private landowner in the state only owns a few thousand acres. The irony is that large landscape conservation is in at least one sense not really about large landscapes. Of course it is easier to put together a jigsaw puzzle with a few large pieces, but it can be done with smaller pieces as well. The point is to connect one piece to another.

The rhetoric of conservation often reeks of despair, and for good reason; there is much in the onslaught of industrial culture to despair over. The point of The Wildlands Project is not to paper over the bad news but to offer an alternative, without apology. "Timidity in conservation planning is a betrayal of the land," write Michael Soulé and Reed Noss. "The greatest impediment to rewilding is an unwillingness to imagine it." Imagination, an appreciation for grasslands full of bison and oceans full of orcas and otters, and concern for the ecological legacy we leave to our children's children: all are prerequisites for realizing a vision for conservation across vast stretches of time and space, and all are lacking. The science, politics, and economics to support that vision are still aborning.

The Wildlands Project is a bold idea, but still incomplete. While a broad-scale perspective on top predators, as The Wildlands Project advocates, may help restore the ecology off Alaska's coast, the science of big conservation goes beyond wilderness areas and fascinating discoveries like the complex dance between great whales, orcas, and otters off the Kenai Peninsula. Actually making bold conservation visions a reality goes beyond science alone. Fundamental to The Wildlands Project—or, for that matter, any attempt at continental-scale conservation—is knowing what we are trying to conserve, knowing why we need to put that park or that bike trail or that housing development in one place and not another, and ultimately knowing what sort of a world we want to leave behind. The last is a question of ethics, and the answer will grow from thousands of breakfast table debates to a national and eventually international dialogue. The first two are questions of science, for which we need a far more systematic approach to conservation than we have used so far. Just such an approach is beginning to gel, based on the oldest conservation method of all, the one Noah used: save some of everything.

CHAPTER 3

SAVE SOME OF EVERYTHING

We abuse land because we regard it as a commodity belonging
to us. When we see land as a community to which we belong,
we may begin to use it with love and respect.
ALDO LEOPOLD

Once upon a time, an intrepid adventurer could hike from Canada to
Tierra del Fuego and never be entirely confident that he was not being
stalked by a puma. Pumas had the widest natural distribution of any mammal in the Western Hemisphere other than humans, living everywhere
from mountains to prairies, temperate zones to the tropics. Though pumas
remain in many areas—to the dismay of many a nervous hiker—their
range continues to shrink. We can "save the pumas" by maintaining them
in some remote corner of the Yukon and letting them disappear everywhere else, but such stilted and miserly conservation leads first to biological and eventually to spiritual impoverishment. For true conservation we
need to save not only pumas but puma-ness: the splendid variety of conditions and relationships that enable pumas to exist and that pumas in turn
help shape across their enormous range.[1]

Puma-ness—or, in more scientific language, representation—lies at
the heart of modern conservation as embodied in The Wildlands Project,
but even more so in organizations like The Nature Conservancy, World
Wildlife Fund, and the Wildlife Conservation Society. These organizations, which are older and more mainstream than The Wildlands Project,
have heightened the credibility of conservation at the scale of an ecoregion
or a large landscape and strengthened the science by bringing in new view-
points and new approaches. In turn the development of the science, particularly the science behind representation, has profoundly altered those
organizations by changing the scale at which they work. Conserving an
entire ecoregion means just that—the whole thing, including parks and
farms and trout streams and suburbs.

A simple but effective strategy for surmounting that daunting challenge may be to make protected areas bigger. Eric Dinerstein, senior scientist with World Wildlife Fund, points out in his book *Tigerland* that preventive medicine may be the best treatment for avoiding extinction: make the reserves or the conservation landscapes big enough and the problems will largely take care of themselves. Dinerstein, an innovative thinker who helped lead the development of ecoregion-based conservation, draws an analogy to a branch of holistic medicine that claims that half of all the symptoms people complain about to their doctors are a result of dehydration. A few glasses of water could cure their ills. Similarly, says Dinerstein, most of the current management problems of wildlife biologists could be avoided if only the landscape or the parks were big enough in the first place. Protecting large blocks of natural habitat maintains the health of natural ecosystems and avoids expensive conservation efforts, just like rehydration solves a multitude of health concerns in humans before they become seriously threatening.[2]

Ecologist Michael Rosenzweig, who teaches ecology and evolutionary biology at the University of Arizona in Tucson, calls this the "tyranny of space." If we reduce the amount of natural area on the planet to 5 or 10 percent of what it once was, eventually we will be left with 5 to 10 percent of the original diversity. "There will be no bargains," writes Rosenzweig. "We'll get what we pay for."[3]

So we need to protect more. But just locking up the land no one wants for anything else will still save at most a sliver of the planet's diversity. We need to think rigorously about exactly what we want to conserve, where we want to conserve it, and how we plan to go about the process.

Noah had it easy; at least when he found dry land all he had to do was open the ark and let the animals fend for themselves in an empty landscape. Would-be modern Noahs have two jobs, as scientists Michael Scott and Blair Csuti have pointed out: ensuring that all species have places to live and that those places will last. In conservation lingo, that means selecting reserves and then designing them appropriately, but in simpler terms it means answering two questions: Where should we work, and how should we work there? Conservation has long had inadequate answers to these questions. The answer to the question of where to work usually amounts to "wherever we can," and that simply is not good enough.

Representation offers some guidance. Representation, simply and powerfully, means saving some of everything. While we need more than two of each species, and need to do our best to ensure that all species are protected, we also need to account for the full spectrum of environmental variation, from highest to lowest, wettest to driest, inside and outside protected areas, and at every level of biological organization, from genes to species to communities to landscapes.

Representation offers the fundamental alternative to opportunism, the far too common method of relying on happy political accidents and scraps from industry's table in gathering enough strictly protected (or at least carefully used) land to ensure the survival of all native species and their habitats. In any given area, maintaining the full array of physical habitats and environmental gradients requires a representative network of reserves large enough to accommodate the disturbances that shape each ecosystem, including fires that cover thousands of acres and wind storms that cover just a handful, and large enough to accommodate many wide-ranging carnivores.[4]

Opportunism is the first refuge of a conservationist. While people have been setting aside land for one reason or another for millennia, in doing so they protected prerogative or spirituality first; nature was an afterthought at most. Until the last half of the twentieth century, decisions about which areas to protect have rarely if ever addressed ecological concerns. Some areas protect water catchments or control soil erosion, but those are exceptions. In the United States, federal assessments of wilderness study areas focus largely on how often people use them for recreation, not how well they protect species or ecosystems.[5] Without either a broad vision or a rigorous plan, and without the political clout that comes from connecting to the values of people who live on and work the land, conservationists have generally settled for whatever land is available. That guarantees minimalism and eventually failure; we cannot save some of everything if we take as a given that all the best land will be used for something other than conservation.

Conservation has for generations focused on those relatively small areas containing spectacular vistas or particularly charismatic species. Island biogeography showed us that most if not all national parks are too small. More recent developments in conservation biology tell us that they often are in the wrong places as well.

In the United States and most other places, opportunism rather than science drove the creation of national parks and wilderness areas. Parks usually become parks for scenery and recreation, and for what they are not —not farms, not mines, not near town. Remote and unusable land costs less to protect, and usually fits at least a generalized notion of what intact and untouched landscapes look like. As a result, protected areas tend to cover high altitudes or wetlands, while productive and diverse low-altitude forests remain outside of the reserve system. Even John Steinbeck, not noted for his expertise in ecology, saw the trend in *Travels with Charley*: "It is my opinion that we enclose and celebrate the freaks of our nation and of our civilization. Yellowstone National Park is no more representative of America than Disneyland."[6]

The lack of ecological insight in the design of protected areas means these areas in fact protect only some elements of the earth's natural heritage. Some environments have large percentages of their total areas protected; others have little or none. Take the Klamath-Siskiyou region of northern California and southern Oregon, one of the biologically richest parts of the United States, as one example. In that region, 65 percent of the current protected areas contain just three classes of habitat types, and represent cool, high-elevation sites and areas with poor soils. Nearly half of the coldest, poorest soil class is protected, but just one-tenth of 1 percent of the low-elevation, warm, best soil is protected. The pattern repeats over and over again: the public owns mountains and ridgetops, but individuals own the rich valley bottoms. The species and communities on the private land have no guarantee of protection. Nationwide, private landowners hold more than 90 percent of the productive, low-elevation land. The most thorough study so far suggests that protected areas in the United States are heavily biased, with the majority of different habitats occurring only rarely in reserves.[7]

For conservation at the national or continental scale to succeed, the design of parks and other protected areas will need to build on their ecological importance rather than their economic irrelevance. Getting beyond opportunism also means understanding which areas are most important and why, and that means seeing the big picture while at the same time not losing the details of which species live in which places.

The incessant cry from industry that most any conservation effort means locking up exploitable natural resources—an exaggeration at best, propaganda at worst—reflects the belief that setting aside productive land or water is a waste, an ideology embodied in water laws in the United States that explicitly define "wasted" as water left in the river for the fish. That attitude, coupled with the political power of big industries, places intense pressure on governments to avoid politically costly confrontation by protecting areas that don't need protection.

The argument that national parks exist where they do because that land was otherwise worthless, made most pointedly by the historian Alfred Runte, can go too far.[8] Political forces that oppose all new protected areas and try to reduce the size of existing ones present a far greater challenge to conservation than having a few too many parks protecting mostly rocks, snow, and desert. Many parks also protect land that had economic value when it was set aside. For example, Kings Canyon National Park contains a prime dam site, Redwood National Park contains over $1 billion worth of timber, and the Gila Wilderness protects some of the finest old-growth ponderosa pine forest in the world. Not all national parks were set aside for scenery, either. Mount McKinley was protected in 1917 as a wildlife reserve, and the Everglades was set aside in 1934 as a biological reserve.

The United States created a nearly unmatched system of protected areas, even if the rationale for selecting the parks—beauty, recreation, inspiration—seems old-fashioned in light of modern conservation biology. Applying rigorous scientific thinking to the creation of parks does not mean ignoring those values, but rather adding to them. The realization that existing reserves cannot carry the whole weight of conservation does not in any way minimize the critical role they play. Existing reserves form the backbone for conservation; identifying their shortcomings merely points out what needs to come next.[9]

ONE STEP BEYOND OPPORTUNISM

Scientists have been advocating a scientific approach to designing nature reserves for over a century.[10] For just about that long, however, politicians have been quite content to ignore them. The first call for a representative system of reserves came from Australia in 1890. Nearly three decades later, the Ecological Society of America began preparing a list of all "preserved and preservable" areas in North America and urged the protection of those areas that were under serious threat.

The society created the Committee on Preservation of Natural Areas for Ecological Study and asked Victor Shelford to lead it. Shelford was among the country's leading ecologists, but few people now remember him. Shelford's committee looked for areas intact enough to lend themselves to long-term research, and reported to the society in 1920. Shelford continued the research and in 1926 published the *Naturalist's Guide to the Americas*, for its time the most detailed and definitive account of natural areas in the Western Hemisphere.

Shelford's work marked some of the earliest applications of biological goals and scientific principles to reserve selection. He argued for more reserves in order to "insure a proper representation of all important forest types," and was an early proponent of protecting carnivores and large, unmanaged wildernesses. Shelford also advocated creating what he called "buffer areas" around reserves, where some strictly controlled human use of resources would be allowed. Some four decades later, that notion would become essential in the global effort to create protected areas, and the term "buffer zone" would eventually be standard parlance in conservation biology.[11]

By the 1930s, Shelford, Aldo Leopold and other wildlife biologists began to see protected areas as part of a larger landscape. Shelford and the preservation committee increasingly became advocates for conservation, putting them at odds with the leadership of the Ecological Society of America, which wanted to keep the organization neutral. The debate dissolved into acrimony by the mid-1940s, and finally the society eliminated Shelford's committee. Undeterred, Shelford and his colleagues founded a new organization, the Ecologists' Union, in 1946. They would later rename the organization The Nature Conservancy, after a British agency that specialized in setting aside open space and wildlife preserves. The Nature Conservancy was incorporated in the United States in 1951.

The Conservancy emerged from a group of scientists interested in research and advocacy. In its early years, however, the organization did little of either. Staffed entirely by volunteers, few of whom had any scientific training, the Conservancy worked purely opportunistically; if land that had obvious natural values came on the market, they bought it, or tried to. As the organization grew and hired fulltime staff, it created state chapters that worked independently, pursuing the best conservation land deals they could find. The organization rightly prided itself on being focused on action rather than reflection and analysis: time was short, so make the best deal you can, protect as much land as you can, and move on to the next deal. Success was measured in terms of money raised and spent, and total land protected—"bucks and acres" in Conservancy parlance. Only later would the organization attempt to determine what species or communities existed on the land it had purchased. The Conservancy's original strategy, if the term even applies, had the virtue of simplicity, but it could only go so far. As the organization grew, it began to buy more and more land, and an effective way to determine what land was actually worth buying became a pressing need.

The Nature Conservancy hired its first staff scientist, Robert Jenkins, Jr., in 1974. Cantankerous, brilliant, and opinionated, he would leave a lasting mark on the organization and conservation in general. Jenkins recognized that buying land and then surveying its species got the process exactly backward. The Conservancy needed to know which species and communities could be found in which places, and target its efforts to protect the biologically most important of those places. Jenkins was building the scientific foundation for a representational approach to conservation, a way to truly save some of everything.

Jenkins also understood that finding every species, or even a fraction of all species, was out of the question. So instead of focusing just on species, he devised a system for inventory and analysis of both species and natural communities. Scientists have devised dozens of definitions of natural communities, most based on the species of vegetation (redwoods versus oaks) that are present, its structure (trees versus grass), or both. The details of how to classify natural communities spawned years of debate. For our purposes, it is enough to understand that natural communities form recognizable places on the landscape; they are categorized with names like "black spruce bog," or "subalpine fir/grouseberry forest."[12] In the mid-1970s, Jenkins termed species and communities "elements of natural diversity," the conceptual equivalent of biological diversity, a phrase that would not be coined for another decade.

His work laid the foundation for a network of scientists who began gathering detailed information on the distribution and status of species and communities, called the Natural Heritage Network. The Nature Conservancy began creating the Natural Heritage Network in South Carolina in 1974. That was just one year after the passage of the Endangered Species Act, so the effort was underway almost immediately to put those species on maps. Natural Heritage programs now gather information in every state—for example, the Florida Natural Areas Inventory, which provided the data that helped refine Reed Noss's map of protected areas in the state, was a Conservancy creation—and across Canada and in eleven countries in Latin America, where they are called Conservation Data Centers. The programs usually operate within state governments, though a few reside at universities or local Conservancy chapters. An independent national organization called NatureServe represents the global Heritage network and develops new methods and tools to help decision makers put the Heritage data to use.[13]

Jenkins developed a methodology for the Heritage effort based on sophisticated classifications of landscapes and vegetation and lists of vulnerable species and communities. In that methodology, natural communities serve as "coarse filters" for conservation: if we protect all major community types, we will protect most of the species found in those communities as well, thus relieving scientists of the impossible task of collecting detailed information on every living thing as a condition for adequate conservation.

The greatest risk of the coarse filter is focusing on the filter—the habitats and natural communities—as objectives in and of themselves, rather than on the species the filters are intended to catch. "At the end of the day, when we are long gone and our descendants are judging us, if we have not preserved the species, they will consider us to have failed," says David Wilcove, now professor of public affairs and ecology and evolutionary biology at Princeton University after years as a scientist with various conservation organizations, including The Wilderness Society and Environmental Defense. "If we become protectors of open space as opposed to protectors of the species within that open space, I don't think we will be viewed as having been good conservationists. You can't say you are interested in saving the short-grass prairie without thinking about prairie dogs, plovers, and ferruginous hawks."[14]

Focusing on the large landscapes in and of themselves, argues Wilcove, is "analogous to preserving the set of a play, the stage, the props, the lighting, and then not really checking to make sure all the actors showed up. The actors are difficult, they are idiosyncratic, they're moody, they get sick, they break their legs. So you end up saying, 'Well, look, what I can do is provide a magnificent set. That is in my control, I can make sure that the stagehands are all there and I am pretty sure I can get most of the actors, but you know, if Polonius doesn't show up, it is still 95 percent of Hamlet.'"

The broad-scale, coarse-filter approach, says Wilcove, must come to grips with the species that fall through the coarse filter, little-known species like the mountain mallow and the Delhi Sands flower-loving fly, the only fly on the endangered species list. The Nature Conservancy estimated, probably overestimated more likely, that the coarse filter would conserve 85 to 90 percent of all species. Neither the Conservancy nor anyone else has definitively tested this assumption, as such a test requires data that are either unavailable or prohibitively expensive to acquire.[15] To account for all species, Jenkins devised a second, finer filter built on identifying and classifying the rare and endangered species and communities one at a time.

In theory, the two filters together should capture the full range of species and communities.[16] The fine filter—focusing one at a time on the species that fall through the coarse filter—should account for the mallow, the flower-loving fly, and others of their unfortunate ilk. In practice, the fine filter is the grunt work of conservation, painstaking and too often unrewarding. "The fine filter is a much more frustrating job, a job with much less likelihood of long-term success," says Wilcove.

The Heritage effort was one of the first steps toward a systematic approach to conservation, but the framework would evolve along with the evolution of conservation science itself. The methods Jenkins devised actually provided too much detail if the Conservancy, or anyone else, was to take a regional perspective. Eventually, the Conservancy would shift from the relatively fine scale dictated by Jenkins's elements of diversity to a far broader approach. In doing so—in moving beyond the boundaries of its own preserves—the Conservancy would need to face the challenge of changing the management of land it did not own, which would inevitably mean finding common ground with people who were not part of what was usually defined as the conservation community.

THE NEXT STEP

High drama in Hawaii in 1982 led to another application of the sort of detailed information about species that the Heritage programs collected.

Mike Scott, an ornithologist with the Fish and Wildlife Service, discovered that the state's rare birds faced imminent threat of extinction, despite a number of protected areas, in a classic case of the parks not protecting the things that needed protection the most. Scott was mapping the distribution, abundance, and habitat associations of the state's endemic forest birds. In the days before GIS and high-powered laptops, he put the distribution maps on sheets of Mylar (the same stuff they use in *Gray's Anatomy* to overlay drawing of muscles, blood vessels, and organs onto a drawing of a human skeleton) and laid these maps on top of maps of Hawaii's protected areas. The maps overlapped by less than 10 percent; Hawaii's birds lived largely outside the protected areas. Scott and a few colleagues carried these simple maps around to The Nature Conservancy and the state and federal government agencies. In another testament to the power of maps, the Conservancy and the agencies looked at Scott's work and set about creating the Hakalau Forest National Wildlife Refuge, the Conservancy's Kona Hema Preserve, and several other reserves to protect the birds.[17]

That experience led Scott and others at the Fish and Wildlife Service to launch a nationwide effort, beginning in Idaho, to map broad classes of habitats—such as mountain big sagebrush or subalpine fir—that occur over wide areas, and from those make a series of hypotheses about which species (mostly but not exclusively vertebrates) are likely to occur where. As in Hawaii, these predictions of animal distribution could be compared to maps of the existing protected areas, and the places where more protection was needed would become obvious. This effort thus was essentially a search for the holes in the protected areas system of the United States, and it became known as gap analysis.[18]

Gap analysis offers perhaps the best example of a conservation program based on representation goals. By using landscape-sized samples of habitat as a coarse filter, gap analysis searches biological regions for areas rich in landscape diversity. The focus on vegetation types can help identify large areas of concentrated species richness across gradients—in elevation or from wetter to drier, for example—and help insure that protected areas contain at least one representative of all species and community types.[19]

Gap analysis has limitations, some highly technical. Most importantly, it does not suggest how to fill the gaps it finds. Even so, gap analysis provides a useful tool for aligning large-scale land use and conservation, and by the mid-1990s some forty states had completed or begun gap analysis projects. More and more scientists at universities and in government agencies saw the importance of the coarse filter, and the concept of representation.[20] Gap analysis represents one more approach to answering a central question of ecoregional conservation: Where should reserves be located?

❧ ❧ ❧

As Mike Scott and his colleagues refined gap analysis throughout the 1990s, a group of innovative (and remarkably prolific) Australian scientists also grappled with that question. They were led by Bob Pressey of the New South Wales National Parks and Wildlife Service, the government agency responsible for developing and maintaining the state's parks and reserve system. Pressey and his colleagues refined the idea of representation into a specialty called systematic conservation planning—the branch of conservation biology that seeks to identify conservation options by making explicit where on the ground conservation needs to happen.

Pressey and his colleagues were not the first to call for systematic planning on a large scale; that idea finds expression in voices as diverse as the Scottish botanist Patrick Geddes, President Theodore Roosevelt, and the historian Frederick Jackson Turner. Most of all, the architect, sociologist, and writer Lewis Mumford and the other founders of the Regional Planning Association of America saw regional planning as a process bringing together climate, soil, vegetation, industry, and culture. In 1925, Mumford described a vision many conservationists could easily endorse today: "Regional planning is the New Conservation—the conservation of human values hand in hand with natural resources."[21] One of Mumford's close colleagues, Benton MacKaye, proposed the Appalachian Trail as an instrument of regional and communal reconstruction, linking conservation with community and regional planning.[22]

Conservation planning, far from being something to rush through in order to get to conservation action, transforms the very idea of conservation: instead of reacting to local threats, conservationists can clearly identify what conservation will require across whole regions. The only way to reach the goal of representation—to save some of everything—is to follow such a structured, systematic approach to conservation planning.[23] Conservation plans offer visions of a desirable future.

The conservation plan that Reed Noss and Larry Harris developed for Florida in the mid-1980s set an early example of how to make explicit recommendations about what land to protect. Since then, the science of conservation planning has deepened significantly, and now includes sophisticated tools for identifying conservation targets, setting goals, and designing networks of reserves, a process that Craig Groves, a leader in the field who works for the Wildlife Conservation Society in Bozeman, Montana, calls "drafting a conservation blueprint."[24]

Drafting a blueprint involves some fundamental tasks: compile the available information, identify conservation goals, review existing parks and other protected areas, select new areas to protect, think big, and get to work. Applying the principles of conservation planning across regions that cover thousands of square miles gives planners the commanding viewpoint to see how important biological areas lie on the land and to separate them from considerations of ownership or jurisdiction. From that high point, planners can see the connections on the landscape (or the lack of those connections), and how things like housing developments or logging concessions or new roads threaten important areas or ecological processes. They then can plan whole systems of interconnected, complementary conservation areas on an ecoregional or continental scale, and begin to account for dynamics such as the movement of animals and natural disturbances that individual areas cannot accommodate.[25]

* * *

Representation as a goal of such networks is about the location and number of species and natural communities, that is, the pattern of life on the land. A suitable conservation plan will ensure that the broad natural pattern remains in place, while recognizing that the details will shift. Like a kaleidoscope, the pieces move—patches of forest burn and meadows appear; oxbows become lakes; floods scour riverbanks—but the whole does not shatter.

Regional conservation networks would be complicated enough if pattern was the only important consideration, if natural systems really were just like kaleidoscopes. But pattern is only half the story. Conservation must also account for the evolutionary and ecological processes that maintain existing species and enable new ones to emerge over time, the reshuffling of genes among populations of plants and animals, and the fires, floods, and droughts.[26]

Systematic conservation planning produces a system of conservation areas that represent a hypothesis about the maintenance of both species and processes. The prediction is that a given system of reserves will maintain more of both the patterns and the processes in the long term than alternatives based only on pattern representation. Unfortunately, for the most part this hypothesis cannot be tested; the scale and nature of the problem rule out experiments. Scientists can monitor species and processes and adjust conservation priorities accordingly, but time is not on our side. Conservation biologist Mark Shaffer, who has held nearly every kind of job possible in conservation, puts it like this: "We are conducting a test on the planet for which there will be no replicate."[27]

Even if scientists could devise the ideal experiments, science alone falls short. Conservation planning can only reveal the consequences of choices that are driven far more by social, economic, and political imperatives. Taking a conservation plan, in all its scientific detail, from conception into action requires a land ethic that guides and informs society's decisions.

Conservation planning articulates nature's bottom line and fits people into the landscape. It provides a basis for understanding ecological variation, and if we understand that variation perhaps we can learn to accommodate it—or relearn, since many cultures live with ecological variation as a matter of course. Those cultures do not live in a state of nature, but they remember what modern, technological society has forgotten: how to learn from the land, and use it appropriately and according to what the ecology will allow. Wes Jackson, founder and president of the Land Institute, a Kansas-based organization dedicated to developing ecologically and culturally enduring agriculture, writes that "nature provides the measure, the standard, the lesson." Jackson writes about farming as the forest does, and fitting farming to the land, but he draws from agriculture much broader lessons about how the unique mosaic of each landscape defines how we should use, or not use, that land.[28]

Conservation planning demonstrates what we need to do to ensure the survival of other species. Planning enables us to get out of the endless debate about human versus nonhuman interests and land uses and recognize that the issue is not only human aspiration but the survival of Creation.[29]

THE TYRANNY OF THE RAINFOREST

Representation or puma-ness offers a subtle, complex answer to the questions of where to put reserves and focus our conservation efforts, but it cannot answer all questions. A representational approach alone will not capture particularly rich areas, important migratory stopovers or breeding areas, patches of old-growth forest, or roadless areas, nor will such an approach conserve vital ecological processes. Simply ensuring that reserves represent all the species and communities of an area says nothing about the efficiency of those reserves, or whether those species and communities face grave risk or no risk at all—whether they are, in scientific terms, viable. Will the grizzly bears in Yellowstone or the jaguars in Manu National Park in Bolivia survive for a hundred years? A thousand years? A system of reserves could represent all the species and ecological processes of a region, yet offer no assurance that any given species would survive long enough to be really considered conserved.[30]

Another approach, far simpler and more intuitive than representation, rose from the ashes of burned tropical rainforests. Public awareness of the importance of tropical rainforests and the threats to them grew throughout the 1980s, helped by the tireless efforts of scientists like E. O. Wilson. Extensive news coverage of the horrifying yearly fires that consumed huge swaths of forest, as well as tragedies such as the murder in 1988 of Chico Mendes, a rubber tapper and grassroots environmentalist from the Brazilian Amazon, also helped sear the South American rainforest into the global environmental consciousness.[31]

The destruction of the rainforest spawned a huge popular and scientific literature. In the public mind, conservation came to mean literally putting out the fires in the Amazon. Since tropical rainforests harbor an astonishing number of species they came to be equated with the word biodiversity, which a group of scientists led by E. O. Wilson coined in 1988 essentially as a marketing tool, to capture in a word all of life on Earth and the processes that support it. Wilson and others, particularly the British ecologist Norman Myers, provided the scientific foundation for a global movement to save the rainforest, providing grim statistics of deforestation and the consequent realization that only five other times in the history of life on Earth have as many species vanished as are vanishing now.[32]

Myers then took another step. In 1988, he identified ten areas in the tropics that contain a high concentration of species, many of them endemic—that is, found nowhere else on Earth—and that are disappearing rapidly. He called these areas hotspots and suggested that the way to get the biggest bang from the conservation buck, at least in terms of number of species saved, would be to concentrate protection efforts on those areas— among them Madagascar, western Amazonia, and Brazil's Atlantic Forest. Myers and others would expand that initial list to twenty-five hotspots (including fifteen tropical forests), which together contain 44 percent of the world's plant species and 35 percent of the vertebrates, and cover just 1.4 percent of the land surface of the planet.[33]

With its focus on the tropics, the hotspots approach fits with the general perception that the terms "tropics" and "conservation" are synonymous. As the hotspots concept attracted more and more attention, it reinforced what Kent Redford calls "the tyranny of the tropical rainforest." He began pointing out the dangers of an exclusive focus on rainforests in 1990, at a time when the most advanced research into conservation planning remained little known outside of Australia.[34] "Before I knew about representation I was a representation advocate for moral, ethical reasons," says Redford from the Wildlife Conservation Society international conservation headquarters, an unimposing set of trailers just off a parking lot at New York's Bronx Zoo. He would soon have a chance to put those beliefs to the test.

❋ ❋ ❋

Other scientists shared Redford's concern over the tyranny of the tropical rainforest and hotspots. Two of them, Eric Dinerstein and David Olson, dramatically reshaped the way World Wildlife Fund (WWF) applied conservation science soon after Redford began publishing articles about the need to conserve more than rainforests.

In 1993, Dinerstein and Olson joined forces with Russian and American biologists to assess the condition of protected areas in Russia, which has a network of strictly protected nature reserves called zapovedniks.[35] Russia's seventy-six zapovedniks form one of the oldest and largest networks of protected areas in the world.

Russia provided a great opportunity for conservation, even if it lay far outside the tropics. Though the collapse of the Soviet Union raised the risk of sudden and uncontrolled development across the country, most of the zapovedniks remained intact, with little or no human settlement. "The Wildlands Project is great," says Dinerstein, "but the experiment has already been done. It's called Russia. Half the country is still wilderness, so if you want to see how a wildlands network would function, study the old system of nature reserves there and see how effective that is."

Dinerstein and the others found that while the Russian system contains areas large enough to maintain viable populations of large mammals and ecological processes, it still misses some important areas. The lesson for Dinerstein and Olson was that even having what Dinerstein calls "whopping big reserve systems" offers no guarantees that you are conserving everything that needs conserving. WWF's analysis provided even more evidence of the need for a coherent framework for making decisions about conservation that worked at every scale, from postage-stamp parks to huge zapovedniks to national reserve networks to whole continents to the entire planet.

The work in Russia started Dinerstein and Olson thinking about how to build such a framework. They drew heavily on biogeography—not island biogeography, with its focus on extinction, but biogeography more generally, with its theories of why a plant or an animal occurs in one place on Earth but not another. While biogeography has a long and noble genealogy, conservationists had not yet plumbed its depths. "We had this whole science of biogeography just floating along out there," says Dinerstein. "How do we bring it into conservation? We had this understanding that there is all this amazing stuff out there on all the continents: How do we put it into a coherent framework to make sure that the most amazing stuff gets addressed first?"

The emergence of hotspots as an organizing principle also provided a counterpoint. "We love rainforests, we all did our Ph.D.s there," says Dinerstein, "but we also have studied enough biology and biogeography to know that a comprehensive strategy is going to have some tundra and boreal forests and other things that may have low diversity but still have to be part of some global strategy. We need a coherent framework that allows us to make the right choices for our portfolio." Dinerstein and Olson wanted a system that would not allow the rainforest to reign supreme and that would include dry forests and deserts as well. This would be the science to complement Kent Redford's moral and ethical concern about the focus on tropical rainforests at the expense of nearly everything else. "Here is a place where the science caught up with the morality," says Dinerstein.

❖ ❖ ❖

In 1993, Redford left a faculty post at the University of Florida to join The Nature Conservancy as director of science for its Latin America and Caribbean Program. In that capacity, he participated in an effort, led by WWF and the World Bank, to map the conservation regions of Latin America and the Caribbean and assess their status. This project was a turning point for Redford, The Nature Conservancy, WWF, and the whole idea of broad-scale conservation.

WWF's priority-setting exercise for Latin America and the Caribbean was the next step after the work in Russia. The WWF scientists sought to move beyond evaluations that were based largely on species lists to a new framework that also incorporated maintaining ecosystem and habitat diversity. The study elevated representation of all ecosystem and habitat types to a first principle, and recognized landscape-level features as an essential guide for effective conservation planning. The fundamental goals of the project were (1) representation of all distinct natural communities, (2) maintenance of ecological and evolutionary processes that create and sustain biodiversity, (3) maintenance of viable populations of species, and (4) conservation of blocks of natural habitat large enough to be responsive to large-scale periodic disturbances and long-term changes (e.g., global warming). Unlike the Russia project, the work in Latin America and the Caribbean did not identify a system of protected areas, though it considered degree of protection as one variable.[36]

In Russia, scientists had divided the country into fourteen large bioregions. In Latin America and the Caribbean, Dinerstein, Olson, and their colleagues took a more rigorous approach. They decided they needed a biological hierarchy, from broad ecosystem types down to specific ecological regions, to organize their efforts and get past the reliance on political boundaries that more often than not have no ecological significance. First, they identified five major ecosystems: tropical broadleaf forests, conifer/ temperate broadleaf forests, grasslands, deserts and other dry formations, and mangroves. They further classified those ecosystems into eleven kinds of habitat, which they termed major habitat types. Finally, they identified 191 discrete examples of those habitats, which they called ecoregions—distinct assemblages of natural communities that share a large majority of their species, ecological dynamics, and environmental conditions, and whose ecological interactions are critical for their long-term persistence.

Delineating the ecoregions of Latin America and the Caribbean took two years. Once the map was complete, the next step was for a team of scientists to determine how much habitat remained in each, whether that habitat was distributed in several large blocks or many small fragments, how fast humans were converting it to other uses, and how much was formally protected. The scientists also looked at how distinctive each ecoregion was—only comparing forests to forests, and deserts to deserts —based partly on the hotspot criteria of richness and endemism but also based on how rare the habitat is globally, the size of the ecoregion, and the occurrence of unusual biological phenomena, like the forests in the Amazon that flood and where fish leave the rivers to live for a time among the trees.

This analysis provided the information necessary to then rank each ecoregion by distinctiveness and threat. The most distinctive areas facing severe threats would be the highest conservation priority; those less distinct and less at risk would be lesser priorities. Finally, within these priorities, the scientists chose ecoregions that represented all of the major habitats and biogeographic zones of Latin America and the Caribbean.

In designing the work in Latin America and the Caribbean, WWF settled on the ecoregion as the fundamental unit for conservation. In 1944, Aldo Leopold wrote that "thinking like a mountain" was essential to conservation. In 1997, David Olson and Eric Dinerstein wrote that ecoregional planning "is simply trying to think more like an ecosystem." They would go on to map all the ecoregions on Earth and, using the methods developed in Latin America, set priorities among them for conservation. The result was called the Global 200 (though the list grew to include 238 ecoregions).[37]

WWF's approach provided a way past the tyranny of the rainforest. The Nature Conservancy was also ready to begin thinking more broadly about how to do conservation, largely because of pressure from its California program. By the mid-1980s, Steve McCormick was director of the California program, and he began to see the limitations of the data the Heritage program in the state was collecting. Those data, he believed, did not provide guiding principles for determining where the organization would work.[38]

In California, McCormick says, most of the Heritage data show that collection efforts were biased toward the easy-to-reach places and the easy-to-collect species—maps of places where species are collected cluster around universities and roads, leaving large areas untouched. As a result, the Conservancy's California chapter oriented its work toward sites with many plant species. "It just occurred to me in California our work was missing an element of the system scale," says McCormick, who became president of The Nature Conservancy in 2001. The Conservancy often chose to work in particularly localized natural communities, such as those on serpentine soils, an unusual soil type found more often in California than anywhere else in the United States, or in the unique Monterrey pine forests of California's central coast. Overlooked in such an approach were other habitats, such as blue oak woodlands. Blue oaks, unique to California but widespread, are too common to justify a classification of endangered or threatened. As a natural community, however, blue oak woodlands are in terrible shape, as they usually occur in valley bottoms, the same places favored by developers. So blue oak woodlands bear the brunt of development, but conservationists had designed not a single large-scale protected area specifically for them.

As a first step in developing an alternative, the California chapter took a hierarchical list of natural communities in California, picked a mid-level classification—not too big, not too small—and asked about a dozen academics who had sufficient understanding of the state to identify at that mid-level which natural communities met three criteria: threatened, unique to California, and not sufficiently protected in some existing or planned park. This was one of the first attempts to plan for conservation across the whole state. It led to the development of what the Conservancy called the California Critical Areas Program, which identified the eleven most critical ecosystems in the state.

The Critical Areas Program moved the Conservancy toward working at a broader scale, but was still an incremental change. "I was struck by the fact that the Conservancy had been working in California for thirty years and I had a very hard time getting anybody to do a tally of how much biodiversity we were protecting," McCormick says. "When we got a fairly accurate representation based on all the past deals we had done—all we were doing at that time was buying land and managing it—it was a very, very small fraction of the state, even if you use the Heritage information. If we stayed on the same trajectory, we were going to lose 90 percent more. That is what got me thinking about scale."

In the early 1990s, the debate within the Conservancy revolved around whether to focus on the few shards of habitat that remain in southern California or on the relatively intact areas in the northern part of the state. In the end they decided to do both, but that required more information about the state of things in the south. As the basis for the assessment, the California chapter chose a system of bioregions, the boundaries of which were partly ecological and partly political. The California bioregions would serve as the prototype for the Conservancy's ecoregional plans.

While the California chapter experimented with bioregions, others in The Nature Conservancy looked at different ways to work at broader scales. In the early 1990s, the Conservancy launched the idea of bioreserves, areas large enough to encompass intact examples of as many as possible of the ecosystems typical of a geographic region. To begin with, Bob Jenkins simply asked the state Heritage programs and Conservation Data Centers to think bigger, to start coalescing individual sites into larger complexes, and to look for large and intact areas.

"The goal of our Bioreserve program is to make the landscape more livable for people as well as for other organisms. This is the essence of the Bioreserve idea," Jenkins wrote in 1991. "It is not a trivial experiment, for if we can develop our scientific management capacity to a sufficient level of competence, we can provide examples of human interaction with the environment that can serve as models for the world."[39]

A GEOGRAPHY OF HOPE

The bioreserve concept never became a dominant organizing principle for the Conservancy, but it marked another step in the evolution of broad-scale conservation. In 1994, the Conservancy took the next step when it created a twelve-member conservation committee consisting of scientists and leaders of some of the state chapters. John Sawhill, then president of the Conservancy, chose Steve McCormick to lead the committee and gave him the charge of coming up with a new strategy for the organization. Sawhill gave McCormick three months to finish the job. It would take two years.

Once again, maps would play a key role. A map of all the Conservancy preserves in the United States, a mass of tiny green dots, came to be known internally as the "green measles." When he first saw the map, Eric Dinerstein said it looked like an infestation of mites. For Dinerstein and the Conservancy scientists, this was an epiphany: *We have got to start doing conservation on a different scale or else we are in big trouble. Some of these pinpricks are going to disappear.* Some of the dots might have been two thousand square miles in size, but most were tiny. Steve McCormick noted that when flying over California, it was impossible to see most of the places where the Conservancy was working. If the places were too small to see, could they be having much of an impact?

Nearly all the places the Conservancy worked were the result of the same ad hoc process that led to the creation of most protected areas. In the Conservancy's case, this was partly the accumulation of land that various owners had bequeathed and the Conservancy had to manage. The organization's goal at the time was to conserve "the last of the least and the best of the rest." Some of those tiny reserves indeed protected the last examples of rare and endangered species and communities. Such clear-cut cases were themselves rare, however. The Conservancy—and every other organization attempting to carry out conservation on the ground—needed a means of determining which were really the last places and which were places that were already conserved elsewhere many times over and were too small and expensive to maintain. Without a plan, conservation could be locally effective but a global failure.

At one of the early meetings of the conservation committee, held at Muleshoe Ranch in Arizona, the scientists on the committee discussed how the Conservancy had moved into working on a broader scale with the bioreserves, but how they struggled to get beyond looking at things project-by-project. The organization needed to really get behind the broader approach and develop a new filter through which to look at its investments. "I will never forget, Kent Redford was squirming in his seat," says Brian

Richter, a biohydrologist with the Conservancy who was a member of the committee. "He had this huge roll of maps, and we had no idea what these things were. He said, 'I'm sorry, but I'm just too frustrated and I have to show you something.' He unrolled the maps, which were WWF's ecoregional maps of Latin America and the Caribbean. He said, 'This is what I want to talk about. This is what I want to do.'"

As Redford explained that he did not want to treat each ecoregion as a separate project, the other scientists began to see the potential of the system. "Once we understood what ecoregions were, which took a little while," says Brian Richter, "we started thinking about how to use that kind of a classification of the world as a guide for conservation. That was the day."[40]

The scientists' vision fit Steve McCormick's desire for a framework for defining what successful conservation would look like, a clear map of the task at hand. McCormick, Redford, and the rest of the conservation committee put together a document called *Conservation by Design*, completed in 1995, which redefined how The Nature Conservancy would do business. Instead of working state by state and site by site—even large sites like the bioreserves—the Conservancy would use ecoregions as the organizing principle. Ecoregions would provide the framework for identifying the individual places—some small enough to contain a remnant population of an endangered species, others large enough to support grizzly bears and once-in-a-century fires—that taken together would spell success: the conservation of all viable, native species and communities.

Conservation by Design is short, in its first version just five pages of heavily footnoted text and a few rather blurry maps. Yet it represented a sea change for one of the country's largest and richest conservation organizations. Land acquisition, the Conservancy's bread and butter for four decades, would not be sufficient; there were other dynamics of the landscape, like depletion or pollution of groundwater, that conservationists could not address by just buying land.

Now The Nature Conservancy had a new goal. What it needed next was a way to get there. For that they again enlisted Kent Redford to lead a team of scientists, this time to develop the methodology for translating general principles into specific conservation actions. Redford drew on Wallace Stegner for inspiration: "Wilderness can be a means of reassuring ourselves of our sanity as creatures, a part of the geography of hope."[41] *Designing a Geography of Hope: Guidelines for Ecoregion-Based Conservation in The Nature Conservancy,* unveiled in 1996, provided the first guidelines of any sort for actually saving both pumas and puma-ness at the scale of an ecoregion.

The choice of the title was no accident; it was not simply the attraction of Stegner's well-turned phrase. For Redford, McCormick, and the other leaders of this effort, an ecoregional approach really is about hope. By taking an ecoregional view, the picture of ultimate success would come into focus. "If we could protect all these places we would capture, and this was another breakthrough, not only the rare and unique and endemic and locally restricted and endangered, we would get the best examples of characteristic community types, of biodiversity," says McCormick.

Redford and the rest of the team had initially used "ecoregional planning" in the subtitle of the report, but for many longtime staff brought up in the culture of fast-paced deal-making, "planning" was a sign of paralysis. After the document was printed and ready to be distributed at a Conservancy conference in Florida, the word came down to change the title. When the conference attendees picked up their packets of materials, in addition to the usual name badges, agendas, and list of participants they found a small sticker (nicely designed to match the front cover of the report) that replaced the word *planning* with the word *conservation*. Science was making inroads, but old habits die hard.

Such resistance should come as no surprise, as taking a broad view actually reshapes conservation itself. "We have been practicing medicine at the emergency room door for too long," says Redford. "We need to be able to say, 'This is the plan.' We have to be able to offer a vision of the costs and benefits of conservation."

PART II

SCIENCE AND COMMUNITY

CHAPTER 4

CONSERVATION IN EXURBIA: FLORIDA AND CALIFORNIA

We have met the enemy, and he is us.

POGO

Okefenokee Swamp, one of the best-preserved wetlands in North America, sits atop the Georgia-Florida border. From it flows the languid Suwanee River. The swamp provides a home to over a thousand species of plants and animals, but its most famous resident was fictional: Pogo, Walt Kelley's wise possum. In the 1950s, when Kelley began his career as a cartoonist and political commentator, Okefenokee seemed as remote as the moon—though in true American fashion, speculators had a scheme to drain, log, and then farm the swamp as early as 1890. By the late 1960s, however, no place was remote. In 1970, Pogo's most quoted phrase appeared on a poster for the first Earth Day, as the forlorn possum looked over his swamp strewn with trash.

Earth Day heightened public awareness of pollution, but in 1970 no one recognized a more insidious threat to Okefenokee. The swamp itself, now a national wildlife refuge, protects one of the largest undeveloped areas on the East Coast, but it is just one part of an ecosystem that covers more than 7 million acres. Roads, subdivisions, power lines, shopping malls, canals, and fences now chew up habitat and chop greater Okefenokee into ever smaller pieces.

The habitat loss and fragmentation of Okefenokee provides yet another entry in the long list of indictments of humanity as its own worst enemy. Florida offers dramatic examples of fragmentation—in North America, perhaps matched only by California. Yet with help from scientists and people willing to think beyond their narrow self-interest, those two fast-growing states may also show the way out, and the way to reestablish ecological connections.

On their original 1985 map of a reserve network for Florida, Reed Noss and Larry Harris envisioned the entire Okefenokee ecosystem as a core reserve. That first map skimped a bit on the details, but six years later The Nature Conservancy, Florida Audubon Society, and the Florida Natural Areas Inventory developed a revised map that revealed the central challenge. The wildlife refuge protects the heart of Okefenokee, and the Osceola National Forest, about sixty miles to the south, contains another two hundred thousand acres of pine trees, swamp, and wiregrass. In between these two reserves lies about sixty thousand acres of private land called Pinhook Swamp, most of it owned by a forest-products company. Protecting this swamp, Noss and Harris realized, would connect Pinhook, Osceola National Forest, and the Greater Okefenokee ecosystem, forming an expanse of wetlands known, appropriately enough, as POGO.[1]

The state government and a coalition of private organizations eventually got together and bought most of Pinhook Swamp. Using Pinhook to tie together two existing reserves was one of the first practical applications of wildlife corridors, or linkages. The corridor concept has sparked vigorous debates among scientists and caused no end of confusion and mistrust among the general public; the property-rights crowd believes The Wildlands Project will turn everything in the country into either parks or corridors connecting them. Yet the idea that animals, particularly large carnivores, need to be able to move across the landscape and not be trapped in small reserves surrounded by increasingly hostile land uses—the most striking revelation of island biogeography—is central to any attempt to carry out broad-scale conservation. Dozens of grassroots efforts are putting the idea to the test. Core wilderness areas, says Michael Soulé, are the organs of a regional wildlands network, and the linkages between them are the arteries.[2]

YOU CAN'T GET THERE FROM HERE

The theory of island biogeography stimulated hundreds of studies of isolated habitat remnants, which collectively demonstrated that small fragments of habitat lose species rapidly, predictably, and permanently unless migrants from other areas can reach those fragments and take up residence. Michael Soulé calls this one of the strongest generalizations in the field of ecology.[3]

Isolated populations of animals can become inbred, and if the populations are small they can be wiped out by a drought, a flood, some other natural disaster, or the vagaries of reproduction. If the last two females of, say, a population of parrots lay clutches of eggs that all turn out to be males, for example, and if that population of parrots is the last one on Earth, then they are doomed.

If being isolated is harmful, it follows that being connected is beneficial. In more formal terms, island biogeography also emphasized perceptions of islands of suitable habitat in a hostile sea of nonhabitat. Concepts of habitat corridors providing linear connections through this sea developed from the application of island biogeography theory to conservation problems.[4] If other parrots of the same species can reach that habitat, then they may be able to recolonize it, and their numbers may grow. A connected landscape also permits daily or seasonal movements of animals and facilitates dispersal, as young animals leave the territory where they were born to strike out on their own. Linkages across many miles will be necessary for some species; grizzly bear populations in the northern Rockies in British Columbia need to be connected to those in Idaho and Montana to accommodate gene flow and dispersal. Linkages at that scale also offer the best hope of adapting to climate change.[5]

The final argument for the importance of large, connected landscapes —as much an aesthetic and moral argument as a scientific one—is that connection, not fragmentation, is the natural order of things. Most species evolved in heterogeneous but connected landscapes, so it makes sense to conserve or recreate them. Restoring connectivity heals the wounds of development and agriculture.[6]

Fragmentation leads to habitat and species loss as well as changes in ecological processes that can result in further decline in habitat and species. Fragmentation leads to changes in the physical and chemical fluxes across the landscape; hydrology, nutrient cycles, and wind conditions, among other things, are all considerably different in a fragmented landscape. Even low levels of connectivity in poor habitats are better than nothing, but we may need many wide corridors to help respond to global climate change. Given a choice, we should pick connected over fragmented almost every time.

As with the selection of protected areas, simply connecting areas that are unconnected now with little more to go on than a vague notion that connected is good and fragmented is bad will rarely restore an ecologically viable landscape. That would be like assembling the jigsaw puzzle without turning all the pieces right side up; you might get some pieces to fit together, but the odds of them being the right pieces are pretty slim. The goal is not connectivity per se, but rather to reverse the consequences of fragmentation, allowing species, soil, water, seeds, pollen, spores, and so on to move between habitats, ensuring genetic maintenance, demographic stability, migration, and other ecological processes. As with nearly every issue in broad-scale conservation, one size does not fit all. The kind and scale of connectivity must fit the context and address the goals of the project at hand.[7]

So far, so good. But what, exactly, does being connected mean? On a map, large green blobs with nice, straight green lines running between them like railroad tracks seem connected, and certainly better than the alternative. Such maps are aesthetically pleasing and theoretically compelling. Securing the land to create these tidy packages creates a sense of accomplishment for conservation organizations and donors alike. If conservation dealt only with theoretical tigers and mountain lions, then the tidy packages would suffice.

Unfortunately, real tigers and lions tend to be far less cooperative and predictable. Landscape connectivity, as conservation biologists call it, is a convoluted topic. The same stretch of land looks far different to different species. To a scientist, it may be one of those green lines on the map that connects one reserve to another. To some animals, it may serve exactly that purpose—a place to pass through. To others species, it may be a permanent home, while still others may find themselves in what scientists call a sink, an inhospitable habitat in which they do not thrive and which they never leave. What appears to us to be a wholly beneficial bit of natural habitat may also transmit disease, promote competition with an exotic species, or increase contact with a predator.[8]

Daniel Simberloff, a professor of environmental science at the University of Tennessee and conservation biology's most persistent and effective skeptic, points out that many—if not most—species will not use corridors the way conservationists would like them to. Many species, to move successfully between two patches, need linkages that are themselves good or at least marginal habitat and that can accommodate normal movement patterns. A grizzly bear, for example, may need a corridor several miles wide, with sufficient food, water, cover, and few roads.[9]

Simberloff and others have raised a host of doubts about the idea of corridors, at least in its simplest form. Various researchers have proposed various rules of thumb: corridors should be at least three times as wide as the distance to which edge effects are likely to extend; corridors should be at least one home range in width, lest they funnel carnivores and ungulates into waiting hunters. Scale also matters: a hedgerow makes a fine corridor for a hedgehog or a field mouse; a landscape full of barriers impassable to a bear has countless small habitats suitable for a beetle. So if the species most in need of conservation are beetles, then the strategy will be very different that if they are bears. As Michael Soulé says, "The answer to every question in ecology is 'It depends' or 'I don't know.'" So if we are to understand anything about corridors, we need to view the world's natural connections through the eyes, ears, and noses of animals.[10]

Much of the debate over corridors is at the human or grizzly bear scale, but key ecosystem functions take place at both finer and broader scales. The benefits of corridors will be realized only if the isolated populations cannot survive for centuries in their present state, and corridors will improve the situation, not simply shuttling animals and plants from good habitats to poor ones. Other considerations include the cost of creating and maintaining the corridor versus the cost of enlarging the reserve, edge effects, and the political costs of creating corridors in rapidly developing areas.

All these concerns are valid, and debate over many of them continues to fill scientific journals. At least one study found no empirical evidence for the hypothesized negative impacts of conservation corridors. Despite the shortcomings of some studies, evidence indicates that corridors facilitate travel by a great many species, though demonstrating that a particular small-scale linkage increases the movement of particular animals has proven difficult.[11]

The biggest problem with corridors may actually be the word itself, which conveys the image of a hallway, straight and narrow and not a place to dawdle, but something that lets you go from here to there without getting your feet muddy. The word *corridor* also suggests a sharp distinction between what is inside and what is outside; when you step into a corridor, you know it. Such corridors certainly exist, but Simberloff and other skeptics have questioned the empirical evidence that they provide landscape connectivity.[12]

The science of landscape ecology formally defines corridors as linear habitats that differ from the surrounding vegetation.[13] But this does not resolve the problem that the same corridor may be a pathway for one species and a habitat for another. Some meanings of corridors are independent of population connectivity; both the Isthmus of Panama and highway underpasses have been called corridors, as have greenways and buffers, which are essentially aesthetic amenities. The greenways movement, which originated in the nineteenth century with Frederick Law Olmsted's "park and parkway" idea, has traditionally focused on recreation and aesthetics.[14] The word *corridor* has been applied to many features that have little if any ecological value, like greenbelts, hike and bike paths, utility corridors, and railroad rights-of-way.

Given the rapidity and global extent of habitat fragmentation, scientists are focusing on the role wildlife corridors and linkages can play in keeping fragmented islands of habitat connected and wildlife populations viable. In North America, few places are under as great pressure as Orange County, California, and it is there that the idea of a connected landscape has had a true test.

THE PUMAS OF ORANGE COUNTY

The debate over corridors raged among conservation scientists for years before Paul Beier entered the fray. Now a professor of conservation biology and wildlife ecology at Northern Arizona University at Flagstaff, in 1988 Beier was fresh of out graduate school at Berkeley and looking for work. With a doctorate in wildland resource science, he naturally expected a post someplace relatively untamed. He confidently told his wife, "I don't know where I am going to get a job, but don't worry, it won't be in L.A." He would have to eat those words in short order.[15]

Not long earlier, a five-year-old child had been mauled by a mountain lion (*Felis concolor*, also called puma, cougar, catamount, or nittany lion) in a park in Orange County, in southern California. Orange County claims two notable distinctions: it is California's most populated area, as well as the most threatened hotspot of biodiversity in the United States, with over four hundred species that government agencies and conservation organizations consider to be at risk.[16]

Orange County lies within the South Coast ecoregion, which encompasses 8.4 million acres, or roughly 8 percent of California. The transition to the Sonoran and Mojave Deserts bounds the ecoregion to the east, and the Santa Ynez and Transverse Ranges bound it to the north; the ecoregion extends approximately two hundred miles south into Baja.[17] In the late 1980s, state and local governments needed to show that they were doing something about the mountain lion problem, so they decided to fund a study of the big cats in the county. In 1988, they hired Paul Beier, whose gentle mien and fondness for tie-dye and sandals belies his activist's passion and his scientist's acuity. Beier's superiors told him bluntly that given the rapid growth of southern California, his job would be to document the demise of a puma population. If county officials expected Beier to accept this undertaker's task and then quietly go away, they would be sorely disappointed.

"That phrase 'document the demise of a puma population' stung like a slap to the face and rang in my ears. I don't remember my verbal response, but I do recall my immediate mental response: I'll be damned if I am going to document the demise of a puma population!" writes Beier.[18] Somewhere between three hundred and five hundred mountain lions remain in Orange County, slightly down from when Beier began; any given mountain range supports about fifteen to fifty. According to Beier, this population size guarantees extinction if these areas become fragmented, but the populations have a very high probability of surviving in perpetuity if they remain connected.

"It became real obvious that it is not a favorable place for the long-term survival of mountain lions unless we really started to think big," Beier said in an interview from his office in Flagstaff. "This was my opportunity to do some research on thinking big: How much do animals need connectivity in the landscape? And let's really demonstrate it with data." Beier saw immediately that he had to think across boundaries when he realized that his study area sat amid seventeen incorporated cities and straddled five counties.

When Beier began his research on pumas, thinking about connectivity and linkages was just starting to come into vogue. "Corridor was a buzz-word, and I was a little skeptical about jumping on a bandwagon," he says.

But Beier recognized that if pumas were going to survive in this land-scape they needed linkages, and he needed to know if they would use them. His sponsors, Orange County and the California Department of Fish and Game, set no real goals for him, says Beier, and just wanted to look like they were doing something, so he could shape his research how-ever he wanted.

Given free rein, Beier decided to document how mountain lions moved from place to place in the crowded southern California landscape. He could take one of two approaches: experimental or observational. Carry-ing out actual experiments with corridors would provide the most conclu-sive evidence one way or the other, but it would be difficult, expensive, and, in cases where the experiment would require destroying an existing con-nection in order to examine the result of the isolation, ethically objection-able. In only a few instances have researchers been able to compare two subpopulations of animals, one in an intact landscape and the other in a fragmented one, and then recreate a corridor to see if the population in the fragmented landscape begins to look more like its intact counterpart.[19]

Beier chose the second approach—to observe whether individual ani-mals in fragmented landscapes used corridors to move from patch to patch. If they did use the corridors, the next step would be to establish that with-out corridors lions would not move around enough to maintain the popu-lation. His first challenge was that adult mountain lions really don't move around that much. Lions prefer to stay home, in territories averaging 50 square miles for a female and 150 square miles for a male. Beier put radio tags on some adult lions and found they did not travel between subpopula-tions. Young lions, on the other hand, leave their home range at about one year old to find their own home range. In Orange County, these juvenile dispersers, as they are known, would have to negotiate among the only three remaining paths from one block of good habitat to another.

Beier monitored each female until she had cubs, put radio tags on the cubs when they got to be about twelve months old, and then hoped the cubs did not die before they tried to disperse or shortly thereafter, a com-mon fate among mountain lions. In three years, Beier was able to docu-ment the travel paths of just nine dispersers, not many but enough to provide some of the first documented evidence that corridors would work as a conservation strategy for a species of conservation concern living in a real landscape. Most of the dispersers successfully found and used the potential corridors, and each of the three potential corridors was used. On the other hand, no lions managed to find their way between habitat patches through the hostile ground of urban and suburban development.[20]

Beier had shown that mountain lions will travel through corridors that would never provide adequate habitat; the corridors they used were narrow, scrubby places, with little cover and less food, but no buildings. Each corridor was crossed by one or two roads, which presented serious obstacles but did not prevent movement. If lions used these linkages—which survived the development onslaught by chance—they would do better with ones we could actually design on purpose. "We should not be designing corridors like these three accidental linkages, but even these things were usable," says Beier. "Take that as the worst we would ever accept. The more you can make the corridors habitat of value, the better they work."

This conclusion highlights the importance of knowing precisely which species will use a corridor and how. In the case of Beier's lions, dispersers are using them to get from one place to another, and they do so many times over. Other species—say a kangaroo rat or a wood rat, other common residents of Orange County—might take twenty generations to get from one core area to another, so for those species a corridor would have to be livable habitat as well.

Armed with hard evidence that pumas would use corridors and that they were important to the survival of the species in Southern California, Beier became a spokesman for the idea. He gave interviews, made speeches, testified before planning commissions, and even filed suits to block a toll road and a housing development in a place called Coal Canyon. He helped found an organization called South Coast Wildlands to promote conservation planning based on The Wildlands Project model. His advocacy nearly cost him his job, and while it showed some short-term success, the long-term prospects remained dim unless his broader vision for the South Coast ecoregion engaged not just scientists and some conservation activists but government agencies and local communities as well.

This broader engagement got a boost in November 2000, when a coalition of organizations sponsored a conference at the San Diego Zoo entitled "Missing Linkages: Restoring Connectivity to the California Landscape."[21] In this context, a missing link was a highly impacted area currently providing limited or no connectivity function (due to intervening development, roadway, etc.), but, based on location, one for which it is vital to restore connectivity function. For example, a missing link might be a critical section of a major highway that bisects two larger habitat blocks but that animals cannot get around or under. More than 160 scientists from universities, public agencies, and private organizations identified and mapped some 220 linkages throughout the state, with annotations for each that included target wildlife species, threats to the linkage, and viability of the linkage. The conference highlighted the critical need for conserving existing linkages in the South Coast, the most fragmented ecoregion in the state, if viable populations of key species were to be maintained.[22]

At the conference, Beier realized that the shift toward thinking at a large landscape scale had occurred among both scientists and land managers in government, academia, and both rich and not-so-rich conservation organizations. "I remember being overwhelmed at that whole meeting, thinking this is not new frontiers, this is mainstream. All these guys from the Bureau of Land Management, Park Service, Forest Service; this wasn't the tie-dye crowd, this was mainstream management. Everybody saying it is high time, it is past time, let's go."

This attitude probably began to emerge in the mid-1990s. By the time of the Missing Linkages conference, a combination of state agencies and citizen activists in California had purchased three parcels of land to conserve Coal Canyon as a linkage between the Santa Ana Mountains and the Chino Hills. The same month as the conference, the state dedicated the three parcels as part of Chino Hills State Park. The Riverside Freeway crossed through the parcels, complete with an interchange at Coal Canyon. The interchange had been planned to serve urban developments—developments that would now remain unbuilt. Recognizing that the best use of the interchange would be to convert it to a wildlife underpass, the California Department of Transportation reconfigured the interchange, closed the ramps, and turned the underpass over to the state park.

In February 2003, the California Department of Transportation began unpaving the Coal Canyon interchange and converting it into a wildlife crossing, thus making it the first freeway interchange in the United States to be relinquished for conservation purposes. Beier has documented that three lions have attempted to use the Coal Canyon underpass as a corridor, and two were successful; one lion crossed under the freeway more than twenty-two times in eighteen months.[23]

＊ ＊ ＊

The interest in corridors flowed directly from the theory of island biogeography, which emphasizes the relationship between the size of an area, be it an island or an isolated park, and the number of species it contains. Extinction, according to MacArthur and Wilson, is the result of largely random changes in demography—like those hypothetical parrots with the clutches of eggs that hatched out all males—and in such cases there is only one possible outcome.

Other theories provide insights into how populations of plants and animals become established, thrive, and go extinct. One way to understand how populations work is to see them as groups of distinct, smaller populations—called metapopulations—linked by individuals dispersing from one group to another. In this view, small populations occasionally go extinct, but reappear as new colonists arrive. Ecologists refer to this process as "blinking out" and "blinking on." Metapopulation theory emerged as a successor to island biogeography in the 1980s, as it appeared to explain the behavior of many populations, and seemed to become even more relevant as human activity split what were once large populations into several smaller ones separated by some inhospitable land.[24]

Classic metapopulation theory tells us that the long-term survival of a species that exists in just a few places across a large area, like the spotted owl, depends on the rate of extinction in each of the patches and the rate of movement between the patches. Simply put, if the rate of movement between the patches counterbalances the rate of extinction within the patches, the metapopulation (the group of population patches) should persist over time. If, however, the rate of movement between the patches does not keep up with the rate of extinction within the patches, the entire metapopulation will eventually become extinct.[25]

Metapopulation theory helps scientists build abstract models of the survival and extinction of species. Most species in nature, however, are not structured as metapopulations in the strict sense.[26] Paul Beier's mountain lions, for example, most likely are not, since scientists have found no evidence that the local populations of lions blink out and blink on—though perhaps studies lasting hundreds of years might alter that conclusion. Instead, many scientists believe the question should be not whether some species fit the theory, but how vital is it for individual members of a population to cross from one core habitat to another. In many cases, what happens closer to home, within the populations, may be more important than the ability to cross large areas of the landscape.

Unlike Beier's work, which focuses on the linkages among populations, many metapopulation studies simply assume the linkage exists, because the research concerns the dynamics of the populations—how they fluctuate, and when they blink out and blink on. From a conservation perspective, it is the linkages that matter, and the emphasis is on retaining those linkages to promote dispersal, ensuring that human-created barriers will not add to the natural barriers that limit connectivity among areas of suitable habitat.[27]

Regardless of whether the theory works in many places or only a few, it has forced ecologists and conservation biologists to begin thinking about how populations of both plants and animals interact across the landscape. "We need to pay more attention to spatial dynamics of populations, whether they are metapopulations or something else," says John Wiens, a landscape ecologist who taught for years at Colorado State University before taking a position as one of The Nature Conservancy's chief scientists in 2001. "No one is asking the questions about what types of spatial dynamics are more prevalent for certain species, in certain systems."[28] Conservation scientists and planners need to think about where species are dispersing to, take the linkages into account, and look at areas within reasonable dispersal distances for given species.

The idea of metapopulations applies to conservation in other ways as well. The theory teaches the key lesson that just because an area doesn't have a species at a particular moment does not mean that it never will. Conversely, just because a species lives in an area does not mean that it always will; we may be looking at a sink, and it may take years to recognize that fact.

"We are not good at thinking about the dynamics of landscapes," says Wiens. "We usually think about the dynamics of populations, while considering the places to be static. We are cognizant of succession, and of disturbance at the local scale, but not across whole landscapes," he says. We need to think about all of this in the context of climate change. The assumption that those places are static is never valid over the timeframe—centuries at least—necessary for lasting conservation.

✦ ✦ ✦

The theories of metapopulations and island biogeography both lead to a focus on the patches of habitat rather than what lies between them. That makes sense, as most species spend most of their time in those patches, and should the patches disappear the species would most likely disappear as well. But such a focus is too narrow. Even a casual glance at an ecoregional map reveals how much land is not green (the industry standard for land under some sort of conservation management) and likely never will be. The amount of white space on the map—the farmland, woodlots, and open space waiting for some developer to come along—in many ways defines the scale of the conservation task. Conservationists usually assume that the white space is uniform and hostile—perhaps the most overused metaphor in conservation biology portrays parks as "islands in a sea of human development"—but it actually varies widely, and often presents opportunities to conserve the entire landscape.[29]

Ecoregional maps convey the vital message that conservation efforts need to consider the entire range of land uses and landowners, not just the traditional wilderness. "Success defined as the portfolio of protected area would be Pyrrhic," says Kent Redford. He advocates instead a range of conservation categories, from the familiar parks to ancient downtowns, with corresponding ranges in how humans use those areas.[30]

The impossibility of relying solely on the traditional protected areas comes into focus by looking at a map of California. In that state, one of the biologically richest areas in North America, 15 percent of the land has been entirely converted to urban or agricultural uses, while 12 percent is in some form of conservation management. The remaining 73 percent, mostly desert and mountains, has multiple land uses. Conservation cannot neglect that land. Future generations will not lightly forgive the folly of conservationists spending all of their effort on the 12 percent while the 73 percent disappears under the asphalt or the plow. Nearly any human use of

land exists on a continuum between compatible and incompatible with nature—the intensity, duration, frequency, and timing of that use all contribute, as does the life history of the organisms that share the land with
human communities. Conservation cannot be carried out in isolation from
all the other uses of the land; it must be incorporated into the overall management of the landscape.[31]

Part of that overall management means enabling animals to pass
through land that is not managed primarily (or even partly) as wildlife
habitat. The latest conservation biology lingo calls this increasing the permeability of the landscape. In other words, for some species and in some
places, core habitats do not need to be physically connected with corridors
so long as the species that move between the core areas can surmount
whatever obstacles they find in their way, from logged forests to freeways.
This requires rethinking the notion of boundaries so they become uncertain and permeable, defined in ecological rather than legal terms.[32]

" 'Permeability' is an attractive term because it focuses on the process itself, which is movement, the movement of things in space," says Michael
Soulé. "Everybody has a different picture in their mind when they think of
a corridor—power lines, highways, recreation corridors. It means so many
different things to different people. Landscape permeability for natural
processes is much more precise a term. It draws the attention to the process
on the landscape rather than focusing people's minds on some sort of linear pathways. With corridors, the next question is always, how wide does a
corridor have to be? When you talk about landscape permeability, the
question that leaps to mind is what are the obstacles, what are the processes
or barriers in the landscape that slow down or affect permeability?"[33]

RECONCILIATION

While insuring permeability across a wide connective swath of habitat
avoids the problems associated with hard-line corridors, it is not always an
option. Back in Florida, an aggressive campaign to buy land for conservation may succeed in protecting a significant portion of the state, but everything not specifically set aside for conservation will be heavily used. "Land
use planning in Florida means buying all you can and letting the developers have the rest," sighs Reed Noss, sitting barefoot in his office at the University of Central Florida in Orlando. "Land will be either protected or

subdivided. The good news is that we are going to have more than one-third of the state in protected areas, much more than other states." The bad news is that Florida needs more area protected because the land between the reserves is so poorly managed. In fact, it is hardly managed at all; if is it not protected it is going to be trashed. An ideal ratio would be one-third protected, one-third developed, and one-third in well-managed, less intensive uses. The way things are going in Florida, that ratio may be out of reach.[34]

"In places like Florida and southern California, the idea of a well-managed landscape outside a reserve is not going to happen, unless we have a truly radical change in politics," Noss says. Limits on growth and sprawl basically do not exist in Florida, which leaves planning to the counties. Most counties plan poorly, largely because county commissions are completely pro-development, refusing to bite the hand that pads the property tax rolls.

The assumption that suitable habitat will survive outside of reserves is dubious. In southern California, the landscape is basically impermeable to mountain lions outside of the few well-defined corridors that Paul Beier and others are working to protect. In many instances, we probably have only ten to twenty years to acquire and protect these landscape linkages.[35]

Ecologist Michael Rosenzweig has another solution. Rosenzweig calls the traditional approach to saving natural habitats reservation ecology. A second standard method, restoration ecology, seeks to repair human-caused damage and return areas to something resembling a natural state. Rosenzweig adds a third R, which he calls reconciliation ecology. He also calls it "win-win ecology," as he believes there are environmentally sound ways to continue using land for our own benefit. In his book *Win-Win Ecology*, Rosenzweig quotes a Chinese proverb: "The careful foot can walk anywhere."[36]

Reconciliation ecology, Rosenzweig argues, can end the bickering and legal skirmishes that characterize modern conservation. Humans are going to use most of the land on the planet, but we can learn to use it better, and in doing so can help unite disparate groups in pursuit of common goals. No one wants to reduce the world to a sterile and lonely place, writes Rosenzweig, and no one wants to force mass rejection of modern standards of living.

Rosenzweig defines reconciliation ecology as the "science of inventing, establishing, and maintaining new habitats to conserve species diversity in places where people live, work, or play."[37] Given the unforgiving species-area relationship, we simply cannot protect pieces of ecosystems; as soon as we begin chopping them up, they begin to lose species. So we must look across the whole range of land uses, from parks to subdivisions, and make all of them as hospitable as we can to species other than ourselves. Reconciliation ecology seeks a science for working in the white spaces on the map.

Not all species will tolerate cohabitation with humans; by some estimates only half of all species will survive in a reconciled landscape.[38] So we will always need protected areas, in most cases the bigger the better, to conserve those species that thrive only in our absence. The overwhelming emphasis of conservation science on those areas, however, may not be enough. Rosenzweig and a handful of other scientists, like Wes Jackson and Australian researcher Richard Hobbs, are attempting to find more of a balance, directing more research to discovering how humans can share their land with at least some wild species, so that conservation takes place everywhere, not just in the tiny fraction of land set aside specifically for that purpose.[39]

Reconciliation ecology updates Aldo Leopold with modern conservation biology. In the early 1930s, Leopold wrote that "conservation is not merely a thing to be enshrined in outdoor museums, but a way of living on the land."[40] The idea of reconciliation offers insights into how we can live on the land without spoiling it (to paraphrase another of Leopold's insights), but we also need to apply the lessons in connectivity learned in Okefenokee, southern California, and elsewhere, and use the discipline of conservation planning to fit the pieces of the puzzle back together.

Reassembling the puzzle requires more than a network of activists and preserves, no matter how well planned or well intentioned. Getting people to think about doing things bigger and bolder is far different from making real progress in real places. Successful conservation requires not just a big vision and good science, not just gaining the tacit support of people who send in the occasional check, but making common cause with those supporters and their neighbors. The tag line for The Wildlands Project is "big, wild, and connected." But a connected landscape cannot just refer to patches of forest linked one to another; it must also refer to the people who are connected to that landscape and to each other. In southern Arizona, conservationists, scientists, ranchers, city dwellers, and suburbanites are beginning to learn how that can happen.

CHAPTER 5

APPOINTMENT IN SONORA

But the care of the earth is our most ancient and most worthy and,
after all, our most pleasing responsibility. To cherish what remains
of it, and to foster its renewal, is our only legitimate hope.
WENDELL BERRY, The Unsettling of America

Cienega Creek rises in Arizona's Sonoita Valley and flows north toward Tucson, between the Sky Islands of the Santa Rita and Whetstone Mountains. Near its source, Cienega Creek flows through high desert grasslands, some of the best examples of native grasslands that remain in Arizona and ideal habitat for a host of native species. Three native fish species, all officially endangered, call the Cienega Creek home, and nearly two hundred species of birds have been identified nearby. Cattle, introduced here in large numbers in the 1820s, also roam these arid lands.[1] From the Civil War era until the late 1980s, much of the Sonoita Valley was private ranchland, including two huge operations, the Empire and Cienega Ranches.

Just twenty miles southeast of booming Tucson's borders, where Cienega Creek flows under Interstate 10, the situation changes. The state of Arizona owns most of the land just north of the highway and leases it for cattle grazing, largely to raise money for public schools. By law, the state must generate the highest return possible from these lands; in some cases that might mean selling to a developer who would replace the cattle with houses. Beyond these state trust lands, further to the north, lie Saguaro National Park and the Rincon Wilderness, two parts of the Coronado National Forest. So while land around the creek to the north and south is protected, the area where the creek runs along the interstate is ripe for development. A piece of the puzzle is missing.

The story of how the Empire and Cienega Ranches became the Las Cienegas National Conservation Area, how the missing link may finally be found, and how these ranches came to be seen as pieces in the conservation puzzle in the first place has much to tell us about science, community, and the need to plan for and carry out broad-scale conservation. The intersection of science and community may be the most hopeful place in modern conservation.

* * *

The key to understanding the larger story lies in starting small, with Cienega Creek and one of its smallest inhabitants. The creek provides habitat for the southwestern willow flycatcher *(Empidonax trailii extimus),* a tiny and rather drab songbird that prefers dense streamside vegetation in Arizona as well as New Mexico, southern California, and parts of Utah, Colorado, and Texas. Easy to miss, even expert birders have a hard time distinguishing the various flycatchers of the genus *Empidonax* by sight alone and usually rely on catching the southwestern willow flycatcher's distinctive song. Even if you are sharp of both ear and eye, however, you may still have a hard time finding a southwestern willow flycatcher, as only a few of them remain, fewer than one thousand breeding pairs across its range.

By the early 1990s, the decline of the southwestern willow flycatcher was clear. In 1993, the U.S. Fish and Wildlife Service (FWS) formally proposed listing the flycatcher as a federal endangered species and designating critical habitat, an important step under the Endangered Species Act that prevents damage to specific areas. The task of writing the rule that listed the bird as endangered under the act fell to Rob Marshall. Marshall, a Yale-trained biologist with FWS in Arizona, was becoming disillusioned by the overall implementation of the Endangered Species Act. The FWS was highly politicized by powerful, moneyed interests that saw species listings and particularly habitat designations as a threat to business: if a species is listed but no critical habitat is designated, a now-common pattern, then restrictions on business are far fewer. This created an atmosphere in which it was extremely difficult for technical biological staff to maintain their integrity, says Marshall. For example, the process to list the flycatcher as endangered began in 1992, the proposed rule didn't come out until 1995, and it took until 1997 to produce the final ruling to list it. The FWS only completed the listing because the watchdog organization Center for Biological Diversity sued them.

Habitat loss poses the gravest threat to the southwestern willow flycatcher. As a combination of livestock grazing, dams, water withdrawal, and urban and agricultural sprawl fragment the bird's habitat, the flycatcher also becomes more vulnerable to nest parasitism by brown-headed cowbirds and nest predation by other species. Rather than looking just at the flycatcher, Marshall wanted to take a broader perspective that would include addressing these threats at a scale that would be meaningful for conservation across Arizona.

Marshall got his chance not long after the flycatcher gained official endangered status. In 1998, some officials from the Department of Defense, like Marshall, yearned to look at the big picture—partly to understand the ecological importance of the immense Goldwater Range, a U.S. Air Force base covering 1.7 million acres of the Sonoran Desert in Arizona, and partly to avoid any further restrictions on military actions on various bases in the Southwest due to problems with the Endangered Species Act.

The Department of Defense gave The Nature Conservancy $750,000 to come up with an ecoregional plan and some pilot implementation projects for the Sonoran Desert. Rob Marshall, who by then had left FWS, headed the effort.

As the Conservancy took to ecoregional planning—haltingly, awkwardly to be sure, like trying to parallel park a cruise liner—staff scientists like Craig Groves struggled to make it part of the everyday work of the organization. An organization that had long prided itself on its can-do self-sufficiency needed to believe that success lay in convincing others, including government agencies and private landowners, to take on much of the work of conservation. The Conservancy had adapted to a new role as a creator or facilitator of detailed visions of conservation success for a particular region or country. The audience was the entire community of individuals, agencies, and organizations on whom conservation success would depend.[2]

The Conservancy hardly boasts of much expertise in such public processes. The Sonoran Desert plan was one of the first testing grounds, and here the Conservancy hired the Sonoran Institute, a small nonprofit organization based in Tucson that specializes in bringing diverse interest groups together for conservation, to facilitate the many meetings—nearly one per month for two years—the ecoregional plan would require. Since the Sonoran Desert, nearly 120,000 square miles in size, crosses the border into Mexico, the Mexican state of Sonora also became involved in the planning, through IMADES, the state environmental agency. While the end result of the project would be a map of conservation areas in the Sonoran Desert—a map that would highlight the importance of Las Cienegas—critical to the success of the effort was all the work the Conservancy, the Sonoran Institute, and IMADES did prior to completing that map.

The plan for the Sonoran Desert ecoregion began with the coarse-filter/fine-filter approach that the Conservancy had developed years before. Marshall and his team decided to focus their attention on all terrestrial natural vegetation communities native to the Sonoran Desert. The list they made captures the marvels of this place, even if the terminology seems to belong to the realm of specialists: mesquite woodlands, desert riparian woodlands, saguaro cactus–velvet mesquite shrubland, jojoba–yellow paloverde shrubland, cattail marsh. These communities formed the coarse filter. The planning team then identified all of the region's rarest amphibians, fish, invertebrates, mammals, plants, reptiles, and birds, including the southwestern willow flycatcher. They also selected a number of common animals, including wide-ranging species that required large areas for dispersal, such as bighorn sheep, or migrated long distances, such as Sonoran pronghorn antelope.

The flycatcher, the riparian woodlands, and all the species and communities highlighted in the Sonoran plan are examples of conservation targets—the things that conservation science tells us are important. Conservation has always selected targets, be they endangered species, scenic landscapes, or all of nature. Like much else in the history of conservation, however, selecting targets has been an ad hoc process, driven by local concerns and preferences, and often with a narrow focus. Only recently has science developed tools for selecting targets carefully. These tools can then be used to set explicit goals for how many examples of each target need to be conserved and how these examples are distributed. All of these are crucial steps in making conservation planning more rigorous.[3]

LET A BEAR BE YOUR UMBRELLA

In a perfect world, every species and every community would be a conservation target. But given our ignorance about most species and the threats they face, the best we can do is focus on a few carefully chosen species or characteristics and hope that they can carry the weight of all the rest. Choosing targets is risky but unavoidable business, guaranteed to spark vigorous disagreements among scientists. As Craig Groves points out in his book *Drafting a Conservation Blueprint,* all conservation targets, at whatever scale, are actually stand-ins or surrogates for all the other species we know little about. Since we can't enumerate all the species in a particular area, let alone all the populations or individuals, we must accept this incomplete knowledge.[4]

Scientists have found no magic bullet, no single best surrogate. For a long time, conservation biologists held out the hope that if a particular place was rich in some relatively easy-to-measure groups of species—like butterflies, vascular plants, or vertebrates—then that place was likely rich in other, harder-to-measure species as well. They also hoped that rare species would tend to occur in areas of high biodiversity. If true, these assumptions would have made the lives of conservation planners far easier, but unfortunately neither seems to hold up under scrutiny. The presence of one species or group of species does not necessarily indicate the presence of any other.[5]

Without an obvious best choice, conservation planners generally consider four types of targets: species; natural communities and ecosystems; abiotic variables like soils, geology, or hydrology; and special elements such as roosting or breeding sites. Classes of biodiversity such as individuals, populations, species, communities, and ecosystems are heterogeneous —each member is different from every other. Accounting for those differences requires clear choices about targets that are based on explicit goals.

Targets, therefore, will be different in the Sonoran Desert than in the Brazilian Amazon, and will vary as well depending on the available information and the resources on hand to analyze that information. Rob Marshall's team chose ecological communities and a range of different species. They also considered how these species were distributed: Were they endemic to the Sonoran, limited to the Sonoran and adjacent ecoregions, or were they widespread? In other places, other combinations of targets and surrogates would be best—climate, landform, geology, vegetation types mapped from aerial photography, known locations of endangered species, and so on.[6]

The longstanding focus of conservation on rare and endangered species means these species are often the targets for ecoregion-based approaches, in the Sonoran Desert and elsewhere. That makes perfectly good sense when you have data that identify the threatened species, but such data often do not exist. Just as scientists look for shortcuts to finding the particularly rich places on Earth, they also look for species that could provide conservation shortcuts—species that play important ecological roles or whose protection would protect many other species as well, without our having to know all that much about every one of them. And just as the search for indicators of species richness has proven disappointing, so the other shortcuts have been full of false hope.

Conservationists have a large capacity for wishful thinking. They have pinned their hopes on particular species that come in a variety of shapes and sizes, have given them a host of often confusing labels, and have usually but not always tied their reasoning to sound scientific principles. What conservation biologists call a flagship species, for example, rallies public support for conservation through sheer charisma. The giant panda is the archetype of the flagship species, embodied in the World Wildlife Fund's famous logo. While flagships certainly help raise money, and one can't sneer at a good fundraiser when conservation must compete with all sorts of worthy causes for the philanthropic dollar, charisma says nothing at all about ecology.

Ideally, conserving a flagship species would also conserve all the other species that share its habitat. The flagship, in other words, would double as an umbrella, spreading protective cover over those nearby. The idea of an umbrella species, while largely untested, is intuitively attractive and lends more credence to the idea of working at broad scales: we may have some chance of preserving field mice if we plan for grizzlies, but we have no chance of preserving grizzlies if we only plan for the mice.[7]

Most umbrellas, unfortunately, leak rather badly. First of all, ecology offers no reason why a flagship species, basically a pretty face, would be a good umbrella. Second, conserving any single species, charismatic or not, actually conveys little benefit to most others. The requirements of each species for habitat and food overlap only occasionally.

Labels such as flagship, umbrella, and keystone, while simplifications, reveal something about a species. Some species may be all of the above; grizzlies, for example, could be keystones as top carnivores and umbrellas because of large area requirements, and they are certainly a flagship species for people in North America. Conservationists use keystones, umbrellas, and other species that represent larger ecosystems for setting conservation and management priorities despite their shortcomings, because they lack information and resources to manage every species individually.[8] Scientists and resource managers resort to such simplifications precisely because they understand too little about the systems they are trying to manage and protect, and because they lack the time, money, and know-how to learn all they need to know.

At the Wildlife Conservation Society (WCS), Amy Vedder, Eric Sanderson, and their colleagues have added a new twist to the notion of an umbrella species: take a jaguar's-eye view of the landscape. Not just a jaguar, actually, but any large animal that uses landscapes over distances and through times comparable to human management regimes and resource-extraction activities—hundreds to thousands of square miles, representing population dynamics measured in years and decades. WCS calls these "landscape species" and uses them to define the landscape in which conservation must occur, both the extent of the landscape and the important variation within it. A landscape species is the lens through which to view the landscape to determine where human activities impinge on the ecological integrity of an area.[9]

The theory of island biogeography treated islands as featureless plains, with no internal habitat diversity, and saw species as characterless features with no genetic or geographical variation. The landscape-species approach focuses reserve design on heterogeneity, species interactions, local- and regional-scale population dynamics, and the effects of habitat modification. The way a species perceives the landscape will be quite different from the way we see it. We may see a uniform forest, but a jaguar will see travel paths, hunting grounds, and watering holes.[10]

Amy Vedder leads the WCS Living Landscapes Program. Vedder and her husband, Bill Weber, worked for a decade with the mountain gorillas in Rwanda, where they founded the Mountain Gorilla Project, and Vedder comes at the question of doing big conservation with a distinctly practical perspective. At the University of Wisconsin in the 1970s, Vedder studied and taught classical wildlife biology, where she recognized that the animals most at risk of extinction were the big ones that needed lots of room, food, and a variety of habitats, from open meadows to dense forests. Between teaching the course and working in Africa, where animals routinely cross park boundaries, Vedder began to think more formally about how to design conservation strategies for larger species.

At the same time, Vedder's work with the mountain gorillas made her keenly aware of the need to work with the people living in and around protected areas (unlike Dian Fossey, with whom Vedder and Weber worked for a time and who had a palpable distrust of local people). But Vedder wanted to keep the focus on the wildlife. "There is a tension in solving human problems and assuming that conservation will result," says Vedder, now based out of the WCS headquarters at the Bronx Zoo. "How do we sort out all of these factors in a clear way?"[11]

The landscape-species concept provides a means of selecting a few species for conservation attention with the belief that meeting their needs will achieve conservation of other species and of the landscape as a whole. But landscape species are more than umbrellas, because conservation of the landscape species will lead not only to conservation of other species in the same habitats, but also to conservation of the very structure of the landscape and its ecological functions. Many species that do not interact with the landscape species may be conserved through maintenance of the functional landscapes themselves.

Many biologists have recommended using a suite of species as surrogates rather than just one, an approach that attempts to integrate ecological patterns and processes by identifying species that are most demanding of room and board—food, water, large connected areas, complex and heterogeneous habitats, and so on—and targeting them for management. In the Sky Islands Wilderness Network, for example, Dave Foreman and his colleagues identified more than two dozen species as the basis for the preserve network, including the Mexican wolf, black bear, pronghorn, prairie dog, southwest willow flycatcher, and Mexican spotted owl (a close cousin of the northern spotted owl). Even with such an extensive list, Foreman argues that using a variety of surrogates to protect representative ecosystems is quicker, less expensive, and easier than other approaches.[12]

❖ ❖ ❖

Deciding what to conserve is the first step in a conservation plan. Then you need to decide how many of those targets to conserve, and where you should try to conserve them. The idea of setting specific, measurable goals for conservation seems rather obvious—how else do we know if we are doing the right thing?—but it is actually a rather recent phenomenon. Recovery plans for species under the Endangered Species Act, for example, for years lacked any clear goals for population numbers.[13] Explicit, defensible goals give credibility to broad-scale conservation. Without clear goals, the entire idea of setting priorities for conservation—a process that has led to heated debates among conservation scientists and organizations—has no meaning.[14]

The scientific community has not yet reached a consensus on how to set such goals, though the process generally involves estimating how many individuals or populations of target species and communities are needed in an ecoregion and how they should be distributed. For the Sonoran Desert plan, The Nature Conservancy convened a workshop to set goals for the region. For two days, over one hundred academic researchers and representatives of federal, state, and municipal agencies, Native American tribes, conservation organizations, and private corporations from Arizona, Baja California, California, and Sonora pored over maps, compared notes, and argued over what areas to conserve to meet conservation goals for birds, invertebrates, fish, mammals, reptiles, amphibians, plants, and natural vegetation communities.

Setting appropriate goals for conservation requires accounting for, among other things, the natural history of the region, the amount of remaining habitat and what size the pieces are, and the distribution of the species and communities, as well as gathering information and recommendations from a variety of sources, such as recovery plans (keeping their weaknesses in mind). Calling this process complex and uncertain seems inadequate; opaque may be closer to the truth. The process remains for now as much art as science, with countless exceptions to every purported rule and no universal truths.[15]

Still, without goals broad-scale conservation teeters on the edge of meaninglessness. The goals must be based in science, but they cannot be set in stone, as social and economic conditions will change.[16] Setting explicit goals and targets for broad-scale conservation also means creating measuring sticks for assessing progress. This is commonplace in business, engineering, and medicine, but still unusual in conservation, which too often retains a piece-by-piece, museum collectors' approach in which it is easy to lose sight of the bigger picture. Keeping your head down and your focus narrow often results in being unable to distinguish approaches that work from those that fail. Civil engineers can quantify their mistakes, and people generally agree that such mistakes are serious and are to be avoided —no one wants a bridge to collapse. But conservation planning differs from the many well-funded and well-organized activities that destroy biodiversity. "Conservation planning is out of its league," writes Bob Pressey. Mistakes tend to be both difficult to define and far less dramatic in this field (though no less serious) than a bridge collapse; extinction happens silently.[17]

Setting unattainable goals makes as little sense as setting none at all. Conservation planners can lay out detailed maps that fully represent all the species and communities of an ecoregion, but if those species and communities will not survive even another decade in the face of ongoing development or other threats, then the planners have failed. While early researchers focused on representation, now scientists face the challenge of defining conservation plans that are both representative and persistent. The concept of representation forms the foundation of broad-scale conservation. But simply ensuring adequate representation of species and communities would make for little more than an elegant plan, sort of like a lovely table-setting without the meal.

PRIORITIES AND POLITICS

In 2000, once Rob Marshall's Sonoran Desert team had identified their targets and set their goals, they then had to find the places across the Sonoran Desert that collectively would spell successful conservation. This process, called reserve selection, has been around since the early 1970s, and measures success in terms of numbers of reserves and their total extent. By the mid-1990s, Reed Noss and his colleagues from Australia and South Africa had developed a much more rigorous approach that would become a sub-discipline of conservation biology all its own.

Based in part on this new work, and using both computers and expert opinion, the Sonoran Desert planning team identified one hundred large landscapes and seventy-nine smaller areas, covering more than 40 percent of the ecoregion, as conservation priorities. They ranged in size from over 6 million acres in a complex of areas straddling the Arizona-Sonora border (including the Goldwater Range and Organ Pipe National Monument) to just over four hundred acres in Ramer Lake on the lower Colorado River.

The Conservancy's plan for conserving the Sonoran Desert will not go from the drawing board to the ground with the stroke of a pen. These plans happen piecemeal, as governments and policies change, as money or land become available, and as conservation agencies and organizations develop the capacity to work on them. All the while, habitats that were on the original map of the conservation region—a map that the experts had so painstakingly compiled and hung in their offices with rightful pride—are being lost to development.[18]

More than half of the land in the Sonoran plan is publicly owned, much of it in the hands of the Bureau of Land Management (the federal agency that manages public grazing and mining land in the western states), the Department of Defense, or the state of Arizona. As a result, most of the landowners do not consider conservation a top priority. Resolving competing reservation agendas requires systematic procedures to compare alternatives.

Conservation planning is riddled with uncertainty—over the use of surrogates, the setting of targets, decisions about which kind of land tenure can be expected to contribute to targets for which features, and decisions about how best to locate, design, implement, and manage new conservation areas in the face of limited resources, competition for other uses, and incursions from surrounding areas. New scientific developments—such as more precise measurements of biodiversity and advances in mapping patterns and monitoring rates of spread of threats—will reduce but never eliminate these uncertainties. Species and communities must be able to survive for hundreds if not thousands of years, to say nothing of the practical difficulties of implementing even the most comprehensive conservation plan in the face of competing uses of the land.

Biologists and ecologists must participate in the real planning process, as that is the only way to understand the need for new ecological and biological knowledge and what the social and political constraints to effective planning really are. Ideally, however, the entire conservation planning process will work its way into the political process. Conservation biology can define a biological vision for an ecoregion or for a portion of one, an approach World Wildlife Fund (WWF) pioneered, but decisions about whether that vision is the right one and about how to get there are social choices not rooted exclusively in science. "Our job is to present the consequences of choices," says Kent Redford. This does not imply that scientists cannot be advocates for their visions—only that the choices will be among competing values, not competing theories or interpretations.

The question of how much to conserve comes down to how much land we are willing to set aside for species other than ourselves, and that boils down to a moral decision. Even different approaches to conservation, like hotspots and ecoregional planning, often and passionately compared and contrasted, differ not so much in the quality of the science as in the underlying principles. Preference for one approach over the other—for representation of a broad range of species and ecosystems on the one hand, or particularly rich collections of tropical species on the other—reflects a value judgment, not a choice of right versus wrong.[19]

The major organizations working on broad-scale conservation all generally agree that the process begins with a scientifically based vision for a region. WWF arrived at that point after vigorous internal debate. "There was huge debate about whether or not the scientifically based biological vision is pure, or whether or not it is legitimate and in fact coequal to modify it by socioeconomic human needs and values," says Bill Eichbaum, vice president at WWF, who was in part responsible for institutionalizing ecoregional planning at the organization.[20]

The resolution, at least for WWF, was to recognize that while the science base is important to start with, it rapidly gets modified by social, political, and economic factors. WWF came up with a theory of how to carry out ecoregional conservation that is captured on a one-page flowchart, starting with a biodiversity vision and a socioeconomic analysis, then moving on to a situation analysis and eventually a conservation action plan.

Bill Eichbaum came to WWF from state government positions in Pennsylvania and Maryland. In Maryland he had worked extensively on the Chesapeake Bay, which in the late 1970s and early 1980s was among the first examples of a broad-based approach to conservation. Eichbaum took over WWF's U.S. program in 1995, just as Eric Dinerstein's and Dave Olson's scientific work was beginning to show results. Eichbaum decided to pick a place in the United States and focus on getting conservation done at a broad scale. "I thought we ought to do it in the Everglades because that brought together a series of skills that we had: we knew something about wetlands, we knew something about water quality and species management. Adding the voice of WWF in the 1994–95 timeframe to that debate could be a useful addition to making things come out right." The Everglades would become one of the most visible examples of a broad-scale approach to conservation (see Chapter 7).

The Wildlands Project takes a similar tack. "First ask, what does nature tell us, what does the biology tell us about how to protect the system, the place, the region. Then let's look at land use and politics and economics, but let's not mix the two, because if you mix the two you end up not knowing what you are talking about," says Michael Soulé. "Our philosophy is to first ask the question, what does nature tell us? and then, through a different process, engage the community."[21]

In the southern Rockies, where Soulé now lives, he is working with the Southern Rockies Ecosystem Project on a wildlands plan. The strategy there focuses on a suite of species—beaver, wolf, marten, bighorn sheep, black bear, grizzly bear, lynx, cutthroat trout, and pronghorn—and, at the outset, the conservation community. Once there is a general agreement on the vision for the region among conservationists (though you will never reach consensus), then they will reach out to the broader community. "We start to engage the agencies and the public as a whole," says Soulé. "Getting the wolf back is a key, and that will be political and educational, for the schools, the legislature, the media, and everyone in between."

This kind of thinking represents a shift within the wilderness movement. Many wilderness advocates draw bright lines between nature and humans, and argue that conservation should focus exclusively on the former. People are the problem, in that view, and should be excluded from both the wilderness and conservation efforts. Soulé, for one, now disagrees. "I think very differently about these issues now than I did twelve years ago when [The Wildlands Project] began, when I was much more anthropophobic than anthropocentric. I have come a long way since then, though some people might say down the wrong path," he says. "I now recognize that it is all one system, and if we don't take care of humans we are not going to take care of nature either."

In the Sonoran Desert, broad public participation helped move the science of conservation planning from theory to practice. In 1998, at about the same time that The Nature Conservancy was finishing its plan, Pima County, Arizona—which includes the city of Tucson, most of south-central Arizona, and about 850,000 people—began its own plan, called the Sonoran Desert Conservation Plan. Officials and residents wanted to manage the explosive growth of the county—Pima County grew at a rate of 27 percent in the 1990s, more than double the national average. By 2010, the county's population may climb to more than 1 million, many of whom will be moving to new developments southeast of Tucson, in the Cienega Creek watershed. Unplanned growth means losing those unique Sonoran Desert values, as well as gaining more traffic congestion and related problems.

Residents and officials of Pima County also wanted to avoid conflicts between development and eight federally listed species, particularly a tiny, rare bird called the cactus ferruginous pygmy-owl *(Glaucidium brasilianum cactorum)*. One of the world's smallest owls, standing just five inches tall and weighing less than three ounces, the cactus ferruginous pygmy-owl has caused quite a stir. Once found along wooded streams from southern California to central Arizona and along the Gulf Coast in Texas and northeastern Mexico, the owl's range has dwindled as groundwater pumping has dried up streams and washes. Only a few of the birds remain in Arizona, mostly around Tucson and in Organ Pipe Cactus National Monument, about 125 miles west of the city.

Pima County had to shelve plans for a school and other developments northeast of Tucson in 1997 when scientists discovered that only a dozen owls remained in the county and several were nesting nearby. That same year, FWS listed the owl as endangered. In 1998, the Pima County Board of Supervisors initiated comprehensive land-planning efforts "with the goal of combining short-term actions to protect and enhance the natural environment and long-range planning to ensure that our natural and urban environments not only coexist but develop an interdependent relationship, where one enhances the other.... The Sonoran Desert Conservation Plan is a form of growth-management plan that will guide future urban growth and expansion by ecosystem-based planning principles. A successful Sonoran Desert Conservation Plan can, in fact, be the cornerstone of conservation as well as economic expansion."[22]

A COMMUNITY FOR LAS CIENEGAS

The Sonoran Desert Conservation Plan, ambitious and far-reaching, addresses natural and cultural resource protection for several decades into the future. The plan has two parts. The first addresses six elements: Ranch Conservation, Cultural Resources, Mountain Parks, Riparian Protection Management and Restoration, Habitat Protection, and Corridors Protection. The second part will be a multi-species habitat conservation plan under the Endangered Species Act that will cover the eight species in the county already listed under the act as well as fifty-five others considered vulnerable to endangerment or extinction.

The county plan integrated the priority conservation areas that The Nature Conservancy, the Sonoran Institute, and IMADES had identified. The first part of the process has gone well: early results of the Sonoran Desert Conservation Plan include the designation of the Ironwood Forest National Monument and the Sonoran Desert National Monument in 2000. Together the two monuments cover almost 640,000 acres of largely intact desert landscapes. The American Planning Association selected the Sonoran Desert Conservation Plan as the 2002 winner of its national Outstanding Planning Award for a Plan.

The county's habitat conservation plan under the Endangered Species Act, on the other hand, will not win any awards. "After four years of work, there is still a misunderstanding of what a habitat conservation plan is," says Rob Marshall. Part of the problem stems from a seventy-member steering committee that Pima County created to advise the county commissioners on the habitat conservation plan. Such an unwieldy group has led to delays and confusion about what the plan should accomplish. "This has been a real eye-opener about how to run a public process," says Marshall.[23]

"The county process has been an exercise in obfuscation," says Roseann Hanson, who directed the Sonoran Institute's Southeast Arizona Program until 2004. The huge steering committee may have been an effort to slow the process, "almost like it was set up to fail," she says. The science in the proposed habitat conservation plan, while high-quality, was done in isolation—in an effort to insulate the scientists from political struggles—with no input from rural communities.[24]

Despite the problems, in June 2003, the Pima County Board of Supervisors adopted the recommendations of the steering committee, including placing an open-space bond initiative before the voters. "For the first time ever, the citizens of Pima County have mapped out the future of our home, showing a unified desire to preserve the values that make our desert attractive to tourism as well as economic growth: beautiful views, clean air and water, saguaro forests, desert rivers, and amazing wildlife diversity," Hanson and Diana Barnes Freshwater wrote in *Vision,* the Sonoran Institute newsletter. "Supervisors took the first steps toward planned growth, healthy desert lands, and quality of life now and for future generations."[25]

The bond would help maintain working ranches, which play a significant economic and cultural role in Pima County, particularly the eastern portion, defining the borders of Tucson and maintaining open space. The community was concerned it was losing its ranching heritage. Most of the ranches in this part of the country are still family owned and operated, and some were being broken up and developed.

In the late 1980s, the Bureau of Land Management (BLM) acquired the Empire and Cienegas Ranches in Sonoita Valley through a series of land swaps. The BLM leased grazing land in what was called the Empire-Cienega Resource Management Area to ranchers Mac and John Donaldson, father and son, from Sonoita. The Donaldsons would become leaders of an effort to keep the ranch in operation while maintaining its scenic and ecological value. The Donaldsons were eager to demonstrate that the Empire Ranch could be grazed in a cooperative and ecologically sensitive manner. BLM at the same time began to work with the Donaldsons and other local residents. BLM is much maligned, and often justly, for its environmental mismanagement, but here the bureau was open to community input—and that made a difference.

Today, to maintain the ecological integrity of the land, the Donaldsons manage the ranch in a holistic manner, utilizing a one-herd concept to rotate the cattle through numerous pastures in accordance with the ranch's natural topography. The Donaldsons call it a "selective rest/rotation strategy." The ranchers move their cattle according to environmental conditions and other factors in a controlled, deliberate process, while constantly monitoring the health of the land. There are twenty-eight monitoring plots on the ranch, and the Donaldsons study each carefully in order to quantify the impact of the cattle.

Just as important, the Donaldsons work closely with a biological-assessment team comprising range specialists and scientists from federal, state, and local agencies, as well as members of the public. The team meets twice a year, once in the spring and once in the fall, to evaluate the management of the ranch against specific environmental goals.

The Donaldsons were out ahead of most of their neighbors in terms of running an ecologically sensitive ranch, but the rest of the Sonoita Valley community was not that far behind. In the mid-1990s, people from the valley, seeking to maintain both their working ranches and the natural values of their surroundings, approached the Sonoran Institute to conduct a series of what the organization calls visioning workshops. The Sonoran Institute helped a group of community members work through the process of determining what they value the most, and what they want to see in the future. They all wanted to protect the biological diversity of the region, while allowing people to live on and work the land, and keep it from turning into suburban sprawl. "The community—ranchers, retirees, environmentalists, everybody—realized we had the same vision for the future," says Roseann Hanson.

A shared vision did not mean the process was a love-fest from day one. "At the beginning there were environmentalists from Phoenix who were coming down, there was a lot of tension and anger, arguments and shouting matches," says Hanson. "But it evolved into a partnership, which has evolved into friendships. People who wanted to strangle each other now have tremendous respect for each other," she says.

The workshops led to the creation of several community organizations, one of which, the Sonoita Valley Planning Partnership, began working with the BLM on a management plan for the Resource Management Area. In addition to the land leased to the Donaldsons for grazing, BLM managed the area for recreation, mountain biking, and upland bird hunting, but not for conservation.

The idea of allowing communities living near and using public land to have a major say in how that land is managed has become a common approach to conservation in the developing world—with distinctly mixed results—but it remains the exception in the United States. At Las Cienegas, the community-based approach to the management plan began with a focus on the 43,000-acre resource management area, but quickly grew from there. "Because of the visioning workshops, the history of collaborative conservation, and the will of local residents, the process morphed into something considerably bigger—a landscape vision of conservation," Hanson wrote in a case study of the Cienega Creek watershed.[26]

The community wanted to expand their vision for Cienega Creek far beyond the BLM land, across Interstate 10 and all the way to Rincon Wilderness. This land was largely state trust land and, if added, it would enlarge the planning area to about 140,000 acres. The community wanted the whole thing designated a national conservation area (NCA), a congressional designation meant to conserve particularly important BLM land for its exceptional natural, recreational, cultural, wildlife, aquatic, archeological, paleontological, historical, educational, and/or scientific resources. The thirteen areas so designated make up the National Landscape Conservation System and range in size from nearly 10 million acres in the California Desert to just over 20,000 acres in Arizona's Gila Box Riparian National Conservation Area, which protects parts of Bonita Creek and the Gila River.

With all the community support for Las Cienegas, the proposed national conservation area got the backing of Interior Secretary Bruce Babbitt as well as Jim Kolbe, a Republican congressman who represented the Sonoita Valley. With such bipartisanship, and endorsements from environmentalists, ranchers, and even real estate developers, the bill to create the Las Cienegas National Conservation Area passed unanimously, an unheard-of event. Even more remarkably, the bill passed at a time when western congressional delegations scowled at the very mention of a new federal land acquisition.

"This is why we are committed to community-driven conservation," says Roseann Hanson. "It is from the bottom up. The community did it, with help. Now this landscape is protected so far into the future we can step back a bit and focus elsewhere. If BLM sidesteps, changes staff, and drops the ball on its management plan, the community will be all over them. This is protection far down into the future, several generations."

But Las Cienegas was not a complete victory. During negotiations over the bill, Congress and the Arizona State Land Department removed the area between Interstate 10 and the national park and wilderness area, thus creating the missing link. They also placed the nonfederal land in an acquisition planning district, which did not provide immediate protection but made it a priority for future acquisition by the state or federal govern-ments. The Sonoran Desert Conservation Plan listed the missing link as among the highest priorities for protection in Pima County.

In early 2003, the Sonoran Institute completed a two-year assessment of the missing link, which they named the Cienega Corridor to make it more recognizable. Their research shows that local wildlife depend heavily on the fifty thousand acres of open desert and grasslands, which also con-tribute to the region's ecological health and to the health of the people of this largely rural area located on Tucson's rapidly growing eastern edge. The area, in combination with Las Cienegas National Conservation Area and the Cienega Creek watershed, provides up to 20 percent of Tucson's groundwater recharge system, which is needed for drinking water in the Tucson basin. Field studies by the Sky Island Alliance also demonstrated that the Cienega Corridor forms an important movement corridor for sky island mammals, especially black bears, mountain lions, coatimundis, and mule deer. The Cienega Corridor also provides habitat for six federally en-dangered plant and animal species and twelve species of special concern, contains numerous archaeological sites up to ten thousand years old, and, in addition to all this, still retains its rich ranching heritage.

Rapid development in the Tucson basin threatens these valuable cul-tural and natural resources. To act quickly on protecting this important landscape and its rural communities, the Sonoran Institute helped form the Cienega Corridor Conservation Council, an ad hoc coalition of more than forty landowners, local business leaders, land managers, and environ-mental advocates. This group is developing a protection plan for the corri-dor, giving presentations throughout the region, developing brochures, and sponsoring media events to spread the word about the corridor and its importance for conservation.

The efforts to protect the Cienega Corridor show promise, but there are no guarantees. "You need a core group of committed people who are will-ing to sit down at a table and work on a consensus basis with their neigh-bors," says Roseann Hanson, "with people who are not necessarily from their community, since this is public land, and keep coming to the table until you get it right."

In addition to public commitment and strong communities, you need a parallel set of organizations and agencies who are also committed, because this whole process costs money—money the community likely does not have. In Las Cienegas, the Sonoran Institute provided organizational and logistic support, and the BLM brought the willingness to have a community process.

"We have the notion that bringing in the community waters down the science and is bad for conservation. Having a strong community group with scientific input is one of the most lasting ways to achieve conservation," says Hanson. "One of the issues that we struggle with here, is we have to bring traditional knowledge to the table and acknowledge that science is not the only way to go."

Broad-scale conservation attempts to address huge, complex landscapes, but its success may boil down to the ability of small communities to come together over a shared vision for the future. The challenge goes far deeper than just getting communities to participate in conservation planning meetings, however. The loss of social capital means detachment between people and their civic role.

In some places, most famously among the Amish or the Mormons but also in other places scattered across the globe, the fabric of community remains intact. The same holds in a corner of Arizona not far from Las Cienegas, where two ranchers named Warner Glenn and Bill McDonald and their neighbors are working together to hold onto the radical center.

CHAPTER 6

THE NATIVE HOME OF HOPE

Angry as one may be at what heedless men have done and still do to
a noble habitat, one cannot be pessimistic about the West. This is the
native home of hope. When it fully learns that cooperation, not rugged
individualism, is the quality that most characterizes and preserves it,
then it will have achieved itself and outlived its origins. Then it has
a chance to create a society to match its scenery.
WALLACE STEGNER, The Sound of Mountain Water

Late in the winter of 1996, rancher Warner Glenn found what he believed to be the track of a large tom lion while hunting in the Peloncillo Mountains deep in southeastern Arizona. His six dogs chased the cat up and down ridges and in and out of canyons, leaving Glenn and his daughter, Kelly, struggling to catch up on their mules and amazed that any lion could run that far, that fast, and not give out.

Finally, Glenn knew from the dogs' short, choppy barks that they had bayed the cat in some large bluffs. After tying his mule to a branch, he walked around some thick trees to get a look at the lion that had led this chase. On top of the bluff, however, stood not a lion at all but a large male jaguar, in the prime of life and full of fight. Glenn was stunned. "God almighty!" he said, out loud. "That's a jaguar!"[1]

Glenn, a fourth-generation rancher, grew up helping his father hunt lions to protect the family livestock. He has a lion pelt and other trophies on his wall. At that moment, facing that jaguar, he stood at a crossroads. Many ranchers, brought face-to-face with an endangered species, even one as beautiful and seemingly out of place as a jaguar in the dry Arizona mountains, would reach for their gun. "Shoot, shovel, and shut up" remains the operating principle here: jaguars have been sighted in this country only sixty-four times in the twentieth century, and sixty-two of those jaguars were killed.[2] But Warner Glenn's love of the land and respect for wild things made it impossible for him to consider shooting that jaguar. "It was a *jaguar*," he says.

Glenn reached instead for his camera. He took a series of jaw-dropping photos believed to be the first ever of a jaguar in the United States. Looking at those pictures—a huge blow-up of one adorns a wall in Glenn's house—reminds you of why people care about preserving open space. More than that, the photos serve as icons for the possibilities of conservation. Perhaps that jaguar ventured north from Mexico's Sierra Madres Occidental into the Peloncillos in search of a new home range, and perhaps his presence marked the first step in the return of the jaguars to Arizona, where they once ranged. That may be unlikely, as better habitat lies to the south, but more jaguars have been found in southern Arizona since 1996. It may not be too late to save the vast and intact desert landscapes the big cat needs to survive.

✦ ✦ ✦

The key to saving that landscape may lie with people like Glenn and his neighbor, Bill McDonald. No one could fairly call Glenn and McDonald radicals. They are ranchers, like generations before them, and they look the part—tall, weathered, unflappable. McDonald was president of the local cattlegrowers association, and Glenn guides hunting trips. They do not want to hold political office or change the world, at least not too much. They want to keep their ranches, plain and simple.

Glenn and McDonald recognized some time ago that maintaining their ranches would be neither plain nor simple. In order to keep their land, Glenn, McDonald, and other ranchers in the neighborhood—a remote, ecologically intact, and biologically rich corner hard by the Mexican border in Arizona and New Mexico—must dramatically recast conservation and land management in the arid West. They have a forward-looking vision for their vast landscapes, what they call "working wilderness." Their vision takes root in science, but these ranchers also look back to a time when cohesive communities worked together to solve common problems.

Ranchers by themselves cannot prevent suburban sprawl and the host of other threats they face. In some parts of the West, however, ranches could be the best way to preserve grasslands and the periodic fires that keep brush and cactuses from taking over. Some recent studies suggest that large, intact working cattle ranches hold together increasingly fragmented landscapes. Other scientists and conservation activists angrily dispute that notion: for pure vitriol, few debates can match the one over grazing on public land. The story of Warner Glenn, Bill McDonald, and their neighbors does not hold all the keys to resolving that dispute—no universal truths apply to every bit of rangeland west of the Mississippi—but their experience offers an opportunity to explore the common values that may allow broad-scale conservation in the region to proceed even as ideologues on both sides continue to lob grenades at each other from their deep trenches.

The public-land-grazing debate, for all its ferocity, misses the point. The fate of public land across the West is tied to private land. The homesteaders who settled the arid land chose to settle, not surprisingly, near water and good grazing. Private ranches, so-called deeded lands, lie at lower elevations and boast richer soils and more water than surrounding public land, and tend to coincide with the greatest ecological value or potential. Federally owned land alone cannot conserve all ecosystems and species in the West, including some of the most at-risk elements of biodiversity in the United States. We will need to learn again how to use land well. In the desert Southwest, the best place to learn that lesson is the region Warner Glenn and Bill McDonald call home, which includes one of the most renowned ranches of all: the colossal Gray Ranch in New Mexico, where five hundred square miles of intact landscapes provide a laboratory for innovative science and conservation.

THE RADICAL CENTER

Bill McDonald may appear uncomplicated, but he is not the Marlboro man. He possesses a keen mind, a degree in political science from Arizona State University, and a MacArthur Fellowship—the "genius award"—for his work conserving open space in the borderlands. "He is one of the smartest people I have ever worked with," says Mike Dennis, for many years the general counsel for The Nature Conservancy and now the organization's director of conservation real estate. "He could run anything; he could run a major corporation, he could run the country."[3]

Making a cattle ranch in southern Arizona a going concern in the twenty-first century may be challenge enough. Small, independent ranchers, a description that encompasses most ranchers in that part of the country, often cannot make ends meet on ranching alone, and must supplement their income by guiding hunting trips (as Warner Glenn does), driving school buses, or running road graders. They could not survive at all without access to land owned by the state or federal governments, and therein lies the rub.

The role of cattle and cattle ranching in the ecological transformation and often outright destruction of the arid West forms one of the most active faultlines in the debate over conservation versus use of natural resources. Stereotypes abound: on one side stand the ranchers, in their own eyes defenders of the great American cowboy tradition and the right to private property, but in environmentalists' eyes presumptuous despoilers of land that belongs to all Americans; on the other side stand meddling tree-huggers, who would be more than happy to see ranchers and their livestock banished from public land. John Muir called sheep "hooved locusts" and was none too fond of cattle, either. The "cow-free" movement is powerful and vocal. Yet ranchers and environmentalists together may be the last levee holding back the flood of suburban homogeneity.

The differences between the two sides run deep. Guy McPherson, an ecologist at the University of Arizona in Tucson, argues the differences stem from neither ideological wars nor scientific debates. "I think that the biggest cultural gap in the West is not between Native Americans and Anglos or Hispanics and Anglos, it's not between ranchers and environmentalists, it's between producers and consumers," he says. "We are such a consumer-oriented society, so the people that produce things for that consumer-oriented society, in the case of ranchers in particular because that production is relatively small, are completely beyond the imagination of most consumers."[4]

Bill McDonald and his neighbors, as well as some scientists and conservationists, have decided that no one can win this battle, so they are seeking another solution. For other landowners in the West, environmental regulation and federal ownership in general inspired the Sagebrush Rebellion and the county-supremacy movement, born in Catron County, New Mexico, not far from Bill McDonald's ranch in Sycamore Canyon, Arizona. Such efforts cause a commotion and stir up activists on either side of the debate, but ultimately change nothing.

McDonald's solution lies in what he calls the "radical center." McDonald did not invent the phrase—it stems from geometry, and the early-twentieth-century Czech playwright Karel Capek adopted it as well—but he has reinvigorated it. True radicalism, as opposed to mindless extremism, means recognizing that neither banning cows altogether nor turning the keys to the public range over to the local cattlegrowers association will solve anything.

For McDonald, anyone who cares about the land has a stake in that land, a community of interest rather than just a community of place. Ranchers tend to get their backs up when strangers try to tell them what to do, so the idea of inviting scientists, federal officials, and conservation organizations to sit at the table with ranchers as equals is another truly radical notion. Love of the land, McDonald believes, transcends the differences. By broadening the definition of who has legitimate interest in the land, McDonald has also broadened the community that must define the future of that land. The radical center rests on a common vision of what the land should be.

At a meeting in New Mexico in early 2003, McDonald joined a group of ranchers, environmentalists, and academic researchers (Warner Glenn and Guy McPherson among them) to write a formal "invitation to join the radical center." A "declaration of interdependence," according to one participant, the invitation calls for an end to the acrimony and polarization of the debate over grazing on public land. "We believe that some lands should not be grazed by livestock; but also that much of the West can be grazed in an ecologically sound manner," the drafters wrote. As an indication of the challenges ahead, the president of the New Mexico woolgrowers association refused to sign the document because of the statement that there are some places that should not be grazed at all. Presumably the woolgrowers believe that every place should be grazed, including national parks, streambanks, steep hillsides, and the courthouse lawn.

The New Mexico woolgrowers stand at one end of the spectrum of ideas about the future of the western landscape. Bill McDonald stands at the other. His vision, broad in both space and time, resonates with Aldo Leopold's land ethic: "A thing is right when it tends to preserve the integrity, stability, and beauty of the biotic community. It is wrong when it tends otherwise."[5] In the desert Southwest, thinking big is not a luxury or an academic exercise, but a necessity. Scientists increasingly recognize that ecological systems in the Southwest or anywhere else are not static, nor do they progress neatly from one state to another. They are far more chaotic, driven by unpredictable events like fires, and shaped to a large degree by changes in climate at the scale of both decades and centuries. At the same time, ranchers, scientists, and conservationists more and more realize that they cannot address human activities, particularly efforts to control fire, graze cattle, and, most recently and perhaps most disturbingly, to subdivide the landscape into smaller and smaller privately owned parcels, with a piece-by-piece approach.

Traditions die hard, however. Many ranchers still live by the old ways, embodied in such maxims as "if a cow is doing good, don't move her," "you've got to run all the cattle you can," and "you've got to use your leased land hard."[6] The emphasis on the condition of the cow rather than the condition of the land runs counter to any land ethic and presents an enormous obstacle to bringing conservationists and ranchers together. Innovative ranchers like McDonald, Glenn, and their neighbors Drummond Hadley and his son, Seth, are working to overcome those obstacles, but the outcome remains far from clear.

These ranchers and about one hundred other people live in an area of roughly 1 million acres, nearly the size of Delaware, which for comparison has a population of about eight hundred thousand. Their ranches and neighboring public land lie within one of the biologically richest areas of North America. Few places on the continent support as many different species and natural communities, and fewer still present such opportunities for conservation. There may not be a better test case for broad-scale conservation, though it may no longer be such a great place to ranch cattle.

MALPAI

The first breeding population of cattle in the southwestern United States arrived in the late seventeenth century with the Jesuit missionary Eusebio Francisco Kino and found itself in cow heaven: a region that essentially had not been grazed for ten thousand years and got a good amount of rain.[7] With a bit of water at the right time, the volcanic soils of the Southwest produce extravagantly—one nineteenth-century horseman reported that his stirrups were never out of the grass from El Paso to the Animas Valley in southwestern New Mexico.[8]

Apart from the relatively large towns of Tucson and Tubac, the Spanish left behind few widespread or enduring impacts on the land. The next wave of settlers would not be so gentle. In 1848, the United States took ownership of the region—along with most of New Mexico, Arizona, Nevada, Utah, Colorado, and California—following the war with Mexico. The United States and Mexico struck a deal regarding the border that created an area that came to be called the bootheel of New Mexico. Remote and sparsely settled—Hidalgo County, the only county in the bootheel, still has fewer than two people per square mile—this arid land straddling the New Mexico–Arizona border would retain much of its natural character for the next 140 years. For much of that time it was nearly lawless country as well. Apaches fighting under Cochise and then Geronimo made this region their last stronghold, but in 1886 Geronimo surrendered at Skeleton Canyon. Nearby, the mining town of Tombstone still rings with memories of the Earps, Clantons, Doc Holliday, and the OK Corral, despite the motels and tourist shops.[9]

One man connects Geronimo, Wyatt Earp, Warner Glenn, Bill McDonald, The Nature Conservancy, and Mickey Mouse. Born in Louisiana in 1841 and raised in Texas, John Horton Slaughter worked his way west and in the mid-1880s bought some sixty-five thousand acres of an old Mexican land grant called the San Bernardino. A former Texas Ranger and Confederate soldier, Slaughter served in the campaign against the Apaches. Skeleton Canyon was on the San Bernardino, and Slaughter witnessed Geronimo's surrender.[10]

Blessed with springs and artesian wells, the ranch was an ideal place to graze cattle, and Slaughter had huge herds, up to one hundred thousand head by some reports. This was the heyday of the cattle rancher—in Arizona in 1870, ranchers held less than forty thousand cattle, but by 1891 the Arizona herd had exploded to 1.5 million head.[11] The good times would not last long.

In 1891, with millions of cows on the range, climate and capitalism collided. Drought hit hard for two years, but heavily indebted ranchers held on, knowing that selling at the bottom of the market meant losing their land. They lost it anyway. Cows grazed the entire region—southeastern Arizona, southwestern New Mexico, Chihuahua, Sonora—down to bare ground. Half to three-quarters of the cows died. You could throw a rock from one dead cow to another, the cowboys said, and they had to strain their drinking water through burlap sacks to get rid of the maggots.[12] Old photos show huge piles of bleached cow bones; ranchers dumped the bones into train cars and shipped them east to fertilizer factories. Arizona had become "a region more completely divested of range grasses than any other in the entire country" wrote a government botanist in 1901.[13] With no vegetation to hold the soil, erosion loomed as the next blow, as soon as the rain came. Rain came in buckets from 1896 to 1898 and again from 1907 to 1911, washing away topsoil and cutting deep, ragged arroyos. Many of the arroyo cuts in the region today trace their genesis to the drought of 1891.[14] The San Simon Valley, east of Tucson on the New Mexico border, lush with grasses when settlers first arrived, became a scrubland with hardly a blade of grass to be seen. So it remains, a global example of desertification.

John Slaughter survived, personally and financially, in part because he also served three terms as sheriff of Cochise County. Slaughter knew Wyatt Earp, who was a U.S. marshal, and his brothers, and he considered the whole Earp clan to be tinhorn gamblers. As sheriff, Slaughter vowed to tame the lawless county and rid Cochise of bandits, and so he did, with ruthless efficiency. Walt Disney would later romanticize Slaughter's exploits in the late 1950s television series *Texas John Slaughter*, one of countless contributors to the myth of the Wild West.

Texas John defined "bandits" rather loosely and conveniently; his definition covered any law-abiding settler who might pose a threat to his cattle empire. He dealt violently with them, too. Some families stood up to him and remained in the territory, among them Bill McDonald's ancestors. The early settlers had other problems as well; they quickly learned that homesteading laws under which they acquired land were designed for the humid East and did not work in the arid West. In the well-watered East, the standard surveyor's unit of a mile-square section—640 acres—would easily support four families. Not so in the arid West. John Wesley Powell suggested a western homestead should be no less than four full sections, 2,560 acres.[15] Despite Powell's efforts, Congress did not change the laws to meet unique circumstances. Other laws prevented fencing of the public domain. In southeastern Arizona and southwestern New Mexico, rangeland fragmentation began with the arrival of Anglo-American ranchers, as settlers claimed areas near water and relied on the public land for the rest. By the early 1900s, settlers had divided the land into parcels too small to be economically or ecologically sustainable for cattle ranching.

Slaughter had put together quite an empire, however, and he kept his operation going until he died in 1922. The government eventually declared his ranch a national historic landmark. The Nature Conservancy bought the ranch and in 1982 conveyed the bulk of it to the U.S. Fish and Wildlife Service to become the San Bernardino National Wildlife Refuge.

❖   ❖   ❖

That maneuver unnerved the neighbors, particularly Warner and Wendy Glenn. The Glenns own a ranch in the San Bernardino Valley that had been carved out of Slaughter's holdings, which are surrounded now by the new preserve on three sides, with Mexico on the fourth. The Glenns hoped The Nature Conservancy would keep the property as a working ranch. The organization quickly became a villain when it turned the property over to the government, crushing any hope of grazing cattle on the well-watered bottomlands.

Warner Glenn responded by seeking the radical center. He could serve as a symbol for that very notion, though his modesty would not allow it. A self-effacing, unfailingly gracious man with a slow drawl, he has deep roots in the dry southwestern soil. Unlike Bill McDonald, who testifies before Congress and makes speeches all across the country and seems completely comfortable doing so, Glenn embodies the land on which he was raised. He dedicated the small book he wrote to accompany the publication of his jaguar photos to his hounds and his mules, a dedication that in other hands might be contrived but for him is sincere and appropriate.[16] "You've heard it said before that someone looks like a million dollars," the journalist Verlyn Klinkenborg wrote after meeting Glenn. "Warner Glenn looks like a million acres."[17]

Glenn's ancestors settled in southern Arizona just after the Civil War, part of the great westward expansion of the United States. He moved to his ranch in the San Bernardino Valley in the early 1960s; his mother still has a place just a few miles to the northwest. When it came time to name their new place they found all the pretty ranch names had been taken, so they chose Malpai, from the Spanish *mal pais*, "bad lands," and also the name of a volcanic rock common to these parts. The Glenn ranch encompasses fifteen thousand acres, roughly two-thirds of which are on leased public land, mostly Arizona state trust land. The Malpai Ranch is one of the smaller in the neighborhood. Apart from the five-hundred-square-mile Gray Ranch, acquired by The Nature Conservancy in 1989, the other ranches in the area range between fifteen thousand and forty thousand acres, at least half on public land, which the ranchers lease for grazing. Out here, with little rain even in good times, a cow and her calf require fifty acres.

In the early 1990s, however, access to grazing on public land seemed at risk. Secretary of State Bruce Babbitt floated a plan that would have nearly tripled the base federal livestock grazing fee from $1.23 per head per month to $3.96, still far below the going rate of about $10.00 per head per month on private land, but potentially the death knell for financially strapped ranchers. Federal land-management agencies also faced increasing scrutiny of their actions from lawsuits filed under the Endangered Species Act. Ranchers, too, felt themselves on the defensive, always resisting some federal initiative or some environmental agenda. The response, Bill McDonald says, produced little: "I've sat through one thousand cattle-grower meetings where everyone complains that everything is going to hell but provide no alternative."[18]

Spurred in part by the range-reform proposal, Glenn, McDonald, and some of their neighbors, along with representatives of The Nature Conservancy and others in the environmental community, began meeting at Glenn's ranch in 1991 to discuss mutual concerns about perceived threats to their culture and lifestyle. They called themselves the Malpai group and continued meeting at various ranch homes for two years. The members of the Malpai group worried about the future of public land grazing in the West, as well as environmental and economic issues, and sought new ideas that would allow them both to live on and protect a million-acre stretch of land.

Glenn, McDonald, and the others quickly identified a common desire to protect the open spaces of the Southwest. One deciding factor in Warner Glenn's decision to tell people about his encounter with the jaguar was his faith in the ability of a small community of ranchers to make it turn out right.[19] "Ranchers, historically speaking, are scared to death to have an endangered species found on their place because they think, well, then they're going to make you quit grazing," he says. "Well, what we're trying to prove is that if there's an endangered species there and it is co-existing at the present time with grazing, then there's no reason why it shouldn't continue to be that way."[20]

The Malpai group focuses on a region that forms a rough pyramid of about a million acres, with the base extending seventy miles along the Mexican border from near Douglas, Arizona, to Antelope Wells, New Mexico, with the apex near Rodeo, on the New Mexico–Arizona border. Ranchers who own or lease 800,000 of those acres explicitly support the Malpai group's efforts. Telephones did not reach the area until 1985, though fiber optic cables arrived in 2003, and ranchers used generators for power until the 1990s. The planning area includes about 53 percent private land (though the Gray Ranch's predominantly private 320,000 acres skew this figure) and 23 percent state trust land. Just under one-fifth of the land falls within Coronado National Forest, and the BLM administers about one-tenth of the land.[21]

The region forms part of what biogeographers call the Maze, a high plateau reaching north from Mexico with mountains forming a basin-and-range topography. To the north and west lies the Sonoran Desert, and to the south and east lies the Chihuahuan Desert—both at lower elevations and both rich in biological diversity. Malpai is higher and wetter than the land that surrounds it, but, most remarkably, Malpai remains filled with native species and virtually no exotics—the result of the lack of roads, the climate, or a combination of the two.

The Malpai group was still an informal gathering until 1993, when concerns over the role of fire in the grasslands pushed the ranchers to take the next step to becoming better organized. That year, the Forest Service suppressed a small brushfire, over the objections of the ranch manager whose land was involved. The ranchers appreciated the role that fire played in rejuvenating grazed land, but the Forest Service generally fought every fire. In order to get more say in how the Forest Service managed fire on land they grazed, the Malpai members requested the agencies join with the landowners to create a comprehensive fire-management plan for the region. They wanted to show the Forest Service and other agencies the places where ranchers wanted fire suppressed, where it should burn, and where they wanted to be consulted when fire broke out. The group also wanted to start experimenting with fire on a grand scale. One result is a fire map that shows where wildfires will be allowed to burn on private property with the landowner's consent.

The Malpai region may be one of the few in the country where a large-scale attempt could be made to replicate frequent natural fires. The relationships among the Malpai ranchers, neighbors, agencies, and rural fire departments have led to more natural fires being allowed to burn, and there have been three prescribed burns, one of which was the largest prescribed burn in U.S. history. Hundreds of thousands of acres have burned since 1994. In the Malpai area, wildfires can burn freely now on most of the land, up to the northern border, where real estate signs on newly divided land signal the end of any chance to keep natural forces at work.

In order to keep their ranches operating while protecting and restoring ecological diversity, Glenn, McDonald, and the others formally launched the Malpai Borderlands Group as a nonprofit organization in 1994. It has a twelve-member board of directors, including nine ranchers who own land in the region. All landowners in the region are welcome to join the group. The Natural Resource Conservation Service and the Forest Service provide liaisons to the group, and two BLM districts work closely with the group as well.

In a bold move, the group also invited the formal participation of The Nature Conservancy, despite the organization's role in creating the San Bernardino National Wildlife Refuge and general suspicion among the ranchers about large, national environmental groups. Although some ranchers pulled out, fearful that the Conservancy would take over the Malpai Borderlands Group, most stayed. The Conservancy made a lasting commitment to the families in the region. "Maybe cattle won't be the answer, but these people will be," says the Conservancy's Mike Dennis.

The Malpai Borderlands Group invited all neighbors in the region to come together for a goal-setting session. With a great deal of community input, the group drafted the following statement: "Our goal is to restore and maintain the natural processes that create and protect a healthy unfragmented landscape to support a diverse, flourishing community of human, plant, and animal life in our Borderlands region. Together we will accomplish this by working to encourage profitable ranching and other traditional livelihoods which will sustain the open space nature of our land for generations to come."

The Malpai Borderlands Group is a new shoot from an old branch, reminding one early participant, Bill Miller, Sr., of what he called "neighboring"—the way things were done when ranchers had only their neighbors to rely upon. The cowboy myth highlights the strong, silent individualist, and ranchers are no doubt an independent and self-reliant group. What the myth obscures, however, is their social capital: the long-standing ability—necessity, actually—for ranchers and other rural communities to come together for collective action. Alexis de Tocqueville commented on the dichotomy between competitiveness and cooperation in the American character in 1835. In the West, stockmen's associations, created to sustain local communities through cooperative land management and livestock marketing and also to bring cattle thieves to justice, date to the years just after the Civil War.[22] In Mexico, ranchers long ago learned the value of *ejidos,* the model that John Wesley Powell wanted to adopt. Wallace Stegner reminds us of his friend and fellow Pulitzer Prize–winning author Bernard DeVoto's remark that the only true rugged individualists in the West generally wound up at the end of a rope whose other end was in the hands of the cooperating citizenry.[23]

Memories of "neighboring" convinced Miller and his son, Bill Miller, Jr., to support the efforts of the Malpai Group. "Seems to me that this group coming together here today is the way it used to be when we all helped each other through tough years,"[24] he said. The younger Miller, a staunch conservative, active member of the New Mexico Republican Party, and owner of the Post Office Canyon Ranch in New Mexico, fits no traditional definition of an environmentalist. He is, however, now the chairman of the Malpai Borderlands Group's board of directors. Bill McDonald is executive director, with more of the day-to-day management responsibilities.

Miller runs board meetings firmly and efficiently. The group holds its meetings in a spacious, high-ceilinged addition that the Glenns put on their ranch house in the late 1990s. The new wing, decorated with some of Warner Glenn's hunting trophies, books, and maps, also provides space for the Malpai group's offices, which Wendy Glenn and Mary McDonald run with energy and zeal. Even with the new space, the room strains to fit the forty-some people who attend a typical meeting. Board members gather around tables, with ranchers from the area and assorted staff, advisers, and guests spread out in chairs across the room.

The topics of board meetings range from mundane scheduling concerns to far more meaningful questions about how to work with the government agencies to manage fire or endangered species. Most striking, however, is that the ranchers who dominate this group—though it has explicit conservation goals, this is clearly a group of ranchers—act as a community. Everyone has a voice, though there is little obvious dissent; the few ranchers in the region who do not endorse the group do not attend the meetings.

"You have to work in one of these community-based projects in order to believe in them," says Bill Weeks, a senior executive with The Nature Conservancy throughout the formation of the Malpai Borderlands Group, and another signatory to the invitation to join the radical center. "I felt at the end of working with these people that although we didn't see the world the same way, they had more in common with my love of the land than most people in society. They knew, lived on, and cared for the land in a way that I felt reflected the same ethic that I had, to a much deeper degree than almost any other element in society, including urban environmentalists, who like the idea of the land but don't know the land. I felt like if we are sitting at the same table, we could come to reasonable decisions for the conservation of biodiversity on the land together, and we had an as good or better chance of doing that right as anybody else."[25]

Whether the lesson of Malpai can be exported remains an open question. The project benefits from heavy subsidies; while a million acres or so is a lot of land, few other stretches of that size have gotten as much attention from either the federal government or organizations like The Nature Conservancy. The Malpai ranchers also have access to the water and vast grasslands of the Gray Ranch, and the financial and political connections of people like Bill Miller and Bill McDonald. While Malpai may serve as a model of how conservation can succeed in working landscapes, if every million-acre landscape requires the same investment, we are going to need quite a bit more money.

SCIENCE IN THE TRENCHES

Conservationists usually assume, with some justification, that ranchers like Miller and McDonald see the world as just so many resources ripe for the picking, and have little patience for the process of science. Yet most ranchers have more than an economic interest in their land, and have insights into how the land works that may allow them to see how they fit into the larger puzzle of conservation and use. In another stroke of good fortune for the Malpai ranchers, scientists have been studying the region for more than a century and have begun to tease apart the mysteries of the deserts.

Science, says Bill Weeks, gives the Malpai Borderlands Group a rudder. "From the beginning, they invested in science, committed to gathering information scientifically." The investment enables the group to defend their decisions, providing a basis for responding to community demands as well as to federal land-management decisions based on the government's own research. The input from scientists gave the Malpai Borderlands Group a systems-based approach that emphasized conservation of natural processes rather than a single-species focus.

Science may be a double-edged sword in the borderlands. Scientific credibility is essential to maintaining conservation efforts because if local people are to play leadership roles in preserving their landscape, they must demonstrate through independent, peer-reviewed science that their efforts are defensible and ecologically sustainable. Yet the insights that science provides will not consistently match the interests of the local community. The benefits outweigh the risks, however, because without science, long-term landscape conservation remains a fantasy.

Ecologist Charles Curtin coordinates the Malpai Borderlands research program from a field office in Animas, New Mexico, and his home in Maine. Curtin argues that conservation advocates should move away from asking how small an area is sufficient to preserve populations of species or their habitats and ask how big an area is needed to preserve the dynamic interactions of natural processes that sustain a functioning ecosystem, including its human inhabitants.

"For so long, conservation biologists have asked what is the minimum viable area, what is the smallest area you need to preserve species x, y, or z. The Malpai group really asks the inverse question. They ask, how big a landscape do you need to preserve the processes that preserve the species?" says Curtin, whose soft voice and rounded features fit oddly in a roomful of thick-skinned ranchers. Posing the question in that way leads to whole new ways of thinking about conservation, a kind of thinking, Curtin argues, that comes naturally to a rancher. "What is interesting to me in terms of science is that people who are based on the land often have an inherently

longer-term, larger-scale view of the world than people who are profes-
sionally trained as biologists."[26]

Curtin and other scientists, as well as the Malpai ranchers, also believe
that conserving ecological processes requires maintaining certain social
conditions. The best way to preserve the open spaces and ecosystems and
diverse biota of the West, this argument goes, is to keep rural people on the
land. If ranching is both ecologically sustainable and economically viable,
then ranchers, government, and the public would be foolhardy to allow
continuing degradation of the range. Wise pastoral stewardship will go a
long way toward maintaining biodiversity and ecological integrity on both
public and private rangeland, according to Charles Curtin.

Good ranching practices by themselves will not be enough, particularly
in the face of a changing climate. Changes in climate have always shaped
the Southwest, a land of cyclic and pervasive vegetation patterns driven by
climate. In the late nineteenth century, for example, a period of unusually
dry winters and cool summers called the Little Ice Age ended, and the climate returned to the pattern we see today—warm summers with monsoon
rains and winters with at least some rain. Under these conditions, the
grasses that had thrived since the fourteenth century suddenly could barely
survive. The changes continue. Tree-ring chronologies show that the
abundant rain (for a desert, that is) that characterized the 1960s to the
1980s had not occurred in nearly two thousand years.

The good rains will not return for some time. According to scientists
who study global climatic cycles, two broad patterns, the Pacific Decadal
Oscillation and the Atlantic Multidecadal Oscillation, are entering a period in which they are aligned as they were in the 1950s—when the Southwest witnessed a truly amazing deep drought. "These data suggest that the
ultra-wet period is behind us, and that terrifying days are ahead for ranchers," says Guy McPherson. The Gray Ranch and Bill Miller completely
destocked early in 2004, hoping to wait out the drought and then bring
back their herd. Other ranchers faced the same dilemma and everyone
prayed for rain.

That the combination of cows and drought can reduce desert grassland to waste seems intuitively obvious, and presents an equally obvious
solution. By its very name, desertification conjures images of barren and
eroded land, of natural disasters compounded by human folly. The desert,

however, confounds both our senses and our intellect. In at least one small part of Arizona, the changes in the landscape we associate with cattle and drought and call desertification may stem, oddly enough, from too much rain.

✦ ✦ ✦

At his long-term study site in Portal, Arizona, just north of the Malpai region, Jim Brown, one of the most highly regarded ecologists in the world, has been studying a fenced area since 1977 and examining the impact of climate change on the native plants and animals and comparing grazed and ungrazed areas. Over the past quarter century, winter precipitation has been significantly higher than the long-term average, with four El Niño events. The unusually high winter precipitation favors woody shrubs at the expense of grasses, in part because the shrubs use a photosynthetic pathway that allows them to use energy more efficiently in cool weather, so they can become established during wet winters and prevent the grasses from ever taking hold. The result has been a threefold increase in shrubs after 1980, with identical increases in shrubs in fenced and unfenced areas.[27]

Similarly, recent climate change has triggered a coordinated syndrome of changes in the Chihuahuan Desert. Previously common animals have gone extinct locally, while rare species have increased. The keystone species in this system are the banner-tailed kangaroo rat *(Dipodomys spectabilis)*, the silky pocket mouse *(Perognathus flavus)*, and two species of seed-harvesting ants. For these species, which store grass seeds in large subterranean larders, an increase in woody vegetation is a decline in habitat quality, and the increased rain may also have soaked seed hoards. Another rodent, Bailey's pocket mouse, which had never before been seen on Brown's study site, colonized the area in 1995, possibly because shrubs provided cover and a decrease in other species had reduced competition. Once-common horned lizards are now rare in the area because there are fewer harvester ants for them to eat. Burrowing owls and Mojave rattlesnakes, two species that depend on kangaroo rats for food or their burrows for shelter, have also suffered.

This work provides a vivid demonstration of the complex dynamics of the desert ecosystems of the Southwest. A slight shift in climate—an increase in winter rainfall—triggered large and unexpected changes in vegetation and animal populations, the kinds of changes that would usually be expected to occur as a result of increased aridity or anthropogenic desertification. Effects on keystone species and biotic interactions amplified the climate changes to alter the entire ecosystem.[28]

The subtle and often confusing ecology of the desert and the passionate debate over grazing form a potent mix, and science inevitably gets caught up in it. The result can be science explicitly used to advance a particular position, or science shifted ever so slightly and perhaps unconsciously by advocacy. The Malpai ranchers engender fierce loyalty, and even the best scientists sometimes stumble while defending the cause the ranchers embody. In one experiment, for example, Jim Brown and Charles Curtin removed kangaroo rats and other rodents from small plots and examined the effects.[29] In all cases, woody shrubs increased and grasses decreased in plots from which the rodents had been removed. Brown and Curtin attribute the increase in woody shrubs to climate change, and argue that the rodents, some of which eat leaves and stems, other just leaves, mitigate the effects of climatically induced vegetation change. Herbivory by native species—birds, insects, small mammals—may be more important than herbivory by cattle. From there, Brown and Curtin go on to argue that cattle may play the same role as the small herbivorous mammals and that having cattle on the range will slow the climate-driven transition from grasses to woody plants, thus helping to keep native grasslands intact.

That argument certainly bolsters the case for keeping cattle on the range. But is it correct? Maybe not. First, the claim that climate change drives the increase in woody plants may be wrong. "Woody plants may have been established before the experiment started and just got bigger because they grew. Woody plants are going to get bigger, especially in the context of what they see as a long-term experiment," says Guy McPherson. McPherson also points out that the experiment has only been running for about one-tenth the life span of the woody plants. Second, and more importantly, the experiment concerned tiny herbivores, and the conclusions concerned huge ones. "The leap is profound," says McPherson. "The results suggest rodents, the conclusion is livestock. Cows good!"

Politicians and the public look to science for definitive answers when often the best it can offer is a better way to deal with inescapable doubt and ambiguity. "Policymakers have to be willing to live with ambiguity a lot better," says Guy McPherson. "The simple-minded idea that fire is good or that fire is bad, both of those are absolutely dead wrong. Asking whether livestock grazing is good or bad is the wrong question." It is both and neither, depending entirely on circumstance. Policymakers for generations have tried to simplify things and come up with policies that can be applied universally, but making the right decisions about how to use or not use land demands specific knowledge about specific times and specific places.

Science offers the best hope of gaining that knowledge, and the communities that live near those places must then find creative and flexible ways to apply it. In the Malpai Borderlands, one of those creative solutions involves a new twist on the age-old tradition of neighbor helping neighbor.

BANKING GRASS ON THE GRAYS

Bill McDonald, Bill Miller, and Warner Glenn unquestionably lead the Malpai Group. Yet at the head of the table, on either side of Bill Miller, at a regular board meeting in 2003 were two other ranchers from New Mexico, Drummond and Seth Hadley, father and son. They said little, but their presence in many ways makes the Malpai Borderlands Group possible. Drum, the elder Hadley—rancher, poet, and heir to the Anheuser-Busch fortune—may also be one of the most enigmatic figures in American conservation.

Drum Hadley owns the Guadalupe Canyon Ranch, Seth the Canyoncito Ranch nearby. But that does not begin to tell the story. Guadalupe Canyon is tucked into a remote corner of this remote corner of the country—while the ranch is in New Mexico, the only way to get there is over forty miles of rough dirt track running east out of Douglas, Arizona. Hadley found his way here in the early 1960s from his Missouri home via a roundabout route that included writing poetry in the Sierra Nevada with poets Gary Snyder and Philip Whalen, working as a ranch hand, and living in cow camps on both sides of the border. He learned the ranching business and by the time he bought his ranch in the early 1970s he seemed like any other rancher in the area. He built his fence posts out of wood just like everyone else, though his neighbors noticed that his house seemed a little more luxurious than most.

Hadley also ran his ranch a little differently. He cut back the number of cows and then ran miles of barbed wire along the ridgetops to keep them out of the streambeds. "The ranch that Drum bought was in tough shape and we all knew there was no way that he could do anything different," says Wendy Glenn. "It needed rest. He could do that for the land." In 1991, the New Mexico chapter of The Nature Conservancy gave him its Aldo Leopold Award for his exemplary stewardship of the Guadalupe Canyon Ranch.[30]

The ranch sits in the Guadalupe Mountains, which, along with the Peloncillo Mountains, form the western edge of the Animas Valley. To the east across the valley rise the Animas Mountains and the Continental Divide. This high valley, some five thousand feet in elevation, much of it an ancient lakebed, has numerous springs and lush grasses. In 1880, former Texas Ranger Michael Gray paid Curley Bill Graham, a gunman, cattle rustler, and yet another foe of John Slaughter, three hundred dollars for his squatter claim on about a thousand acres here. Just two years later, Gray sold it to California mining magnate George Hearst—father of newspaperman William Randolph Hearst—and his partners for twelve thousand dollars.[31] This was the first in a series of land purchases that would extend well into the twentieth century and create the Diamond A Ranch, one of the biggest cattle operations in American history.

The Diamond A would become a legend. Native grasses such as grama, big sacaton, tobosa, and three awn made ideal fodder, and the Diamond A supported fifty thousand head of cattle in its heyday. The herd dwindled after the turn of the century, but the ranch remained intact and under one ownership for nearly a century. With such a huge expanse of land, the Diamond A, still often called the Gray even though Michael Gray had owned just a portion of it for a few years, did not suffer nearly the degradation that plagued much of the surrounding land.

In the 1980s, a wealthy investor from Mexico City named Pablo Brener acquired the Gray Ranch when the previous owners went bankrupt. Though reduced in size from the peak years, the Gray still encompassed over five hundred square miles, including nearly the entire run of the Animas Mountains. Brener continued to run cattle on the ranch, but he wanted to sell out. Rumors ran rampant: several ranchers expressed interest, as did the Kennecott Copper Company and a wealthy Sri Lankan who planned to resettle all her relatives there. Local Fish and Wildlife Service (FWS) officials hoped to acquire the land and create the Animas Mountains National Wildlife Refuge, which they thought could attract up to thirty thousand visitors each year.

The Nature Conservancy had long been interested in the Gray Ranch as well. Conservancy scientists knew it as a largely intact ecosystem with dozens of natural communities and hundreds of species, including some listed as rare or endangered—like Gould's turkey, one of five turkey subspecies, which can be found only on the Gray and in the Peloncillos, where it has been reintroduced. Unable to resolve heated internal debate over whether to buy the ranch and run it as the country's biggest and best private reserve, turn it over to FWS and create a public reserve, or find another conservation-minded private buyer, the Conservancy decided to buy the ranch from Brener for $18 million and take a year to study it and come up with a long-term plan.

The Conservancy ultimately decided that the best course would be to seek a buyer who shared the organization's vision for the ranch. Finding a buyer rich enough to buy the Gray Ranch who would not try to recoup the investment directly was difficult. The Conservancy and media mogul Ted Turner had a deal on the table, and got as far as drawing up all the necessary papers, when Turner walked away. Then they needed a new buyer.

The local communities, meanwhile, harbored deep suspicions about the Conservancy's motives. Many of the Conservancy's new neighbors believed (as some still do) that the organization sought to buy up all of America's productive land. The New Mexico Cattle Growers Association passed a resolution saying the Conservancy had "contempt for local communities—the viability of rural and small town economies, trespass laws and ethical behavior." The cattlegrowers sought an end to the Conservancy's tax-exempt status and asked the state attorney general to investigate the Conservancy on grounds of "conflict of interest" and "conspiracy" with the government.[32]

As with the creation of the San Bernardino Reserve a decade earlier, the notion of the government taking over a working ranch caused a panic among the ranchers nearby, only this time the object was one of the largest and most famous ranches around. "Come back in ten years and see what's happened to this land," one rancher's wife said bitterly at the time. "There'll be people from the East and people from universities who have read some books coming down here telling us how to conserve things."[33]

Despite its reputation to the contrary among local ranchers, the Conservancy never tried to ban cattle grazing on the Gray. They took cows off the forty-four-thousand-acre lakebed pasture, kept cows out of the Animas Mountains, and cut the herd in half, to six thousand, but the longtime manager of the Gray Ranch remained in charge. At this point, the Conservancy still thought of Drum Hadley as a local, environmentally minded rancher, but not as a potential buyer of the Gray Ranch. Hadley did not see himself in such a prominent role, either.

Seth Hadley saw a solution, however. If he, his father, and his grandmother, Puddie Hadley, great-granddaughter of Anheuser-Busch founder Adolphus Busch, pooled their inheritance, they would easily have enough to buy the Gray Ranch and run it right. So the three generations of Hadleys created the nonprofit Animas Foundation with some $47 million.

The objective of the Animas Foundation was to demonstrate sustainable agriculture in harmony with the environment—a goal completely in keeping with the Malpai Group. As its first act, the foundation bought the Gray Ranch from the Conservancy for $13 million. "Let us hope that this story [of the Gray Ranch] points a direction for those still remaining open space lands to become connected to one another in a working rangeland wilderness across the west," Drum Hadley wrote in 1996.[34]

The Animas Foundation paid $5 million less for the Gray Ranch than what the Conservancy had paid Pablo Brener. The difference represents the value of what is called a conservation easement that the Conservancy retained on the property. The Gray Ranch was the first time many ranchers had heard of conservation easements, one of the central tools for the rapidly expanding land trust movement. Under a conservation easement, a landowner and a land trust or government agency reach a legal agreement to permanently limit uses of the land in order to protect its conservation value.

Donating a conservation easement means giving up some of the rights associated with the land. A rancher, for example, might give up the right to build additional structures, while retaining the right to graze cattle. As lawyers say, an easement also "runs with the land," meaning that future owners also will be bound by the easement's terms.

In the case of the Gray Ranch, the easement stipulated that the ranch can never be subdivided, that the rangeland must be maintained in a condition as good as or better than when the land was transferred, and that the Animas Foundation would establish and maintain 114 monitoring plots on the Gray Ranch in order to insure that the latter understanding is honored. No limits were set on the number of animals that may be grazed on the ranch; the number will be determined by the conditions of the rangeland. The Conservancy has the right to make yearly inspections in this regard.

An easement does not change the ownership of the land, nor does it impede the right to sell the land or pass it on to heirs. The most important benefit of an easement, in fact, may be preserving the ability to pass land on to the next generation. A conservation easement removes the land's development potential and thus lowers its market value, which in turn lowers the estate tax. The smaller tax burden can make a critical difference in the heirs' ability to keep the land intact.[35]

Once the right to subdivide has been extinguished through an easement, the value of the ranch depends on its productivity for livestock, which provides a strong incentive to preserve and improve range conditions. These legal tools only cover the land in private hands, however, leaving public-land-tenure issues unresolved. Ranchers won't sell or donate conservation easements if they think they might lose access to public land, as that would eliminate the ranching value and the development value would go with the easement, leaving the rancher with nothing.

Since 1994, the Malpai Borderlands Group has been a part of seven different conservation easements. Three of those easements were purchased for outright cash, and the other four easements were obtained in exchange for access to grass on the Gray Ranch. The seven transactions included approximately thirty-five thousand acres. The ranchers involved in the conservation easements sought out the Malpai group, and the terms of the easement were agreed upon by both parties to meet joint objectives. The group has not accepted easements outside the borderlands area, but has helped ranchers find other appropriate easement holders.

The existence of the Gray Ranch and its colossal pastures enabled Hadley and others to design another ingenious mechanism to promote both conservation and private ranchers. The biggest problem with arid-land grazing is that most ranches are not big enough to capture the regional variation in rainfall. What no single ranch could accomplish, many ranches together could.

"I remember once when it hadn't rained and Grandpa Ira didn't have grass or water and was about to sell his herd," Hadley writes, quoting an old rancher from the region. "Frank Krentz spoke up then and said, 'Ira, it's rained on my place. I've got feed and water, so why don't you bring your cattle over to my place for a while?'"[36]

In 1995, Hadley built on that neighborly approach and developed the idea of a grassbank. In a grassbank, the trick is to leverage the short-term use of grass for long-term conservation. "I'm not that familiar with economics, but I am familiar with metaphor," wrote Hadley.[37] With the Malpai grassbank, Hadley and the other local ranchers have developed a system of moving cattle to where the grass is, so that the ranchland can rest.

❦ ❦ ❦

This kind of communal land management also resembles the pastoralism found in Africa. The Maasai and their pastoralist ancestors of East Africa, for example, have for three thousand years grazed cattle on dry, marginal land. Without fences but with strong community traditions, the Maasai move their herds constantly across the landscape, never staying in one place for too long. Such mobility may not last, however, as one element of the new constitution in Kenya involves subdividing land and granting private title to areas once held in common. In many ways the Maasai are at a point similar to the western United States before the Homestead Act, and representatives from the Maasai have met with the Malpai ranchers in the hope of avoiding the mistake of creating private ranches that are too small from an ecological perspective and are cut off from the surrounding land.

A grassbank loans the use of its pasture grasses to a rancher in return for the rancher placing a land-use easement on his or her land. The easement stipulates that the rancher will never subdivide the land; this keeps the ranch intact, rests the land, improves wildlife habitat, keeps fine fuels available and thus allows the reintroduction of fire, increases forage, and generates increased revenue. If rain falls on resting grassland, there will be significant increase in propagation. Benefits of the grassbank include increased calf-weaning rates, weight at sale, and yearling weights, as well as an increased calf crop.

Innovative ideas, unfortunately, won't change the weather. In January

2004, the grassbank ran out of grass as the prolonged drought hammered the Gray Ranch and every other ranch in the region. Over sufficiently long periods, nature trumps science and management every time.

COWS, CONDOS, AND CONTROVERSY

The land that ranchers use for cattle in the Southwest contains numerous distinct ecological communities, called by a variety of overlapping and similar-sounding names: scrub, steppe, desertscrub, thornscrub, chaparral, savanna, desert grassland, and even, with a hint of the poetic, Apacherian savanna, for the land where the Apaches once ruled.[38] Many ecologists use the term "desert grassland" to describe a highland mixture of grass and shrubs in the North American Southwest—Bill McDonald grazes his cattle on high desert grassland, for example—but "desert grassland" presents a semantic challenge: a desert would seem an unlikely place for grass, especially the kind of grass people think of when they think of grazing cows. Further complicating matters, the most common plants on desert grassland may not be grass at all, but shrubs or small trees.[39] Desert grassland reflects more the economic reality of raising livestock on this land than the ecological reality of the kinds of plants found there.

Whatever you call it, the land itself has been transformed. Nearly half of the land in the southwestern United States may have been covered in grass within the last two hundred years, compared to only 20 percent today. In place of grass, shrubs now grow, at least where cities and suburbs have not replaced the vegetation entirely.[40] During droughts, which have occurred repeatedly for more than one hundred years, and consistently for the past five, occasional tufts of grass a few inches high struggle forlornly amid the mesquite, ocotillo, cholla cactus, and prickly pear. Elsewhere in the arid West, species of grass native to Africa, especially Lehmann lovegrass, introduced to hold the soil after decades of overgrazing, now thrive at the expense of native species, and the invaders differ so dramatically from the natives in their response to climate and fire that they completely change the ecological dynamics of the invaded regions.

Thinking big in the western United States brings you face-to-face with grazing, which is by far the most extensive land use in the region, occupying some 650 million acres—about 70 percent of the eleven westernmost states, excluding Alaska.[41] Any such effort must also deal with the rank

arrogance that has shaped the history of settlement in the West. For generations, ranchers, miners, and loggers assumed that public land meant
private profit, and fought every move to limit their control or cut into the
public subsidies that make ranching possible on arid land. The corruption
and violence that marked battles over public land through much of the
twentieth century leave many environmentalists with little hope for
change. Better, many think, to keep up the fight in the hope that more
land can be secured for conservation through private acquisition, land-use
planning, or conservation easements, than to try to find common ground
with ranchers. The battle lines could not be clearer.

Anyone hoping to conserve, restore, or make a living off of arid land in
the West must come to grips with four major variables: the lay of the land
itself (that is, the soil and the topography), climate, fire, and the behavior
of all the animals that eat plants, from grasshoppers to prairie dogs to
cows. Humans have little direct influence over the first two, but enormous
influence on the last two. Ranchers have witnessed and participated in the
dramatic environmental changes that the Malpai region and the surrounding land have undergone in the past 140 years.

In the most visible shift, mesquite and other woody shrubs and trees
now cover many former grasslands. Cows cannot eat the woody vegetation,
so the shrubs expand and force the cattle out. The collected books and
articles debating the precise mechanism of that change fill many library
shelves. Ranchers, researchers, and activists on either side argue that overgrazing causes the invasion of woody plants by eliminating the grasses, or
that cows keep the trees out by eating the young, tender shoots before they
become established. Is it the cycles of drought and rain, or human-induced
climate change? Or the lack of fire? Blame the kangaroo rats. Or all of
the above.

A debate now rages over how these factors, particularly the human
choices that affect fire and grazing, shape the future of open country, and
hence of broad-scale conservation, in the West.[42] Humans do not make
those choices in a vacuum; history sets the boundaries. The extinction of
North America's large mammals, the end of the Little Ice Age, and the
predictable catastrophe of the cattle boom all contributed to a wounded
landscape. Scientists, ranchers, and policymakers have been searching for
ways to heal those wounds.

One approach was to organize much of the public rangeland into grazing districts managed under a system of exclusive leases, which would provide a means to manage livestock and improve forage while also preventing the development of a quasi-aristocratic class of large landowners. "Without quite realizing it, we have put together an entirely new kind of commons—an American commons—where individuals may go to find resources but which no one can take into his or her exclusive possession," writes the historian Donald Worster. "What is most interesting about this American commons is there is nothing feudal about it; it is the achievement and patrimony of a modern nation that, in some measure, still believes in the dream of democracy and realizes that it cannot be fulfilled through the institution of private property."[43]

The success of grazing leases depended on determining how many cows a particular range could support—the carrying capacity—for range types as the basis for divvying up the range into equitable grazing allotments. Range managers just needed to establish a fixed carrying capacity and then ensure that ranchers put the right number of cows in the right places at the right time. The variability in rain and soils would not matter; fences, water tanks, and other "improvements" to the range would smooth out the irregularities. Banks demanded fixed carrying capacities before they would make loans to ranchers, even though the natural variability of forage production made such figures highly misleading.

Opponents of grazing have equally simplistic solutions, too often falling into the trap that snared most range scientists: cows caused the problems we see today, so removing the cows will solve the problems. The argument that banning cows from public land will by itself reverse the damage caused by overgrazing and lead to fewer endangered species appeals to common sense, but has little basis in science or experience.

Widespread increases in cover or density of woody plants coincident with the development of the livestock industry has led to the conclusion that grazing is the ultimate cause of increased woody plants in former grasslands throughout the world, including the borderlands. The simple solution, one that government agencies that manage public land continue to implicitly endorse, would be to manage the cows or remove them altogether and leave the rest of the ecosystem to take care of itself. The pristine range of the days before the cattle boom is within reach. Simplicity makes for a catchy bumper sticker—"Cow Free by 2003" (or "Cows Galore in 2004," depending on which side you are on)—and is no doubt rewarding for those who would drive the cows off the range, but perhaps it is not terribly effective.[44] As H. L. Mencken said, "for every complex problem there is a solution that is simple, neat, and wrong."

While the number of cows on the range may appear to be the most important consideration, even more significant is what Guy McPherson calls ecological inertia; we set events on their way fifty to one hundred years ago through catastrophic overgrazing, then woody plants moved in and we crossed a threshold, effectively burning the bridges behind us. From this perspective, removing woody plants and restoring the grasslands, a major source of conflict in the arid Southwest, requires a huge human effort; simply removing the cows or adding more cows will have little impact. Once woodlands dominate these dry ecosystems, fires intense enough to kill woody plants become less and less common, as the amount of fine fuel is too scarce and scattered. Fire alone thus cannot recreate the grasslands —barring herbicides or mechanical shrub control, woody plants become permanent. Excluding livestock now will have little or no impact on the abundance of woody plants or non-native herbs over the next several decades; keeping livestock out of areas smaller than thousands of acres will not produce islands of grass in a sea of shrubs.

❧ ❧ ❧

Grazing can obviously be destructive. Grazing decreases the surface area of the grass, thus limiting photosynthesis; increases mortality rates; and decreases seed production and seedling establishment of palatable grasses. Grazing may also increase susceptibility of grasses to other stresses, such as drought, and create gaps between bunches of grass, which increases the amount of sunlight reaching the soil surface and increases germination and the establishment of woody seedlings, especially after drought. Gaps in grass cover also make an area less likely to burn—there is not enough grass to "carry the fire," say scientists—which further accelerates shifts from grassland to woodland.[45]

Cows inflict most of their damage not on grass, however, but on streams. Domestic cattle evolved in the cool, wet meadows of Europe and Asia, so they tend to avoid hot, dry conditions. In the Southwest, this means that left to their own devices, cattle congregate in and around streams, fouling the water, eroding the streambanks, and causing a host of other problems. Vigilance in keeping cows moving may allow some streams to recover, but in other cases the only solution will be to fence cows out altogether, a step some ranchers have already taken.[46]

The grazing debate has become a pitched battle of absolutes. Science offers no simple answers that apply everywhere in the West. Interactions among climate, fire, herbivory, and vegetation play out against a background of evolutionary and human history, and all these factors vary across time and space. The concept of an ecoregion is one solution to the problem of finding the broadest scale at which ecological communities and the processes that shape and support them are roughly similar, without getting so broad that the important variations get lost. Think big, but not too big.

In one sense, the opponents of grazing rightly claim that science is on their side; despite intense effort, little evidence exists for widespread benefits of grazing on arid land. The general improvement in western grazing land over the last sixty years stems not from the creative use of livestock, but from the simple fact that after the destruction of the cattle boom, conditions on that land could hardly have been any worse unless it had been covered in asphalt.

Some scientists and ranchers argue that cows and other livestock serve as a replacement for natural disturbances, such as fire, that have been removed from the ecosystem by human activity. Guy McPherson argues, however, that "to claim that grazing is a substitute for any natural disturbance requires a huge leap of substitution. Fire removes biomass, cows remove biomass, so they must be the same, except that fires don't weigh fifteen hundred pounds and they aren't out there when the grass is wet. Fires remove vegetation indiscriminately, but cows remove the good-tasting grasses and leave the woody things and the poisonous stuff behind."

* * *

McPherson is something of an iconoclast in the grazing debate. He once gave a lecture on the importance of population control, the reasons we should eat less red meat, and gay rights. An interesting mix of topics, but nothing extraordinary, except that he gave the talk to the ranchers and traditional range managers who make up the Society for Range Management, and he was in Salt Lake City, the very heart of Mormon conservatism, at the time. No one heckled him or threatened bodily harm, which McPherson says was more than he expected, or deserved.

Tall, lean, and sharp-witted, McPherson gleefully skewers what he sees as the absurdities in the arguments from each side, particularly when those arguments build on shoddy or incomplete science. One such argument from the supporters of grazing suggests that livestock grazing is a natural process—that ruminants evolved in arid and semiarid landscapes to eat grasses that other organisms have trouble digesting, and that grasses evolved to survive such grazing. Grazing is perfectly natural for the grazers, but not the grazed, McPherson explains. Many other creatures feed on desert grasses, but most of them, like kangaroo rats and prairie dogs, are tiny compared to cows. "Claiming that grazing is a natural process and therefore should be done in these semiarid regions because there are ruminants that have evolved—this strategy completely misses the point," he says. Such arguments may seem the recondite fodder of academic debate, but they become weapons on the grazing war. Says McPherson: "I hear a lot of ranchers saying 'See, grazing is a natural thing. That's what I've been doing. Hallelujah!' "

Ranchers and their supporters also make a cultural and an economic argument for keeping cows on the range. These arguments are as unconvincing as the attempt to muster scientific evidence for the beneficial effects of grazing in the Southwest. The cultural argument revolves around defending the ranching lifestyle in order to protect the cowboy as an American icon. McPherson, for one, scoffs at the notion. "It seems like a kind of funny argument," he says. "After all, it was only two centuries ago that the ancestors of the people promoting this myth were responsible at least in part for eliminating a culture that had been in place for over ten thousand years. And now you want us to save this historical cultural feature that is brand new on the landscape? I don't think so, and you're not going to be able to convince people of that, either."

The economic argument builds on the premise that people need the products we grow on western land. That, too, does not stand much scrutiny. Western cattle account for only about 4 percent of the beef in the

United States; the rest comes from feedlots in the Midwest. Further, depending on the state, between 60 and 90 percent of the people in the western United States live in cities. In Cochise County, Arizona, where Bill McDonald's ranch is, less than a third of farm income comes from livestock, while the county population grew by 88 percent between 1970 and 1990. Neighboring Pima County is growing even faster—138 percent since 1970—and its agriculture sector is crashing.[47]

✵ ✵ ✵

By far the most contentious argument made in defense of cattle grazing boils down to the phrase "cows or condos." If ranchers cannot make a living by raising cattle, they will be forced to sell their land, and there are plenty of buyers: the population of the West is growing rapidly and much growth is in rural areas. In the Southwest, along the front range of the Rockies, and elsewhere in the region, ranchers looking to sell their land most often turn to developers who will build subdivisions or "ranchettes" of ten to forty acres. As developers carve up ranches, land consumption grows at an even faster rate than population. In the West, developed land rose from almost 20 million acres in 1970 to 42 million in 2000. It takes only a few homes to render fire management effectively impossible at the landscape level. With subdivisions come people and their pets, roads, cars, off-road vehicles, and, most importantly, the loss of any hope of restoring the land to anything remotely resembling a natural state, however defined.

Again, generalizations about the West lead to trouble. Developers are not lining up to buy land on the high plains of the Dakotas, and in California's San Fernando Valley and elsewhere, even some of the world's most productive farmland is not enough to keep out the subdivisions. Until 1970, livestock production generated the most income from desert grasslands. Now the value of land is tied to its potential as real estate—at least in the economic terms that do not properly value conservation uses. Some areas are already subdivided. Outside the city of Douglas in southeast Arizona, a few miles from Mexico, just where the pavement turns into a dirt road that leads to the Glenns' Malpai Ranch and eventually to Bill McDonald's place, the signs advertising a forthcoming housing development have already appeared.

The "cow or condos" argument rests on the assumption that whatever harm cows cause, that harm pales in comparison to the havoc of housing developments. That seems a safe assumption, though the destruction wrought by urbanization occurs over relatively small areas, while livestock and agriculture suck up water from streams and aquifers for irrigation, remove or trample topsoil and cause erosion, introduce pollutants, disrupt fires and other natural processes, and remove prairie dogs, wolves, and other species.[48]

Today, suburbs do less harm than agriculture because there are not many of them compared to the scale of the western states. Tomorrow, however, there will be another house, another road, another subdivision, another mall. Opponents of grazing want to remove the cows and farms and replace them with wilderness. Fair enough, but the trend is entirely in the opposite direction. Since conversion of ranchland to suburban sprawl is irreversible, the question then turns on whether ranches form the best or at least an acceptable means for protecting open space. Grazing opponents point to the huge subsidies that prop up most ranchers and argue that we should not spend public money to use public land in destructive ways. "Your Land Is Their Feedlot" shouts the back cover of a massive coffee-table polemic against cows, *Welfare Ranching*. The notion of subsidies makes economists shudder and strikes most people as somehow unfair. As with everything in the debate over conservation in the Southwest, the truth lies with neither ideological camp but somewhere in between, in the radical center.

* * *

Bill McDonald and his neighbors do not run their ranches for the money. "I submit to you that anyone who gets into ranching for only economic reasons is an idiot," McDonald says.[49] Ranchers love the land, though they obviously love it in different ways than ecologists or urban environmentalists. The question, McDonald says, is not grazing or no grazing; the question is open space or no open space, a place for jaguars or endless subdivisions. On that point the most conservative rancher and the most liberal environmentalist can agree, as they both want to maintain the vast, undeveloped landscapes of the Southwest. Such agreement may seem a small thing; after all, actions matter more, and if ranchers won't stop raising cows and environmentalists won't stop hating them, then we will be right back where we started.

Perhaps, but perhaps not. Perhaps by finding common ground and envisioning a common future, the two sides will also find new ways to bring that future about. A hopeful vision for the future builds not on marginal improvements in the way we treat land and its myriad inhabitants, not just on making do and slowing the pace of destruction. Hope lies in making things better, in undoing past mistakes and learning how to avoid them altogether. The cattle boom was one such mistake, and whether the damage it caused can ever be undone remains an open question. Among the many other notable mistakes, more than one hundred years of nearly ceaseless effort to drain Florida's Everglades stands as a testimony to human ingenuity, persistence, and shortsightedness. In a hundred more years, with luck, historians may see the equally ingenious effort to put the Everglades right as part of a revolution that transformed the way we live on the earth.

CHAPTER 7

SAVE ENOUGH TO LAST: FLORIDA AND THE EVERGLADES

The Everglades is a test. If we pass, we may get to keep the planet.
MARJORY STONEMAN DOUGLAS

On December 11, 2000, Florida governor Jeb Bush went to the Oval Office and stood by as President Bill Clinton signed a bill to restore the Everglades. No run-of-the-mill piece of legislation, the bill authorized the largest, most expensive environmental and public works project in U.S. history. That same day, attorneys for the vice president, Al Gore, and the governor's brother, George W. Bush, presented their cases to the Supreme Court in *Bush v. Gore,* thus bringing to a close the bitter and controversial presidential election. While reporters waiting for the president focused their questions on Florida's electoral swamp rather than its real marsh, the process that Clinton set in motion that day will continue long after the political careers of the principals have ended.

The Everglades restoration already serves as a model for huge restoration projects in Louisiana and California, and may also help plan for the conservation of two of the world's other great wetlands, the Pantanal in Brazil and the Okavango Delta in Botswana. Yet in its details, a morass of engineering specifications and a particularly nasty brand of political infighting, the Everglades restoration stands apart. The vital lessons of the Everglades, and conservation in Florida more broadly, that may prove vital to countless efforts elsewhere lie in the experience of integrating science and management—or the failure to do so—and building consensus among people and communities who have often been at odds.

The Malpai Borderlands Group demonstrates that the neat division of conservation debates into the evil despoilers and the virtuous defenders of nature rarely stands much scrutiny, especially at broad scales. The Florida Everglades will make you believe otherwise. Few stories about our dwindling natural treasures feature as malevolent a villain as the South Florida sugar industry. The remarkable power of that industry threatens to undermine the effort to restore the Everglades—an effort that forms a crucial part of the even more daunting undertaking of coordinating conservation across the booming state of Florida.

Despite the looming presence of Big Sugar, Florida's conservation planners in and out of government are applying key concepts in conservation biology to solving the problem of saving fragile ecosystems: ensure that all ecosystems in the state can withstand disturbances such as hurricanes, floods, and fires without being completely destroyed (a concept called resiliency); conserve multiple examples of every ecosystem to prevent catastrophe from leading to extinction (a concept called redundancy); and protect enough examples across a large enough area to last for at least one hundred years. Add to resiliency and redundancy the idea of representation, and you have the three fundamental principles for conservation.[1]

Reed Noss and Larry Harris began thinking about conservation across the entire state of Florida in the late 1980s, and the state has been a leader ever since. That stems in part from the work of good scientists like Noss and Harris, and in part from Florida's ecology. "Florida is so seamless, everything is so connected that it is intuitively obvious," says Jora Young, a Florida-based conservation scientist with The Nature Conservancy. Young moved to Florida after a stint in Ohio, where one of her projects involved restoring a small stretch of the Big Darby Creek for the endangered mussels found there. Florida offered far different challenges. "I went from Ohio, with a few federally listed species, to Florida, with hundreds, and I realized we are not going to be able to work [species by species] here. We have to work on systems; we have to work on a different scale."[2]

"I come all the way back to the first law of ecology, that everything is connected," says Young. "We could manage [The Nature Conservancy's] forty thousand acres in Florida as museum pieces and they could be beautiful, but we will have done nothing for the conservation of biodiversity. I used to say this to everyone I ever hired: if that is all you do you will have done nothing. The Nature Conservancy owns a mere forty thousand acres here; no matter how well we manage these, we won't save the incredible natural diversity of Florida. It is literally going to take changing the way humans relate to every ecosystem in which they are embedded if we are really going to do our job."

That job, says Young, is not just to own and manage land for conservation, but to inspire others to act, to identify the most pressing causes of environmental degradation, and to develop strategies to address them. Most of all, she says, the job requires having "a presence in the community so that we can be real people to the communities in which we live."

Young and other conservationists in Florida realized in the late 1980s that even though the state had one of the best programs in the country to acquire land for conservation, it wasn't nearly big enough to keep up with the pace of development. "You have got to ratchet up the money spent on conservation beyond anything we have ever seen because there is no way we are going to stop the development juggernaut in this state without some substantive money," says Young.

✦ ✦ ✦

In the early 1990s, a Nature Conservancy staffer named Steve Gatewood, who would go on to become the first executive director of The Wildlands Project, convened a series of workshops to gather expert opinions on the scale of conservation for Florida. Gatewood asked the question, What do we need to protect to ensure conservation of all of the state's natural diversity? The result was the next generation of the Noss and Harris map—a map that would identify conservation priorities and areas of conservation interest across the state.

The evolution of the conservation map of Florida continued in 1994, when the Florida Game and Freshwater Fish Commission took a more rigorous approach to determining what the state would need to do to provide adequate habitat for declining wildlife species and rare plant and animal communities. As Rob Marshall and his team would discover years later in the Sonoran Desert, the commission could not assess all the thousands of species in Florida. So the commission scientists blazed a trail that Marshall and others would follow by relying on a set of species selected for their value in indicating the presence of specific habitats and natural communities, or selected because, like the Florida panther, the species needed large amounts of habitat.

Altogether, the commission's researchers examined 179 species of vertebrates, 105 rare plants, and four rare natural plant communities. Under the initial plan, and a second phase completed in 1998, adequate conservation of those species meant providing enough habitat for at least ten populations of at least two hundred individuals. If so many large populations were distributed across the state (rather than being lumped together), Florida might have a conservation system that is redundant, resilient, and representative of the state's natural diversity.[3]

The scientists looked first to see whether existing conservation land, which is mostly in public ownership and accounts for about a fifth of the state, would conserve all 288 species and communities. Not surprisingly, they found some gaps. To fill them, Florida would need to place 13 percent more land under some form of conservation management, bringing the total to about a third of the state. The cost of adding that land would be approximately $8.2 billion dollars, or about 16 percent of Florida's annual budget.[4]

The Florida study represents one of the most concrete applications of conservation planning at the scale of a state or ecoregion. The results of this study have informed Florida's efforts to acquire land for conservation. During the 1990s, Florida spent more money buying land for conservation than the federal government did for the entire country.

The $8.2 billion dollars needed to secure at least a baseline of Florida's plants and animals seems impossibly expensive until you realize that the state and federal governments have already agreed to spend that much to restore the Everglades. The Everglades restoration, just a component of the statewide efforts, captures many of the elements that make doing big conservation so difficult and yet so essential. The restoration targets a vast ecosystem profoundly transformed by more than a century of human ma- nipulation, with topflight scientists still piecing together a complex eco- logical puzzle after decades of research. The effort engages multiple levels of government with different agendas and priorities, as well as diverse human communities who have divergent attitudes about conservation but who ultimately share a dependence on the Everglades for their continued prosperity.[5]

The seed of a consensus among all the actors begins with the recog- nition, shared across the political spectrum, that something needs to be done. Both conservation scientists documenting the decline in dozens of species that once characterized the Everglades and developers worrying about where they will get enough fresh water to supply a burgeoning population along South Florida's Atlantic coast understand that the Ever- glades will not long survive without drastic steps.

Thinking broadly about conservation in Florida brings into focus landscapes that do not just need to be protected—they need to be rebuilt, to the extent that such a thing lies within our limited human abilities. As Marjory Stoneman Douglas saw many years ago, the Everglades provides a test not just of our science but of our will to conserve that which we do not fully understand.

THE ENDANGERED EVERGLADES

Everglades National Park occupies the tip of the Florida Peninsula, but the Everglades ecosystem once stretched from the headwaters of the Kissimmee River, just south of Orlando, to Lake Okeechobee, and all the way south to Florida Bay, a distance of nearly 250 miles. If you include the bay itself and the Big Cypress Swamp in the southwestern part of the state, all told wetlands once covered roughly 14,000 square miles, nearly twice the size of Massachusetts and more than a quarter of Florida's land area. During the wet season, most of South Florida was underwater.[6]

The sheer size of the Everglades ecosystem made it resilient, because it was large enough to tolerate floods, droughts, fires, hurricanes, and even an occasional freeze. The Everglades contained many different habitats—tree islands, wet prairies, sawgrass marshes, swamp forests, the world's largest mangrove forest in Florida Bay—spread out in a mosaic across a vast landscape, which allowed species like wading birds and panthers to move to new habitats as old ones dried, flooded, or burned. So while the Everglades as a whole remained apparently stable, its myriad component parts were actually in a state of constant flux.[7] No one year was exactly like the next. Climate and fire shaped the Everglades at the broadest scale; alligators digging holes, building nest mounds, and creating trails through the marsh shaped it at the finest. While all ecosystems change, in the Everglades change was constant, the system's defining feature.

Since many of the key processes in the Everglades, like fires or hurricanes, occur across wide areas, shrinking the size of the Everglades may have profound effects even if we could reassemble all the other pieces of the puzzle. As Frank Preston predicted more than forty years ago, recreating the Everglades on a smaller scale, a Xerox reduction of the original, may simply be impossible.[8]

The wild species that inhabit the Everglades thrive on the constantly shifting conditions. Humans, on the other hand, crave stability. People and their crops need to be kept dry during wet seasons and well-supplied with water during droughts. The efforts to drain the Everglades and provide that predictability began in earnest in the 1880s and lasted nearly a century. Nearly all the endangered species in South Florida can trace their precarious status to the miles of canals and levees cut into the Everglades to bring the region firmly under human domination. After more than a century of trying, we have drained the Everglades, but at a huge cost. Today, only half of the Everglades wetlands, about 3 million acres, remain.[9]

Agriculture and development have taken over the other half of the historic Everglades, and engineers have replumbed the flow of water from the Kissimmee to the bay with one of the largest and most remarkable systems of public works anywhere in the world. Without that system, the product of some three decades of work by the U.S. Army Corps of Engineers, South Florida could support only a fraction of the more than 5 million people who now live in the narrow band east of the historic Everglades. The engineers took the variability out of the natural system in usually vain efforts to prevent surprises from happening, rather than being prepared to respond to them.

❧ ❧ ❧

The harmful side effects of dredging and draining the Everglades appeared early in the twentieth century. In 1928, a landscape architect from Yale named Ernest Coe began a concentrated effort to create the Tropical Everglades National Park. His persistence paid off when he and others persuaded Congress to designate the Everglades as a national park in 1934. It took Coe and other park supporters, most notably Marjory Stoneman Douglas, at that time a columnist for the *Miami Herald* and a vigorous defender of the Everglades, until 1947 to acquire land and secure funding. That year, Everglades National Park officially opened,[10] and Douglas completed *The Everglades: River of Grass.*

A bit less than half of the remaining Everglades falls within the national park, which may be the most endangered national park in the country.[11] A huge human population growing faster than Haiti's or India's encroaches on the park's eastern and western edges and demands water and flood protection; sugar cane fields and cattle ranches pollute the water; and invasive, exotic species take advantage of the disturbed ecosystems and spread at frightening speed. As a result, many wild populations have crashed. Wading birds have declined by 90 percent, with wood storks *(Mycteria Americana)* and white ibis *(Eudocimus albus)* particularly hard hit.[12] Florida panthers *(Puma concolor coryi)* once ranged across much of the southeastern United States, but today fewer than one hundred survive, most in Big Cypress National Preserve, northwest of the national park. All told, the U.S. Fish and Wildlife Service counts sixty-eight threatened or endangered species in South Florida, from the striking Audubon's crested caracara *(Polyborus plancus audubonii)* to the drab Cape Sable seaside sparrow *(Ammodramus maritimus mirabilis)* to the obscure Okeechobee gourd *(Cucurbita okeechobeensis* ssp. *okeechobeensis).*

Of all the changes in the Everglades, few can match the shift, across huge areas of the Everglades, from sawgrass to cattails. Sawgrass once defined the region—sawgrass marsh formed Douglas's "river of grass"— and thrives in the low-nutrient waters of the intact Everglades. Cattails, also native to the Everglades but usually far more limited than sawgrass, take over rapidly when agricultural runoff enriches the water with phosphorous. When phosphorous concentrations in Everglades National Park increased by an order of magnitude in the mid-1980s, the federal government sued the state of Florida for dumping polluted water into the park, adding legal and political urgency—as well as a public rallying point— to the long, tortuous process of undoing generations of damage to the Everglades.

Water has become the limiting resource in South Florida, despite its being one of the wettest regions of the country. The Everglades restoration plan that President Clinton signed into law seeks, above all else, to solve that problem. Some environmentalists worry, in fact, that the restoration will become simply a water supply plan for South Florida cities and the sugar industry, thus subsidizing more of the development that degraded the Everglades in the first place.

The Everglades restoration seeks to provide water for even more people in South Florida, as many as 6 million more, while also providing flood control and returning more water to the natural system. Doing all three will be difficult—impossible, say some critics—and even if everything goes according to plan, the restoration of the Everglades will take decades.

Everything cannot possibly go according to plan, and from the perspective of many of the scientists involved, that is precisely the point. As with every ecosystem, we have a drastically incomplete understanding of the Everglades, and even a perfect understanding would not prevent ecological surprises. So any plan must be tentative, built on scientific understanding that may shift fundamentally, and this holds whether the plan encompasses just Everglades National Park, all of South Florida, or the entire state. The U.S. Army Corps of Engineers, however, makes its living by finishing huge construction projects on time and under budget. Whether the corps can live with this contradiction will be one of the most closely watched aspects of the restoration effort.

Groups working to restore the Everglades face daunting technical, political, and cultural challenges. No one has ever tried to undo such a large and complicated water-control system, and no one knows if the plan the corps has proposed will actually work, as it relies on largely untried technologies, such as injecting surface water into deep underground aquifers. Stuart Applebaum, who heads the restoration efforts for the corps, likes to say that "the restoration plan isn't brain surgery. It's much more complicated." Politically, the restoration must overcome the entrenched power of big sugar companies and developers, who have usually gotten whatever they wanted. Culturally, each new generation that arrives in South Florida seeks to drain the Everglades, and this remains as true for the most recent immigrants as it did for the early settlers in the mid–nineteenth century.

Yet the Everglades also has some unusual advantages for doing big conservation. The Everglades has a clear identity, even if many people living nearby do not have direct experience with the untrammeled wetlands. Getting people to have some stake in the Everglades does not require a tremendous leap, unlike many other ecoregions. The Everglades lie wholly within a single state, with a single official language, in the richest nation in the world. The state depends heavily on tourism, so one can easily make the case that as the ecosystem goes, so goes the economy. The connection between the ecosystem and people is also readily apparent; Florida has no rivers the size of the Colorado bringing in billions of gallons of drinking water. For drinking water in South Florida, either save the Everglades and the system of limestone aquifers beneath it, or start taking the salt out of the Atlantic.

❧ ❧ ❧

State and federal governments will be spending billions of tax dollars on the Everglades restoration over the next thirty years, but if the tax-paying public expects an unimpaired or perfect Everglades they will be sorely disappointed. No one can predict with any certainty whatsoever that any given point within the Everglades will look and act as it did a century ago. By that definition, Everglades restoration is an absolute impossibility. The mid–nineteenth century was just yesterday in geological terms and not all that long ago in human terms, when you consider that Marjory Stoneman Douglas was born in 1890 (she lived to be 108), yet the Everglades of the era before the ditch diggers and railroaders came is a lost world.

Scientists have only a vague and incomplete picture of how the Everglades functioned prior to European settlement, and even if they knew it in detail they could not recreate it, given the magnitude of the transformation wrought by human ingenuity. The challenge instead is to create a new Everglades that looks and acts more like the real thing than the one we have now. No one knows the original hydrology, and no one knows if bringing back the original hydrology would bring back the biology, because no one still alive saw the pre-drainage Everglades. "We are still wrestling with what we are restoring," says John Ogden, a senior ecologist with the South Florida Water Management District, the state agency responsible for operating the system of canals and levees in the Everglades and one of the lead scientists in the restoration effort. "I have been here since the late sixties and it is a very different system today than it was in the late sixties, and I expect a lot of people would call it success if we got back to the system of the late sixties, with a lot more wading birds and clear water in Florida Bay."

Aside from the obvious political impossibility of removing the farms, towns, and roads that now occupy parts of the former Everglades, ecological reality poses nearly insurmountable problems for restoration. Even the much more modest goal of repairing the system so that water flows again in a fashion that at least roughly approximates what happened before the days of levees and canals requires sophisticated models and even more sophisticated modelers.

Sometimes, though, all you really need to know is which plant to pull out by the roots. Invasive, exotic plants have literally laid siege to the Everglades. Some were introduced intentionally, particularly melaleuca, a fast-growing ornamental tree, which was introduced in the early twentieth century in part as a means to drain the swamp. Elsewhere, ecological changes wrought by engineers, such as changes in the depth and duration of floods, have allowed woody species such as the Brazilian peppertree *(Schinus terebinthifolius)*, punk tree *(Melaleuca quinquenervia)*, and horsetail casuarina *(Casuarina equisetifolia)* to encroach in marshes and sloughs.[13] Teams of field workers and volunteers attempt to beat back the invaders with aerial spraying, biocontrol agents, and picks and shovels. Sometimes they succeed, but then a new and tougher opponent shows up, such as the recent sighting of a nasty plant called the old-world climbing fern *(Lygodium microphyllum)*, which spreads via tiny spores and smothers everything in its path.

Without far broader changes, the alien invasion will continue and likely get much worse. With some luck, those changes may be on the horizon. Not only is the Everglades unique, but so are the efforts to repair it. No other country has spent as much on wetland restoration, and most countries can scarcely imagine spending $8 billion on anything. The Everglades serves as an example and a warning—once wetlands are degraded, most economies will be unable to bear the costs of restoration. Even where the cost is not an absolute impediment, as in South Florida, getting restoration right poses enormous challenges. Ecologist Stuart Pimm, a leading critic of the Everglades restoration plan, believes the flaws in the plan have even larger implications.[14] "If we can't fix this plan, it might not just doom the Everglades. It might doom our chances of getting to do restoration again."[15]

Even with a scientifically ideal restoration plan, the Everglades restoration would only have a fifty-fifty chance of succeeding as intended. Political, economic, and cultural forces that are unsympathetic, uncomprehending, or openly hostile toward the notion of restoration, combined with the inevitable scientific uncertainty, makes the Everglades a treacherous landscape for large-scale conservation.

In Broward County, for example, what little undeveloped land remains sells fast at one hundred thousand dollars an acre. Cheaper land exists elsewhere, but the fantasy of a get-rich-quick Florida land deal has sunk deep roots into American culture. The developers who buy and sell that land have enormous political power, and the landowners who have not yet cashed in want to make sure nothing happens to limit their opportunities. Shannon Estenoz, who ran World Wildlife Fund's Everglades office from 1996 until 2003, sums it up this way: "Scratch a farmer in South Florida and you find a developer."[16]

RESTORE WHAT?

The bill that President Clinton signed will "restore, preserve, and protect the South Florida ecosystem while providing for other water-related needs of the region, including water supply and flood protection. The Plan shall be implemented to ensure the protection of water quality in, the reduction of the loss of fresh water from, and the improvement of the environment of the South Florida ecosystem and to achieve and maintain the benefits to the natural system and human environment...."[17] In other words, something for everyone. This may simply reflect the salesmanship necessary to get an expensive bill through a divided Congress, but it glosses over innumerable hard choices. The law by no means guarantees which way those decisions will go.

Drive west on Tamiami Trail, which links Miami with Naples on the Gulf Coast, and the magnitude of the challenge becomes clear. "It is like the housing boom of the 1950s," says ecologist Bill Loftus, who has spent nearly thirty years working in Everglades National Park, first with the National Park Service and then the U.S. Geological Survey. Most striking are the piles of peat by the construction sites. The Everglades sits atop peat, a type of soil formed by the slow accumulation of incompletely decomposed plant material. While bulldozers can scrape off peat soil several feet deep in a matter of minutes, it could take roughly one thousand years to accumulate just one inch of the rich, thick stuff.[18] Peat soils form the foundation of the characteristic Everglades marsh, so these new housing developments sit in what was the former Everglades, on what conceivably could have been restored. Scraping off peat all the way down to the limestone bedrock tends to limit the options for restoration.

The pattern of development across South Florida, and indeed the whole state, has been one of intensive development right up to the edge of protected areas, with little or no open land in between—hence the importance of identifying the important land for conservation, the effort that began with Reed Noss and Larry Harris. Around Everglades National Park, the only buffer is the agricultural areas in southern Dade County, and that may soon disappear. "Right along the park boundary, real estate signs are going up all over, they're sprouting," says Loftus. "It's like developers are finally keying in that this is the last open land in South Florida, and we better get it and start doing something with it. Any sensible planning would keep that land in some sort of low-density agricultural buffer, but money talks."

Nearly everyone in South Florida, with the exception of those who make their living fishing in Lake Okeechobee or Florida Bay, gain their economic benefits from an intensively managed Everglades. So the Everglades will remain a managed ecosystem. The goal now, says Shannon Estenoz, is to "preserve that firewall between an ecosystem that is destructive to people and people who are destructive to the ecosystem."

People, however, operate on far different scales than South Florida's ecosystems. The Army Corps of Engineers has a long tradition of funding relatively straightforward, discrete projects, like the dozens of separate dams, canals, and levees that led to the situation we find ourselves in today. The corps planned those projects on much different physical and temporal scales than the Everglades restoration requires, and with much more limited objectives, which were generally hydrological rather than ecological. In the Everglades, it will take years if not decades to determine the effectiveness of restoration efforts, but the colonels in charge of the corps move on after two or three years, the water management district reorganizes itself nearly as often, and the governor and legislators stand for election regularly.

This mismatch between the scale of the problem and the scale of the human institutions intended to address it makes restoring the Everglades feel like fighting a forest fire with an eyedropper. Yet, while the corps may not be the ideal agent of environmental restoration, only the corps can undo what the corps itself has done. To its credit, the corps has made significant changes in the way it works in order to take on the restoration, one of the most collaborative federal/state/local research activities in the nation.[19] Whether the changes are real rather than cosmetic and whether they will be sufficient will remain topics of intense debate for years.

Scientific research will be a crucial element in determining the course of restoration, but conservationists and planners cannot wait until all the data are in, as that would amount to simply documenting the death of the Everglades rather than determining how to heal it. While the Audubon Society has a history of surveying wading birds dating back to the 1930s, and individual scientists had been gathering data from various parts of the ecosystem for nearly that long, the idea of applying research findings to conservation was as slow to reach South Florida as the rest of the country. "In the 1970s, with Everglades National Park, it was hard even to justify surveying wading birds outside the park boundaries," says John Ogden, who worked as an ornithologist in the park before moving to the South Florida Water Management District.[20]

At that time, the park spent its research dollars on hydrology, with the goal of determining how much water the park needed and how to get it. So while scientists have some idea of what the hydrology should be, the understanding of the ecology of the Everglades lags far behind. "The link between the ecology and hydrology had to have been there all along, but people didn't understand what it was," says Ogden. Science was scattered among various agencies—the academic community showed relatively little interest in the Everglades until the late 1970s—and cooperation was limited, but some people began to sense an opportunity to pull all the research threads together and develop a solid understanding of the ecosystem.

The turning point for science in the Everglades came at a conference convened in October 1989 that brought together scientists from federal and state agencies. Among the questions the conference addressed was what, exactly, we should restore. As far back as the 1930s, scientific assessments of the Everglades found substantial degradation that would require at least fifty years of wise management to undo. "Long before anyone was measuring anything or asking questions the place had been substantially changed," Ogden says. "We had to figure out what we were trying to get back to, characterize what was important about the pre-drainage system."

By the mid-1990s, a scientific consensus had emerged. The most important features of the Everglades were its size, the slow flow of nutrient-poor water from Lake Okeechobee in a vast sheet, and the variation across the landscape in terms of how long certain areas remained flooded (the hydroperiod, in hydrologists' terminology) and to what depth. Everglades restoration cannot succeed if the hydrology of the system remains in its current state, but it will also fail if hydrology is the only consideration. Scientists continue to expand their understanding of how water depth and flow shapes the biology of the Everglades, but this understanding remains far from perfect.

❦ ❦ ❦

The Everglades seems a simple place, an enormous, placid marsh. A little investigation, however, reveals apparent contradictions. Take wood storks and snail kites, for example. Wood storks, North America's largest wading birds and only native storks, eat fish and depend on periodic dry spells to concentrate their prey in shrinking pools. On the other hand, snail kites—crow-sized hawks—feed exclusively on a species of snail that lives in permanently flooded marshes. Despite the seemingly divergent habitat needs of these two birds, the Everglades once supported thriving populations of both. How is that possible?

An even more fundamental puzzle centers on how the Everglades generates enough food for all of its residents. Ecologists call the Everglades a low-nutrient, low-productivity system, which basically means that few plants you could survive on grow here. Sawgrass, the botanical icon of the Everglades, is an evolutionary marvel, with razor sharp, silica-edged blades and a unique ability to survive in an environment almost totally lacking in phosphorous, usually a key nutrient for plant growth. But no animal eats just sawgrass. So how did the Everglades support so many animals? "If you can answer the question of how could a low-nutrient, low-production system support a quarter-million wading birds and a million alligators, you have made a major step in understanding how the system works," says John Ogden.

You also need to know some basic hydrology. Before the Corps of Engineers started digging, Lake Okeechobee had no direct outlet to the sea. When the water rose, it simply overflowed the lake's shallow banks. Some water eventually reached the St. Lucie River and then the Atlantic, or the Caloosahatchee River, which flows west into the Gulf of Mexico.

Most of the water from Lake Okeechobee never reached those rivers but spilled instead into the marshes and formed an enormous sheet of water, miles wide and inches deep. This sheet flow, as hydrologists call it, distinguishes the Everglades from nearly all other wetlands on Earth. And restoring sheet flow across as much of the remaining Everglades as possible will be perhaps the central challenge for the Corps of Engineers and the South Florida Water Management District.

The seasonal progression of the wet and dry cycle dominates the Everglades ecosystem, with 60 percent of rain falling between June and September. This hydrologic pulse keeps the Everglades alive. Reversals of the pattern due to dry-season rains or wet-season droughts do not cause havoc, because water creeps through the system, slowed by vegetation, the almost imperceptible slope of the land (under two inches for every mile—slide a piece of paper under a book and you get the idea of how infinitesimal a drop this is), and the large water-storage capacity of the marshes. The result is a lag of many months between when the rain falls and when it finally reaches the southern tip of Florida, and hence prolonged flooding throughout the system. Certain parts of the system never dry out, even during severe droughts.[21]

As the sheet of water inches south, nearly all phosphorous in the water binds tightly to the limestone bedrock. The smallest but most widely distributed plants in the Everglades, species of microscopic algae that grow into large, floating mats called periphyton, may also help account for the lack of nutrients, by taking up whatever are available and creating an environment that removes even more phosphorus. As a result of all this, plants rely on rainfall to deliver nutrients.[22]

Such a thin diet means little plant growth and reproduction, at least per unit of area, like an acre or a square mile, which is how ecologists measure productivity. While productivity in the Everglades may be low per square mile, in its unaltered state it covered thousands of square miles. "The sheer size of the system was the real driving force in having enough biomass to support large numbers of big predators like alligators and wading birds," says Bill Loftus.

The tiles in the habitat mosaic of the Everglades range in size from a few square feet to hundreds of square miles. Ecologists have identified seven broad types of landscapes that occurred in the early-twentieth-century Everglades, including sawgrass plains, swamp forests, and a jumble of tree islands. Of the seven landscape types, three—a cypress forest that grew along the northeastern edge of the marsh, a forest of custard-apple trees that occurred around the shores of Lake Okeechobee, and a wet prairie that occupied parts of the Atlantic ridge—have vanished. A fourth landscape—the dense stands of sawgrass that once covered the northern Everglades—has been almost entirely replaced by agriculture, mostly sugar plantations.[23]

TRANSFORMATION

The Everglades restoration represents the latest in a long series of attempts to transform South Florida that date back to the early nineteenth century. Most of the transformation occurred in response to crises, like too much or not enough water for the farms and towns. The responses usually resolved the immediate problem, but at the expense of the integrity of the entire system. The people formulating the solutions rarely had visions big enough in either space or time to do much but delay the ultimate reckoning, and they inadvertently set in motion events that exaggerated future crises.[24] "You've got flooding issues, you've got nutrient problems, you've got water supply problems," says Mark Kraus, a biologist and senior staffer with the Audubon Society in Florida. "They were never looked at in a comprehensive way. [The approach] was, what is our crisis of the week and how do we deal with it without significantly addressing the structure that is in place?"

When Florida became a state in 1845, it had fifty thousand people (not including the uncounted Native American population), half of them slaves, and 90 percent of the population lived north of Gainesville. From the earliest inhabitants, people who settled in South Florida chose the exact spot where today you find Miami, Ft. Lauderdale, and Palm Beach, on the high ground along the Atlantic coast, high enough to stay dry through all but the worst floods. Before the railroad reached Miami in 1896, only fifteen hundred people lived in South Florida outside of Key West, where a deep water port had long supported a thriving settlement.[25]

In Florida as throughout the country, the federal government sought to divest itself of the land it owned by giving the individual states as much of that land as they were willing to take, and it gave most of the Everglades to the state, which then sought to make use of it. The early efforts to drain the Everglades sought to clear land for agriculture and settlement.[26] They focused on the area near Lake Okeechobee, where the richest soils could be found. Most soils in the Everglades are poor, as they derive from decomposed sawgrass. Soils near the lake, however, are distinctively different and much more fertile, a rich, complex mixture called Custard Apple Muck. This muck (a technical term, believe it or not), while rich in organic matter, lacks certain essential minerals. Once farmers learned the right fertilizer to add, the soils produced exuberantly.[27]

Floods in 1903 devastated crops in South Florida, and the gubernatorial election the next year became a referendum on the Everglades. Napoleon Bonaparte Broward ran on a drain-the-Everglades platform, and claimed it would involve a simple bit of engineering. Broward won and took personal responsibility for the drainage project, acting as planning engineer, construction superintendent, and tireless promoter. By 1917, four major canals dissected the Everglades from Lake Okeechobee to the Atlantic. These canals remain the backbone of the drainage system, capable of removing more than twice the annual precipitation of the Everglades.[28]

The drainage efforts spurred an unprecedented land boom in Florida. Regional growth rates in South Florida exceeded 100 percent between 1900 and 1930, and were among the highest ever recorded by the Census Bureau. After the Depression ended the frontier era, the Army Corps of Engineers undertook a project to build a navigable waterway from one coast to the other, which entailed connecting the Caloosahatchee and St. Lucie Rivers to Lake Okeechobee, enabling boats to travel from the Gulf up the Caloosahatchee to the lake, and then down the St. Lucie and into the Atlantic. The spoil from digging the channels became the Hoover dike (named for Herbert, who was president at the time), an enormous structure three stories tall and as wide as a football field that runs for more than eighty miles, nearly encircling the lake.[29] The dike cut the Everglades watershed in two, separating the Kissimmee River from the marsh.

While the dike marked the beginning of the end for the natural Everglades, it opened a new era for development in South Florida. Attention shifted from drainage to flood control around the lake, which, coupled with subsidies, allowed farmers to double sugar cane production. The seeds of what would become one of the most powerful agricultural interests in the country had been planted.

Congress began propping up the sugar industry in 1934. Soon thereafter, the other shoe fell on the Everglades. Three major hurricanes hit South Florida in 1934 and 1935, dumping over one hundred inches of rain and swallowing millions of acres for up to six months. The Army Corps of Engineers decided that only a comprehensive plan would solve this latest crisis, and Congress authorized the corps to begin building what would become the Central and South Florida Flood Control Project for Flood Control and Other Purposes, a mouthful mercifully shortened to the C&SF Project. Today that system includes seventeen hundred miles of levees and canals, 150 control structures, and sixteen pump stations, some powered by nuclear engines cannibalized from submarines.

The first step, in 1952, was a series of levees and canals running roughly one hundred miles from Palm Beach to Dade County, parallel to the coastal ridge. This system created an essentially floodproof strip of land about twenty miles wide and opened the door to explosive urban growth: between 1950 and 1990, the population of Dade, Broward, Palm Beach, and Monroe Counties grew from 750,000 to close to 4 million. If the region was an independent nation, it would be one of the fastest-growing in the world.

While the levee protects Miami and Ft. Lauderdale from floods, it also serves as the last line of defense for the Everglades. With the notable and contentious exception of an eight-and-one-half-square-mile area in Dade County just south of Tamiami Trail, the sprawl does not extend west of the levee.

All that plumbing enabled the corps to drain the northern Everglades in the 1950s, creating 550,000 acres of fertile farmland called the Everglades Agricultural Area (EAA). Its potential remained largely untapped until 1959, when Fidel Castro came to power in Cuba and a host of sugar growers suddenly needed someplace new to plant their crop. That year, farmers planted less than 50,000 acres of sugar cane in the EAA; by 1986, they planted over 400,000 acres of cane there, producing one-fourth of the country's sugar. To keep the cane dry, the corps turned the remaining central Everglades into five isolated wetlands called water conservation areas to be used as sumps and reservoirs. A federal program props up sugar prices; this costs $800 million to $1.9 billion each year. The government also buys sugar the industry can't sell, which costs hundreds of millions more, while the cane growers use hundreds of billions of gallons of water and pay minimal water taxes.[30]

By the early 1960s, much of the replumbing of the Everglades had been completed, though work on portions of the C&SF Project would continue for another decade. The crises the engineers had designed the replumbing to avoid did not end, however; they just changed shape. The project focused exclusively on controlling a single variable—water—and smoothed out, to the extent possible, the impact on people of Florida's unpredictable weather. Regulating the water conservation areas to minimize flood risk during hurricane season means keeping the reservoirs low when they would normally be high (June to October), and emphasizing water storage during the dry season means keeping them high when they would normally be low (November to May). We are standing the Everglades on its head.[31]

Once the corps had constructed the water conservation areas, they had to be filled with water so they could act as reservoirs. So the corps cut off all water to the area south of Tamiami Trail, including Everglades National Park. For two years in the mid-1960s, no water flowed through the marsh and into the park. Huge areas in the park dried up and caught fire. The sight of America's most famous wetland in flames powerfully conveyed the message that something had gone terribly wrong.

All this means that growing sugar cane in South Florida is as sure a thing as you can find in farming. During a severe drought in 2000, water district managers decided that Lake Okeechobee was too low to allow any water for irrigation. The sugar growers demanded a meeting, and Governor Jeb Bush reversed the decision without public hearing. Lake Okeechobee dropped below nine feet for the first time ever, and a third of the lake dried up. Governor Bush declared an economic state of emergency, but sugar growers had their fourth-largest harvest ever.

"Sugar takes on no risk. They take no climate-related risk at all, and here they are agriculturalists," says Shannon Estenoz, still amazed at the power of the industry after years of working on environmental causes in Florida. "Crop yields over the last twenty years have been increasing every year. Whether it is flooding, whether we are in the middle of an El Niño year, or the worst biblical drought you can possibly imagine, sugar keeps making money. Why? Because of flood protection and price supports— and we operate the second largest freshwater lake in the United States for their purposes," she says. "It is almost as if they want something written down in the Constitution that says they must be guaranteed a profit every year." On her computer, Estenoz had a sign, only half in jest: Big Sugar Is Watching.

Sugar cane is a dryland crop, which makes growing tons of the stuff in what used to be a swamp all the more bizarre. The dike keeps the cane dry, and to keep the dike intact, every day water managers dump billions of gallons of fresh water into the Gulf and the Atlantic. These pulses of water destroy the balance of fresh and salt water in two of America's most diverse estuaries. According to one environmentalist, fresh water has become a pollutant in South Florida. So much fresh water gets dumped into the Atlantic that fishermen have caught freshwater bass two miles out to sea.[32]

If South Florida's population keeps growing at the current rate, cities like Miami and Naples will need to drink much of the water now being dumped with the tides. The amount of water is not an issue; the South Florida system contains plenty of water under most circumstances to meet the present and prolonged future needs of urban society, agricultural industry, and the environment, if there was anyplace to put it. A glance at a map reveals the obvious place to put the water: south of the lake, where it always used to be. That would put water right in the middle of the sugar cane, and that remains an unspeakable thought among most Florida politicians. At some point, however, the cities will confront the sugar growers in a battle over water.

＊ ＊ ＊

The sugar industry cannot last forever, though it will undoubtedly try. Scientists, activists, and politicians have long predicted the demise of Everglades agriculture and yet it remains, so betting against it may be unwise. However, the industry would seem to be bucking some fundamental geological processes. All organic soils subside when drained, partly due to physical compaction and burning, but mostly due to oxidation—water protects soils from aerobic decomposition. The soils in the EAA are no exception. In 1912, over 95 percent of soils in the EAA were deeper than five feet. Today, most of the soils are less than three feet deep and nearly half are less than one foot deep. Homeowners in the area have had to add new steps to get from their doors to the ground because they have lost so much soil. Some farmers continue to grow sugar cane on soils less than one foot thick, but those areas will be productive for only a few more years. Since soil depths vary, and growers can change practices, subsidence will not completely end all agriculture, but the cattle industry may reemerge, because pasture grasses can grow on shallower, wetter soils. Scientists are also attempting to develop strains of sugar cane that can grow in those conditions.[33]

The subsidence of soils has another, even more important implication: it is the definitive nail in the coffin of the pre-settlement Everglades. Even if you removed the dike around Okeechobee, the water would flood the EAA and stay there, since the loss of soils means that the EAA now lies below the rest of South Florida. Releasing water into the EAA would create Lake Okeechobee South. It may still be worthwhile to restore at least parts of the EAA to a wetland, using it as water storage and wildlife habitat, but water will never again flow from Okeechobee to Florida Bay without a lot of help from a lot of engineers and quite a bit of energy to run the pumps.

The EAA could remain in cane or become pasture, or it could return to a wetland. There is also a third option, worse even than sugar cane: suburban sprawl.[34] If developers replace the sugar cane with houses and malls—most of which would need to be constantly pumped dry—any hope for the Everglades would likely disappear. Since the restoration plan works around the EAA altogether, it remains silent on this troubling possibility. Big Sugar rules in the EAA, and if the industry determines that greater profits are to be found in selling the land to developers than growing cane, then the process will be hard to stop. The state and federal governments will need to find far more resolve than they have shown thus far in confronting the abuses of the sugar industry.

RESTORATION

In the summer of 1981, water levels in Lake Okeechobee hit an all-time, post-drainage low following a one-in-two-hundred-year drought that lasted sixteen months. The next year, heavy rains and floods threatened the deer population in Everglades National Park. The years of crises and the growing environmental awareness in the country generally, and in South Florida in particular, meant that the public would no longer settle for limited and ultimately ineffective responses from the corps and the water management district—responses that focused on flood control and water supply at the expense of the natural system.

This time, the responses would be different. Conservationists like Arthur Marshall and Marjory Stoneman Douglas had talked for years about restoring the Everglades. This notion at last became part of the public debate.

Among the first to talk about undoing what the corps had wrought was Jim Webb, regional director of The Wilderness Society. Webb began lobbying Congress to reauthorize the C&SF Project in the 1980s, arguing that there is no solution but to redesign the whole system. "We can't defend the Everglades—or Yellowstone—just at their boundaries," said Webb. "We have to deal with the whole ecosystem."[35]

Bob Graham, then Florida's governor, gave the restoration movement a huge boost when he launched his Save Our Everglades program in 1983. The program sought, by 2000, to restore the system to its condition one hundred years earlier, at the turn of the twentieth century. The plan included restoration of natural water flow to the park and restoration of the Kissimmee (which had been discussed since the mid-1970s), among other things. That the state and the corps did not succeed in restoring the Everglades by 2000 does not detract from the boldness of Graham's vision.

In the mid-1970s, the state had studied how to restore the Kissimmee, which the corps had transformed from a meandering river to a concrete-lined ditch to reduce flooding. The corps in general focused on how water moves through the Everglades rather than on the quality of the water itself. Scientists had worried about the impact of nutrient-rich water flowing down the Kissimmee and into Lake Okeechobee and the Everglades marshes for years, but the issue did not reach the public consciousness until 1986, when a 120-square-mile algal bloom covered a fifth of the lake's surface.[36] The polluted water flowed into the water conservation areas and on down into Everglades National Park, eventually turning the sawgrass marshes into dense plains of cattails.

In 1988, the federal government sued the water management district, the state environmental authorities, and the sugar industry for violating a suite of state and federal laws, as well as water quality agreements between the state and federal governments.[37] The lawsuit led to years of complicated litigation, but the state finally offered to settle the case in 1991 and recognize the severe harm the park and the adjoining Arthur R. Marshall Loxahatchee National Wildlife Refuge had suffered and would continue to suffer if the state and federal governments (primarily through the Corps of Engineers and the water management district) did not take steps to reduce the amount of phosphorous in the system.

The Florida legislature codified the settlement of the federal water quality lawsuit in 1994 as the Everglades Forever Act, which mandated an increase in flows of fresh water and established a maximum phosphorous concentration of 10 parts per billion (ppb) in the water conservation areas, the refuge, and the national park. The act also required the construction, funded in part by the sugar industry, of forty-five thousand acres of stormwater treatment areas, basically artificial marshes to remove phosphorous from water leaving the EAA. The artificial marshes have indeed reduced phosphorous concentrations, from over 100 ppb to under 30 ppb in some areas. Getting from 30 ppb to 10 ppb everywhere in the system may cost billions more, mostly to acquire additional land, take it out of production, and build even more sophisticated stormwater treatment systems—a daunting task the state government is not fully prepared to acknowledge, let alone achieve by the dates set forth in the act. In any event, the Everglades Forever Act did not address the fundamental hydrological problems of making sure the right part of the Everglades received the right amount of water at the right time, leading some observers to conclude that under the act, the Everglades would not be "forever" at all.[38]

* * *

Just as the litigation over water quality wound down, the broader restoration issues heated up. In 1992, the corps and the state began filling in part of the Kissimmee Canal and purchasing land from willing sellers in the areas that would be flooded. That same year, concerned about the amount of money being spent on many separate water projects in South Florida, Congress authorized the Corps of Engineers to begin restudying the entire Everglades drainage system. The next year, a group of the leading Everglades scientists compiled a report spelling out the federal objectives in any restoration. The report essentially restates the fundamental principles of broad-scale conservation: larger is better than smaller, connected is better than fragmented, and natural is better than managed.

In 2000, the corps and the water district began blowing up the dams on the Kissimmee River, and now fourteen miles of the river again twist and wind south, attracting largemouth bass and black crappies along with great blue, tricolor, and black-crowned night herons, glossy and white ibis, and roseate spoonbills.

The restoration approach for the Kissimmee is simplicity itself: buy out the ranchers, blow up the dams, and let nature take over from there. With a price tag of $518 million, or about twenty thousand dollars for every acre restored, it is also inexpensive, at least compared to the overall restoration. As the Kissimmee project progressed, the idea of taking the next step and restoring the entire Everglades ecosystem no longer seemed outrageously ambitious.

"The problem in the 1980s was that the restoration seemed too big. The Kissimmee restoration was beginning, and that also seemed too big, but once that seemed doable, and got some powerful allies, it allowed people to start making connections. In your mind, in your imagination, the blinders came off," says Shannon Estenoz. "We are fixing the Kissimmee, we need to fix the bay, we are trying to fix the park—people began to think, 'maybe this is all connected and there is a problem, and it's the corps and all their works.' It was more an issue of limited imagination than limited science or lack of scientific consensus," she says.

A broad vision for the Kissimmee and the Everglades helped convince then-governor Lawton Chiles to launch the Governor's Commission on a Sustainable South Florida, an assortment of homeowners, home builders, sugar and citrus growers, business and tribal leaders, water managers, and environmentalists intended to assist the corps's analysis. The commission developed alternatives and finally adopted a set of recommendations for the corps that included many of the ideas raised by the scientists, such as preserving large contiguous areas to enhance surface water sheetflow, creating water storage areas in various locations to hold and release large quantities of water to simulate more natural hydroperiods, creating water preservation areas and other buffer functions along boundaries between natural and human systems, and increasing water deliveries to the southern part of the system, especially Florida Bay.

Allison Gromnicki, an attorney for the Florida Audubon Society, dates public interest in broad-scale restoration of the Everglades to the 1995

Governor's Commission Report. "The report said South Florida is not sustainable. We need to restore the entire ecosystem, and the environment, economy, and society are integrally linked."

John Ogden helped lead the process of making science more relevant to the water managers at the corps and the water management district. "We were thinking that we have one shot at this," he says now. "We wanted to sell the message that science has two roles; the role of learning, gathering new information, and the obligation to maximize the usefulness, the effectiveness, the focus of existing knowledge. We are going to quit crying that we don't have enough research funds, and look at the years of research we have that was seriously scattered in time and place."

+ + +

The Corps of Engineers took seven years to compile all the results from research, weeks' worth of public meetings, and many volumes of engineering studies into an $8.4 billion plan to revamp South Florida's plumbing. Codified into law in 2000 as the Comprehensive Everglades Restoration Plan, or CERP, the plan identified four key hydrological factors in the Everglades: the quantity, quality, timing, and distribution of water. A complex scheme with sixty-eight components, four governments (federal, Florida, Miccosukee, and Seminole), and more than a dozen government agencies, the plan proposes a variety of methods to deal with quantity, timing, and distribution of water. It does relatively little about water quality, as it rests on the rather shaky assumption that the state will actually meet the water quality goals it endorsed in the consent agreement that arose out of the 1988 federal lawsuit.

The Corps of Engineers talks about the environmental benefits of its efforts, but the first and most critical projects in the plan are constructing numerous and various types of storage reservoirs and wetland-based treatment areas for the water supply, and preventing flooding through more extensive control of water seeping under the levees. Much of the plan relies on experimental techniques: advanced treatment and reuse of wastewater, which could then be released into the Everglades and Biscayne Bay; using limestone quarries as reservoirs; building seepage barriers underneath the levees; and riskiest of all, pumping water one thousand feet underground into the enormous aquifer that lies beneath the Florida Peninsula. Aquifer wells rather than reservoirs are necessary because undeveloped land can cost one hundred thousand dollars per acre in Miami-Dade and Broward Counties, sugar growers refuse to sell land in the northern part of the Everglades, and high evaporation everywhere in the region limits the effectiveness of more surface reservoirs.

These gambles account for nearly half the price of the restoration. If they pay off, the additional storage space will mean water managers won't have to use the central Everglades and Okeechobee as storage tanks, and then dump billions of gallons into the marsh and estuaries during floods. In theory at least, this will enable the water management district to manage the natural system for nature, prevent flooding, and at the same time capture enough new water to serve 6 million additional South Floridians.

Beneath all of the official formality, the bureaucratic processes, and the political salesmanship of such a massive governmental undertaking lies fundamental uncertainty. No one knows if this will work. One might see this as a scientific failure—despite years of research, we still don't know the answer—but that would be a mistake. The plan is not uncertain despite science, it is uncertain because of science. "Basically we took a plan to Congress that is based on seventy-five or a hundred working hypotheses, and we don't know if any of them are right," John Ogden says. "On the one hand, we need to convince Congress and the world that we have a plan that can pay off. On the other hand, we are not really certain what the system is going to look like once we build this. We don't want to say that too loud, but we are hammering away on the uncertainty and the unexpected."

If Congress fully comprehended the depth of uncertainty beneath the restoration plan it might have slammed shut the cash drawer rather than fork over billions of dollars, but no matter. The fact remains that the United States will be spending those billions on a series of experiments. They may not always be the experiments conservationists would choose, and politics will muddy the waters, but the framework exists to do the restoration right. If the various agencies carrying out the restoration think big, learn from their actions, and are flexible enough to change in response to new information or new situations, then there is hope.

The something-for-everyone approach certainly made the plan politically palatable. Many environmental organizations, including World Wildlife Fund and the Audubon Society, lobbied Congress to pass the bill. Yet the ecological benefits of restoration will not be evident for years, as most of the early projects focus on flood control and water supply for human uses. The most striking example of this pattern concerns the plan to allow miners to dig limestone out of thousands of acres of Everglades wetlands along the so-called Lake Belt, on Miami's western edge. The limestone will last for the next thirty-five years, at which point the corps will spend $1 billion to convert two of the pits into reservoirs—one for drinking water and one for additional flows to Biscayne National Park. The reservoirs may implode, burst, or leak and thus drain the wetlands to the west, but by that point the miners will have already reaped the economic benefits.[39]

The restoration plan that Congress approved was long on vision and short on details, with just a few paragraphs describing each of the sixty-eight projects that make up the plan. Many of the projects depend on feasibility studies that are either just underway or not even begun. While it makes sense from the corps's perspective to omit the details of projects that will not begin for years, the lack of details leaves ample room for backsliding and conflict.

The restoration will test the stamina of the conservation community on an almost daily basis. Most fundamentally, the corps's plan provides for both restoration and water supply and takes as a given the land-use pattern that obliterated so much of the Everglades in the first place. "We are never going to have a situation where Everglades National Park will have the water it needs *and* anybody over on the East Coast will be significantly flooded or not have enough water," says Mark Kraus of the Audubon Society. "If the needs of the urban population are not taken care of, you cannot do the restoration."

✦ ✦ ✦

As just one example of the challenges ahead, in 1989 the corps developed a plan to provide flood protection to the so-called 8.5 Square Mile Area, the community of 350 homes and small farms west of the protective levee. Building more levees to protect the area would dry out thirty thousand acres of marshes. The plan set off a flurry of more lawsuits. The National Resources Defense Council sued to protect the Cape Sable seaside sparrow. The residents of the 8.5 Square Mile Area sued to keep their homes. The Miccosukee tribe sued to stop flooding on their land in the central Everglades.

After years of litigation, the corps proposed a partial buyout of the residents of the area. The difficulty in resolving that issue raises a broader question: If the government can't get a few families to move, how can they restore the entire eighteen-thousand-square-mile ecosystem? "The decision was that it is in the public interest to move people out of there, but it was a twenty-year fight," says Shannon Estenoz. The process was frustrating, she says, "particularly when the same nation would put a football stadium there and condemn them in a heartbeat, and not even give them more than two public hearings, let alone twenty years of a voice. This is not a nation that struggles to put the public interests above the individual. That happens every day. The question is whether it is willing to do so in the name of ecosystem restoration."

WORKING LANDSCAPES

Slowing Florida's explosive growth presents an enormous challenge, one far beyond the ken of civil engineers, so the conservation community must take up that responsibility and send the message that restoration cannot rely exclusively on technological fixes. The restoration plan dramatically expands the spatial scale of typical corps efforts, but it is not enough to just consider water flowing over a larger area. The plan addresses just one thread in an intricate ecological, social, and political web. How do you reach a population that does not have ownership of the Everglades?

"The implementation framework has thirty-year goals, but the state has been fighting this whole effort from the very beginning," says Shannon Estenoz. "The state wants to do it more piecemeal, project by project, making the Everglades fight for its water sixty-eight separate times. You have a better chance of making the moneyed interests happy if you don't have these overarching goals that restrain your ability to do large-scale water development projects," she says.

The restoration plan and the politics surrounding it provide endless ammunition for skeptics. The odds of the plan living up to the challenge indeed seem long. Yet the plan offers reasons to be hopeful as well. The legislation authorizing the restoration includes some innovations, such as mandating a role for both the state of Florida and the Department of the Interior, the first time the Corps of Engineers has been required to share some of its authority with anyone. Often called the "imperial corps" for its high-handedness, this marks a major change. The corps has been looking for ways around the requirement through implementing regulations, however, so eternal vigilance may be the price of working with the corps.

Some in Florida would certainly want to avoid the whole restoration effort, and just grab enough water to meet most needs for the next twenty years and worry about the consequences later. On the other side, some environmentalists say that if the state reneges on its commitments, the strategy should be to pick a handful of the sixty-eight projects, file lawsuits under the Endangered Species Act, and shut the system down altogether. If an organization like the Center for Biological Diversity demonstrates that one of the restoration projects threatens the Cape Sable seaside sparrow, for example, "the corps would not be able to open a gate or a culvert for the next twenty years," says Shannon Estenoz. "Voilà, you have paralysis."

This strategy would not likely do anyone, including the sparrow, much good in the long run, and Estenoz does not endorse it. The paralysis would only affect the corps and the restoration effort; Florida's development would continue apace. If the restoration can proceed as a series of experiments, as John Ogden foresees it, scientists and managers can actually learn from their actions and improve as they go along. Admittedly, that is a mighty big if, but even so it seems more hopeful than the alternative.

The current trends simply cannot continue in the Everglades or Florida as a whole. If they do, the state will end up with two kinds of land: protected and developed. That won't work. Even with all the money the state and local governments spend on land acquisition, only 25 to 30 percent of the state will end up in some sort of protected status. Rather than develop the remainder into the strip-mall and traffic-jam hell that is Greater Orlando, Florida needs to leave about a third of the state in some sort of relatively benign use, like well-managed timber operations or cattle ranches. That would leave Florida roughly divided into thirds—one-third heavily developed, one-third protected, and, one hopes, one-third well-used.

"If we don't have a mix that looks something like that, we are going to lose," says Jora Young. That means finding ways to keep the large, working landscapes like cattle ranches free from more intensive development and thus serving at least some of their long-established ecological functions. Otherwise, the protected areas will become places to store stormwater, as already happens in the Everglades. "We have to keep the large agricultural land uses to allow flexibility if some of the key hypotheses driving the current restoration experiments don't work," says Young. If, for example, the aquifer storage wells fail either completely or by degrees, what will we do with all that water? "What will we do, especially if all the open lands that exist in the landscape today become cities and suburbs? Probably the key reason to try to maintain the open-space structure over large spaces in the landscape is to prudently, conservatively plan for such an eventuality," says Young.

❊ ❊ ❊

An alternative, as in Malpai, is to keep people living on and working the land, as long as they do so in a way that is not abusive. The Nature Conservancy is working on such a concept in the Kissimmee-Okeechobee basin. Across this vast agricultural landscape are hundreds of thousands of isolated wetlands embedded in a flat prairie landscape, all draining slowly toward a network of lakes threaded together by the Kissimmee River. The vast majority of these wetlands are drained. At the same time, state water authorities manage the chain of lakes that form the headwaters of the Kissimmee in the exact opposite of what nature would have done; they draw them down in the summer so they can take stormwater from the greater Orlando area, and keep them up in the winter to keep up the pressure so there is drinking water in the south.

This kind of water management illustrates the importance of maintaining some open land in central Florida. Years of elevated levels in one of the lakes, Lake Toho, has resulted in muck soil accumulating in the shallows, and the fishery has suffered. The state wanted to lower water levels in the lake and remove tons of the muck, which would cause a cascade of effects: the water would flow into Lake Okeechobee, but to avoid a flood, the water level in Lake Okeechobee would have to be lowered by dumping water into the St. Lucie estuary. This whole scenario raised opposition from managers of the lake and environmentalists concerned about the estuary.

The resolution to the fight over who gets the water came only when two ranchers agreed to retain more water in their systems on their large landholdings. That meant Lake Okeechobee wouldn't need to be drawn down to receive the blast of water from Lake Toho, and the estuaries wouldn't receive a blast from Okeechobee. This is how the balance could work, and it shows why we don't want the cattle ranches to be converted to cities.

While the ranchers and farmers drained most of the wetlands and converted much of the native range to cultivated pasture grasses, the landscape is still largely open and vast. Occasional panthers still range across it. Caracara and burrowing owls nest, and colonies of wading birds still can be found. Much could be done to enhance this area to sustain even more native wildlife and support the restoration of the Kissimmee River, Lake Okeechobee, and the Everglades, as the basin has not yet been overrun by subdivisions. Managing the drained, isolated wetlands as part of the Greater Kissimmee–Okeechobee-Everglades ecosystem would help to provide more flexibility for the water managers, providing them more options for storing and cleansing water and fewer obstacles than if the fields of pasture grass become fields of three-bedroom houses.

With land prices continuing to skyrocket and agriculture continuing to be an uncertain economic enterprise, many of the landowners in the Kissimmee-Okeechobee basin are tempted to sell out to developers, which would eliminate any chance of restoring the wetlands or integrating the landscape back into the greater ecosystem again. So we face the challenge of providing economic incentives to ranchers to protect and restore wetlands and maintain open-space land uses. These things can be accomplished to some extent while maintaining the agricultural productivity of the land and keeping it in private hands. The Nature Conservancy and state and federal agencies are working to buy easements, restore wetlands within the easements, and develop management plans to improve the ecological benefits of the restoration while compensating the landowners for management activities. Often the appraisals for these projects can't compare with the value of the land for development, as no one knows how to appraise water storage flexibility or enhanced wildlife productivity.

Jora Young explains: "If we could restore these isolated wetlands, people wouldn't have to leave, they could still graze cows. It might affect the number of cows you could graze, but you could still grow timber, you could still hunt, but also now you would also be growing clean water and water storage. So we should figure out how to pay you for that. You would be growing what society really needs. Society needs agricultural lands. But in some cases the benefits of water storage, water quality improvement, wildlife enhancement, and open space mean more to us than anything else the rancher or farmer might produce. Society needs to figure out how to value these things and to pay private landowners for growing clean water and helping to store stormwater."

This principle could work in the Everglades. Do we need farmers to grow sugar cane there or do we really need them to grow clean water, to grow wetlands? Asks Young: "Instead of subsidizing them to grow sugar we don't need, why don't we figure out how to pay them to grow what we do need?"

"For the earth's biodiversity to survive, we have got to have the working landscape. We've just got to," Young says. "The government can't manage all that land. We have to figure out how to keep traditional landowners on the land." If we could figure out how to make private-public partnerships work to help keep people on the land and compensate them for any land uses that need to be reduced to achieve conservation goals, we may have a model for what could work in a lot of other parts of the world, Young believes.

"Ultimately, unless humans are aware of how their behaviors affect the systems that give them air and give them water and give them fish and give them soil, we are not going to win this game," Young says. She recalls an article some twenty years ago in which the author argued that saving natural areas is like saving precious works of art; we have to curate them just like you would care for a Da Vinci, keeping the humidity and the lighting just so. "We can do that, we can curate natural areas, but if we want living landscapes that evolve, tolerate global climate change, tolerate hurricanes, support myriad species of fish and wildlife, that is going to require massive change in the human system."

PART III

YELLOWSTONE AND THE BEST HOPE OF EARTH

CHAPTER 8

BLIND MEN AND ELEPHANTS

It was six men of Indostan
To learning much inclined,
Who went to see the Elephant
(Though all of them were blind),
That each by observation
Might satisfy his mind.

JOHN GODFREY SAXE

The fearsome grizzly bear and the scurrying red squirrel make an odd couple. The grizzly dominates northern forests around the globe, squirrels terrorize backyard bird feeders. They would seem to have little in common. Yet in parts of the West, if we had no squirrels, we might not have any bears, either.

Grizzly bears *(Ursus arctos horribilis)*, a North American subspecies of brown bears found throughout Europe and Asia, can kill elk and even bison. What bears in the Rockies like most of all, however, are pine nuts. A class of pine trees known as stone pines produce large, fatty seeds—the Italian stone pine *(Pinus pinea)* gives us the *pignoli* found in grocery stores and pesto sauces—and bears live wherever stone pines grow. Whitebark pine *(Pinus albicaulis)*, the only stone pine in North America, produces seeds about the size of a pea, huge compared to most other pines. The pine seeds average 30 to 50 percent fat. Bears, particularly lactating females, need to accumulate body fat, and only a few other foods, such as adult army cutworm moths, certain ant colonies, and elk and moose late in the year after they have fattened up for winter, provide as much fat as pine nuts.[1]

So grizzlies love pine nuts. They face just one problem: birds and chipmunks love them, too, and make quick meals of any whitebark pinecones that fall to the ground. And adult grizzlies do not climb trees. Enter the red squirrel *(Tamiasciurus hudsonicus)*. These industrious animals spend enormous energy gathering pines nuts and storing them in underground larders, sometimes collecting a thousand or more cones over many years, according to Dave Mattson, a leading bear expert with the U.S. Geological Survey in Flagstaff, Arizona. Bears listen for the sounds of the squirrels at their labors, dig up the larders, and feast on the pine nuts—and occasionally on the squirrels as well. Grizzlies like pine nuts so much that whenever and wherever they feed on pine seeds they feed on virtually nothing else.

The relationship of grizzly bears, red squirrels, pine nuts, and the last player in the drama, a specialized bird called Clark's Nutcracker *(Nucrifraga columbiana)* that is the primary disperser of pine nuts, would be just another entry in the endless, and endlessly fascinating, book of natural history save for two facts. First, when pine seeds are scarce, bears encounter humans more often, and when bears encounter humans, bears often get killed. Second, whitebark pine is in decline as a result of a fungal disease called blister rust, insect infestation, global climate change, and fire suppression. With fewer pines spread further apart, bears may need to expand their already large home ranges in order to survive.

As grizzlies expand their ranges, they will encounter more people, and that's a problem. People have been directly responsible for 70 to 90 percent of grizzly deaths near Yellowstone National Park since the 1970s. In the coming centuries, however, even if no human killed a single bear, they may still face hard times. Unlikely as it may seem, the survival of the whitebark pine may be a key to the survival of grizzlies, the embodiment of wilderness in North America. "Save a pine tree, save a grizzly" makes a catchy new bumper sticker for conservation.

The grizzly, seen by various cultures as a shaman, a tribal elder, and a nurturer, has become an emblem as well for the need to think beyond the boundaries of our national parks. In Yellowstone, grizzly bears have become the single greatest driving force in the movement to protect not only the enormous park itself—in the lower forty-eight states, only Death Valley National Park is larger—but the surrounding land as well. The idea of protecting the entire Yellowstone region dates back almost to the creation of the park in 1872, but has gained both urgency and stronger scientific foundations in more recent years.

✦ ✦ ✦

The history of Yellowstone National Park is intricately connected to the status of the ecosystem-wide population of grizzly bears. Yellowstone was the world's first national park and America's first biosphere reserve, and is a World Heritage Site as well, a designation that recognizes Yellowstone's archeological treasures (other heritage sites include the pyramids and the palace and park of Versailles). Greater Yellowstone is one of the few large areas in North America that still has nearly all the same species as were present when the Europeans arrived, and in nearly their same abundance. All told, ten native and many non-native fish, twenty-four amphibians and reptiles, three hundred birds, and seventy mammal species reside in Greater Yellowstone.[2]

Yellowstone is often called "one of the largest, relatively intact temperate zone ecosystems left on Earth."[3] This claim rings not quite true. For many years, Greater Yellowstone was far from complete; it lacked wolves, and it lacked fire. Both of those have returned, a product of many related factors, one of which is broad-scale thinking on the part of scientists and some forward-thinking land managers. How long they will be allowed to stay is anyone's guess.

Without proactive, collaborative conservation at a broad scale, Yellowstone will eventually fit that most feared of all conservation stereotypes, the island of seminatural habitat in a sea of development. Still, big conservation is still possible—and essential—in and around Yellowstone. Yellowstone and its grizzly bears and wolves have provided test subjects and a proving ground for new ideas in both the science and practice of conservation. These ideas form another thread in an emerging and revolutionary pattern: science can guide the actions of people and communities committed not only to holding the line against creeping ecological destruction, but to reversing the trend in the name of the common good.

GREATER YELLOWSTONE

The pioneering work of researchers Frank and John Craighead made vivid the travels of bears in and around Yellowstone in the 1970s. The Craigheads, identical twins, for the first time brought broad public attention to the ecological insufficiency of national parks, and set new standards for scientific research in them. At a time when few scientists and probably no land managers saw the need to think beyond individual species and small

areas, the Craigheads tracked bears to and beyond Yellowstone's boundaries and showed that the bears in the park formed a single interacting
population stretching over nearly eight thousand square miles of federal,
state, and private land. Frank Craighead's *Track of the Grizzly*, published
in 1979, showed that Yellowstone's remnant population of grizzly bears
required over twice the area provided by the park. With that book, the first
to demonstrate that even a large park like Yellowstone may be insufficient
to conserve populations of large carnivores, the concept of the Greater Yellowstone ecosystem was born.[4]

The precise size of the Greater Yellowstone ecosystem is a matter of
some debate, but in any definition, Yellowstone National Park lies at the
heart of it, and the plants and animals of the ecosystem are identical to
those in the park. In general terms, these plant and animal communities,
along with geology, climate, and physiography, define the ecosystem
and distinguish it from the surrounding plains. In arriving at the most
expansive definition, covering some 27 million acres, Reed Noss and his
colleagues used wildlife migration and habitat use, physical gradients,
topographical features such as mountain ranges and river drainages, the
location of major transportation corridors, and agriculturally developed
landscapes, among other factors, to determine the ecosystem boundaries.

For now, let's assume that Greater Yellowstone covers roughly 20 million acres, or a bit more than West Virginia, 300 miles north to south and
about 150 miles east to west. It includes nearly a dozen mountain ranges.
Forest Service wilderness areas occupy about 6 million acres, nearly half of
the federal land base. The Forest Service manages another 6 million acres
of nonwilderness forest land under a multiple-use mandate.[5] Other federal
agencies manage just under 1 million acres, and Idaho, Montana, and
Wyoming together own about seven hundred thousand acres, with private
landowners and Native American tribes owning the rest, about 6 million
acres. Private land accounts for about a quarter of the land in Greater Yellowstone. Yet here is one of the last places where you can let millions of
acres burn and bring wolves back, a unique opportunity to let nature play
out in a way that has been lost in most of the lower forty-eight states.

In Greater Yellowstone, the answers to the key questions—What are
the proper spatial and temporal scales for managing the region? What is
wrong with the current management? How would a broad-scale approach
work here?—remain within reach.[6] Greater Yellowstone provides perhaps

the ideal testing ground for big conservation. After all, the federal government owns more than half the land, so the task of developing a coherent approach to management would seem greatly simplified.

Unfortunately, the political dynamics of Greater Yellowstone handcuff anyone attempting to carry out relevant research and apply the findings to improving land management. The bureaucratic and political process of incorporating research into management is as complex as the ecosystem itself.[7] Even scientists as renowned as the Craigheads learned the hard way the risks of proposing new ideas that run counter to the accepted wisdom within the federal agencies or the industries that have dominated the West since the arrival of white settlers. The industries, the agencies traditionally tied to commodity extraction, and elected officials at local, state, and national levels—the "iron triangle"—essentially determine what scientists can and cannot learn about Greater Yellowstone. At one time, the Park Service and Forest Service actually forbade its employees from using the term "Greater Yellowstone ecosystem."[8]

Those resource management entities are highly fragmented, bounded by management jurisdictions with no basis in ecological reality, and operate under innumerable and often conflicting policies. Each state in Greater Yellowstone has its own fish and wildlife departments whose systems of management differ from one another and from the federal agencies.[9] More than twenty-eight federal, state, and local government entities manage parts of the region.

These artificial, bureaucratic distinctions so transform the landscape that at one time the impact could be seen from space. From three hundred miles up, the southwestern border of the park looked exactly as it does on a map, as if drawn with a ruler. The edge of vast clear-cuts on the Caribou-Targhee National Forest west of Yellowstone ran with geometrical precision along the park's edge. The Targhee long had a reputation among environmentalists as one of the worst-managed of all national forests, and in 1993 environmental groups filed suit to force changes in management practice there. The Forest Service settled the suit by agreeing to halt logging on 164,000 acres of land, including some prime grizzly habitat.[10] Enough trees have now regrown to provide bears with some minimal protection, and they once again can cross parts of the Targhee that had been laid waste.

Greater Yellowstone's condition has improved over the past few decades. Despite problems such as the growing human population, the conflicted management, and the grizzlies and the fire and the wolves, there has not been the kind of dramatic surprise—like a huge outbreak of disease or pests—that usually accompany long-term, intensive management of an ecosystem.[11] The number of bears and bison are up, and wolves have been reintroduced. An estimated 325,000 acres of private land are under easement, and the land trust infrastructure has been invigorated. Meanwhile, the sale of timber from publicly owned land has nearly ceased. Huge fires burned through parts of Yellowstone in 1988 and attracted worldwide attention, but while certainly dramatic, the fires actually were within historical norms. Yellowstone is the dog that didn't bark.[12]

＊ ＊ ＊

America's most affluent citizens place a high value on Yellowstone. The fringes of the ecosystem have been called the Park Avenue of the Rockies, and the Greater Yellowstone region is a hotspot of potential leadership and wealth for conservation. The opportunity for broad-scale conservation in Yellowstone, the symbolic importance of the park, and the populations of big, charismatic mammals all attract conservation organizations to the region. Some twenty conservation organizations and a host of agencies have offices in Bozeman, Montana, including American Wildlands, the Gallatin Valley Land Trust, the Greater Yellowstone Coalition, the Sierra Club, the Sonoran Institute, The Nature Conservancy, the Trust for Public Land, World Wildlife Fund, and the Wildlife Conservation Society. This small city of under thirty thousand people, home to Montana State University, feels a bit like a company town, where most of the people work for Big Green. That is an illusion, of course, but with so many organizations clustered into a few blocks, it is a comfortable one.

The high density of conservationists in Bozeman offers reason for hope. More and more of the organizations here take broad-scale approaches to conservation planning and action. At the same time, going from one office to another in Bozeman's old but reviving downtown can also be disconcerting. Each organization sees the problems in Greater Yellowstone a bit differently, as each brings a particular expertise and bias to the question. Together, they seem like the blind men trying to describe the elephant. "We need more science," says one. "Pay more attention to the communities and their economic needs," says another. "Focus on government policy," argues a third. The groups do not fall to quarreling like the blind men of the fable, and all of them are correct, but each one is incomplete. Conservation at this scale requires being able to see the whole elephant.

PLEASURING GROUNDS

The idea of a "national park" must have jarred strangely the nineteenth century intellects upon which the words of a Montana lawyer fell as he spoke from the shadows of a campfire in the wilderness of the Yellowstone one autumn night 70 years ago. For Cornelius Hedges addressed a generation dedicated to the winning of the West. He spoke at a time when stout hearted pioneers had their faces determinedly set toward the distant Pacific as they steadily pushed the frontier of civilization and industrialization across prairie and mountain range to claim the land for a Nation between the coasts. His plan was presented to men cast of that die—men whose courage and enterprise characterized the era in which they lived.

But Cornelius Hedges had looked deeply into American character and was not disappointed. He counted upon the altruism which marked that character, and planted in it the ideal which instantly took root and has since flowered as one of America's greatest treasures: the national park system. Thus was a new social concept born to a Nation itself reborn.

So opens *A Brief History of the National Park Service,* a 1940 publication of the Department of the Interior.[13] It purports to recount the creation of Yellowstone National Park; the *dramatis personae,* in addition to the "Montana lawyer" Cornelius Hedges, who in this telling single-handedly created both Yellowstone and the National Park Service, are the nineteen other members of a group called the Washburn-Langford-Doane expedition, among them some of Helena's most prominent citizens and their military escort.[14] The legend goes that on the evening of September 18, 1870, the explorers gathered around a campfire at the junction of the Firehole and Gibbon Rivers, in northwestern Wyoming, and pondered what should become of the land they had traveled through, rarely seen by white men and full of natural wonders. Some at first argued for commercial exploitation, but Hedges said an area so special should be protected, and the others agreed. They sailed downriver the next morning with their mission clearly in mind: to protect Yellowstone, for that is where they were, for future generations. After lobbying Congress and President Ulysses S. Grant for a year and half, this dedicated band of altruists succeeded and the president signed the Yellowstone Act on March 1, 1872, creating the world's first national park, a "pleasuring-ground for the benefit and enjoyment of the people."

The legend, as usual, offers far more heroism and romance and far less insight than the truth. The vision of public land shared for the common good did not emerge fully formed from the head of Cornelius Hedges, nor did it grow from the mountains of the American West, though it may have come closest to perfection there. Countless cultures protect land and wildlife, setting aside areas as sacred groves, royal hunting reserves, or some other designation reflecting religion, class, or aesthetics. Europeans had a long history of creating parks, though they had had no wilderness to protect since the Dark Ages; New England colonial towns had town greens; and New Yorkers set aside Central Park in the mid-1800s.

The members of the Washburn-Langford-Doane expedition also would not have succeeded unless the public rallied to their cause, and for this they needed help. A painter, Thomas Moran, provided it. Ferdinand V. Hayden, administrator of the U.S. Geological Survey, led a survey team to Yellowstone in 1871 and brought Moran and the photographer William Henry Jackson to document the trip. Hayden later displayed Moran's sketches and Jackson's photos in the Capitol rotunda to bring Yellowstone to the public, and through personal lobbying and powerful political connections encouraged congressional interest in the idea of protecting the region as a park.[15] Moran took to signing his paintings "TY Moran," for Thomas "Yellowstone" Moran.

Moran painted monumental canvases—his most famous work, *Grand Canyon of the Yellowstone*, measures seven by twelve feet—of some of the most spectacular scenery on the continent. The grandeur of that scenery, embodying a vision of America, drove the creation of the park.

Hedges, Hayden, and others sincerely wanted to protect Yellowstone for posterity, but theirs were not the only voices. Railroad tycoon Jay

Cooke, founder of the Northern Pacific, saw a park as a way to advance his plans for a rail route through Montana territory. An agent for Cooke, A. B. Nettleton, wrote to Hayden suggesting that Congress ought to "pass a bill reserving the Great Geyser Basin as a public park forever. . . ." Subsequently the Northern Pacific became the principal means of access to Yellowstone and its first concessionaire providing services for tourists.[16]

The geysers, hot pots, and other geothermal wonders of Yellowstone drew tourists, then as now. Congress wanted to protect the geological and geothermal features of Yellowstone, but they had little precise information on the location of those features. The park's boundaries therefore reflect not science but hope—hope that the park would be big enough to encompass the known geysers and hot springs as well as any others that may lie undiscovered on the still-unexplored plateau. Supporters in Congress argued that the area was unfit for anything save a park, but held out the possibility of dissolving the protections should some better use be found. Yellowstone has now reached nearly sacred status, but the park's legislative foundation was initially far from secure.[17]

Early advocates for Yellowstone focused on the panoramas, geysers, and recreation. In the words of the Yellowstone Act: "Hereby reserved and withdrawn from settlement, occupancy, or sale under the laws of the United States, and dedicated and set apart as a public park or pleasuring ground for the benefit and enjoyment of the people; and all persons who shall locate or settle upon the same, or any part thereof, except as hereinafter provided, shall be considered trespassers, and removed therefrom." Still, Congress used remarkably sophisticated language when it created the park. The Yellowstone Act explicitly included biological considerations in addition to scenic and recreational ones. Few others parks would address such issues for more than sixty years, until the creation of Everglades National Park in 1934.

While Congress may have chosen its words carefully, reaching the Wyoming Territory from Washington in 1872 demanded many days of hard travel, and Congress had neither interest in nor money for close supervision of Yellowstone. The park's first superintendent served without pay, and the only authority he had was to expel people from the park. Hunting was legal in the park throughout the 1870s. Hunters killed thousands of elk for their hides in what historian Paul Schullery calls an "ecological holocaust." For good measure they left behind carcasses laced with strychnine to poison wolves (as well as any other scavenger, including eagles and bears) taking advantage of the carnage. The situation got so bad that the U.S. Army took over management of first Yellowstone and then other national parks, and remained on duty until the creation of the National Park Service in 1916.[18] The poisoning of predators on federal land would not stop until 1972, when that unlikeliest of environmentalists, Richard Nixon, banned the practice.

The uproar over the slaughter of elk in Yellowstone led to a ban on hunting in the park in 1883. Poaching continued regardless, often with the support of communities around the park, such as Gardiner, Montana. This enraged William Temple Hornaday, an outspoken opponent of hunting, a crusader for wildlife, and as a conservationist second in prominence in his day only to Teddy Roosevelt. Hornaday, not a man known for tact, had a simple solution: "If the people of Gardiner cannot refrain from slaughtering the game of the park, then it is time for the American people to summon the town of Gardiner before the bar of public opinion to show cause why the town should not be wiped off the map." So much for community-based conservation.

People concerned with Yellowstone also recognized its limitations early on, prefiguring by nearly a century the work of the Craighead brothers and the development of conservation biology. In 1882, Civil War hero General Philip Sheridan proposed doubling the size of the park, moving the borders forty miles to the east and ten miles to the south, primarily to protect the big game populations. That plea fell on deaf ears, but others would take up the cause. In 1917, writer and conservationist Emerson Hough coined the term "Greater Yellowstone" when he exhorted Wyoming to consider enlarging the park to include Jackson Hole and the Tetons: "Give her Greater Yellowstone, and she will inevitably become Greater Wyoming."

Hunter-conservationists like George Bird Grinnell, a patrician New Yorker who grew up in a home carved out of John J. Audubon's Manhattan estate, recognized that protecting the park was good for hunting. Grinnell repeatedly emphasized the role of the park as "a breeding ground for big game which will furnish sport for hundreds of hunters."[19] In modern terminology, he saw the park as a source population, and many of the surrounding areas were likely sinks, depending on the intensity of the hunts.

As long as the source populations continued to thrive, the dynamic could continue indefinitely. Banning hunting in the park connected the fate of the park to the fate of the surrounding land—an act, says Paul Schullery, that should have been the beginning of the effort to manage the park and the surrounding land together as an ecological whole.

It should have been, but wasn't, at least not for nearly a century. Pressures to shrink the park and dam its rivers nearly matched the pressure to enlarge it. But Yellowstone remained as it had been created. In the meantime, protection for the region expanded piecemeal. In 1891, President Benjamin Harrison created the Yellowstone Park Timber Land Reserve to the east and south. Six years later, President Grover Cleveland, at the urging of both Gifford Pinchot and John Muir—perhaps the last time the two men ever agreed on anything—added the Teton Forest Reserve, which protected most of the Teton Range and Jackson Hole.

* * *

By 1980, Yellowstone was a popular destination, and watching bears up close, either at the garbage dumps near the park lodges or by the roads, became a standard feature of a visit to Yellowstone. The park began to resemble something of a zoo, but a highly selective one; except for bears, which always received special treatment, no predators need apply. Yellowstone was not unique: throughout the early twentieth century most people made the common distinction between "good" animals like elk, bison, and songbirds, and "bad" animals like wolves and mountain lions.[20] Killing the bad animals was a moral obligation and a national duty, a contribution to America's westward expansion, and settlers throughout the West gladly took up the cause.

Park managers killed or drove off nearly all of Yellowstone's wolves by the late 1880s. By the time the federal government launched its official predator-control program in the early 1900s, there were few predators in Yellowstone left to control. A photo from 1926 shows two wolves on a bison carcass in the Lamar Valley, in the northern part of the park. By the 1930s no wolves remained in Yellowstone.[21]

The campaign against predators grew out of the Progressive ideology of Teddy Roosevelt and Gifford Pinchot—an ideology that saw the value of nature in its service to humans. Roosevelt and Pinchot occupy a central place in the history of conservation, so it seems more than a little odd to a twenty-first-century sensibility that they essentially presided over the most efficient and well-financed effort to destroy wild animals in human history. Eliminating dangerous animals to make the land safe for settlement made perfect sense to Progressive conservationists on a moral mission, especially with wealthy and powerful ranchers urging them on, and they pursued that policy with all the might of the federal government.[22]

In Yellowstone, the predator hunt drew strength from the belief that wolves and mountain lions kept the elk population down. A comfortable belief in the balance of nature would seem to dictate that if you have more wolves, you will likely have fewer elk. Nothing in ecology is that simple. Add bears, antelope, moose, human hunters, a variable climate, disease, dams, logging, roads, cars, subdivisions, and an untold number of other variables, and the precise dynamics of any particular predator-prey relationship disappear into the fog. Wolves indeed kill quite a few elk, but they actually have little impact on the elk population as a whole.

Following the hunting binge of the 1870s, the elk population naturally began to expand, and park managers began to feed them. The park's military managers assumed such growth was good, at least until there were enough, but no one knew what enough was. They wanted stability above all, unaware that the system never really stood still.[23]

SCIENCE COMES AND GOES

The government spent almost nothing on scientific research into the effects of its campaign against predators, but academic interest grew. That interest, which continues in earnest today, would spawn some of the key ideas in conservation science, involve some of the most influential scientists—including Aldo Leopold and, much later, Michael Soulé—and reveal the need to think beyond the boundaries of the national parks.

Several now obscure but influential researchers addressed the question of predators in the national parks, particularly Yellowstone. Charles C. Adams helped found both the study of animal ecology and the Ecological Society of America. He urged the National Park Service to protect what he first called the "primitive" in the Americas, and in the 1920s promoted the protection of "natural conditions." He was also among the first scientists to refer to "natural processes." This notion would later prompt the

Ecological Society to create the Committee on Preservation of Natural Conditions for Ecological Study, under the direction of Victor Shelford, a classmate of Adams at the University of Chicago; the committee would lead to the creation of The Nature Conservancy. Adams promoted the idea of carrying out research in the national parks before anyone else, and his own research emphasized relationships among animals as well as between animals and their environment.[24] Adams saw the significance of predators, and he believed they could survive in remote areas: "What would be the cost of maintaining one hundred mountain lions in North America? Would it stagger American civilization? We have millions of acres in National Forests. Some of these could be managed in such a fashion that some of these animals could be preserved and eat deer meat!"[25]

Adams spent his career in academia. His younger contemporary, George M. Wright, on the other hand, moved directly from graduate studies at Berkeley to the National Park Service. Wright came from a wealthy family, and in 1929 he proposed a wildlife survey office and program for the National Park Service that he would fund until he could demonstrate its value to the Park Service. Wright hired two scientists, B. H. Thompson and Joseph S. Dixon, packed up a car with supplies, and drove across the country to survey the wildlife of the national parks.

The results, published as *Fauna of the National Parks of the United States*,[26] were revolutionary. The authors proposed that the parks were too small, management should be based on research, and species should be left alone unless threatened with extinction. These ideas meant, among other things, that Yellowstone's managers would have to stop feeding the elk. Park managers should maintain existing conditions and where necessary restore the parks to a "pristine state," though Wright, Thompson, and Dixon understood that nature was always in a state of flux. They defined one of the Park Service's tasks as "preserving characteristic examples of primitive America." The same recommendation, in nearly the same words, would reemerge some thirty years after Wright and his colleagues first conceived it.

Wright, Thompson, and Dixon ascribed many of the problems they found to "the insufficiencies of park areas as self-contained biological units," and recommended acquiring necessary winter habitat to protect migratory animals. "At present, not one park is large enough to provide year-round sanctuary for adequate populations of all resident species," they wrote. "Not one is so fortunate—and probably none can ever be unless it is an island—as to have boundaries that are a guarantee against the invasion of external influences." The size of the park was crucial: "Without adequate territory in our national parks and proper natural boundaries to protect them the whole national-park project must fail to fulfill its purpose."[27]

Wright became the first director of the newly formed Wild Life Division within the National Park Service in 1933. He used his new position to bring more ecological thinking into park management. He recruited two dozen young scientists who published hundreds of reports, including several reports following on his own pathbreaking model. This golden age of research in the National Park Service would not last. On February 25, 1936, Wright and Yellowstone superintendent Roger Toll died in a car accident on their way to Why, Arizona. The ecological approach to science in the parks died with them, at least until John and Frank Craighead arrived in Yellowstone more than two decades later.

Without Wright's vision and his political skills, the Park Service's traditional focus on tourism and single-species management returned to the forefront. By World War II, Wright's most important work was out of print and out of mind, and the Park Service abolished the Wild Life Division and transferred the scientists to the new Fish and Wildlife Service in the Department of the Interior. Scientists took a back seat to rangers, landscape architects, and engineers, a situation that would continue for a generation.[28]

✦ ✦ ✦

The lack of scientific input into park management would have profound consequences. A central task for rangers throughout the 1940s, in Yellowstone and other national parks, was to manage—that is, shoot—elk, deer, and bison to keep the herds in check and prevent overgrazing. They were simply following the bible of the profession—Aldo Leopold's *Game Management*. In that work, Leopold saw game animals as a farmer saw crops, and he sought to understand the factors that encourage growth of the crop and those that inhibit it.

Like the relationship of predators and prey, the effect of grazers on grass seems self-evident: too many mouths chewing the same grass leads to trouble. Yet all of the clearest examples of overgrazing, and they are not hard to find, involve humans, usually trying to ranch too many cows. Demonstrating that elk were overgrazing the good grazing land in Yellowstone's northern reaches posed far more difficult challenges.[29]

A Wyoming cattle rancher may have looked at the northern range and immediately declared it overgrazed, and it may have been, for cattle. But Yellowstone was not an elk ranch, and elk are not cattle with antlers. The range has good years and bad years. Instead of supporting research and scientific debate, however, park managers simply adopted the conventional wisdom of range management and stifled anything that might pose a challenge: in 1943, the superintendent of Yellowstone denied Aldo Leopold a permit to conduct research on the elk herd. Leopold had by that time shifted his focus from the game animals themselves to the land on which they depended, but instead of allowing a prominent scientist to gather more information, the superintendent reaffirmed, based on no new evidence, the need to continue culling elk in the park.[30]

The decline of science in the parks continued through the 1950s, and by the early 1960s the Park Service was essentially flying blind. The hunts of Yellowstone elk continued nonetheless; their ferocity even increased. In late 1961, rangers killed or trapped more than forty-five hundred elk from the northern herd in an operation of military precision and devastating effectiveness, using helicopters and Sno-Cats. The public outcry, from hunters who wanted the elk for themselves, conservationists, and people just horrified at the carnage, forced the government's hand. The rather uninspiring response, following a time-worn and by now rather tattered tradition, was to commission several new studies of the Park Service's wildlife management policies. This time, however, the studies would not pass unnoticed into the heap of turgid government reports.

A PRIMITIVE VIGNETTE
The wildlife-management review panel convened under the guidance of Aldo Starker Leopold, Aldo Leopold's eldest son (his youngest son, confusingly enough, was also named Aldo, but went by his middle name, Carl). Starker Leopold had more than a famous bloodline to recommend him. He had established a solid reputation as a wildlife biologist in his own

right and taught biology at Berkeley. The panel issued its report, *Wildlife Management in the National Parks*, in 1963. The title has been forgotten; it is now and forever known as the Leopold Report. Fewer than twenty pages long and mercifully free of bureaucratese, the report had a lasting impact on the national parks, and contains some seeds of the idea of conservation at broad scales.

The Leopold Report appeared nearly fifty years after the creation of the National Park Service. In all that time, despite the advances in understanding of the ecology of the parks, the service had never revisited its founding principles, which focused on the parks as pleasuring grounds for tourists and gave no weight to either science or wilderness. The Leopold Report changed that: "As a primary goal, we would recommend that the biotic associations within each park be maintained, or where necessary recreated, as nearly as possible in the condition that prevailed when the area was first visited by the white man. A national park should represent a vignette of primitive America."[31]

That recommendation echoed the work of George Wright and others in the 1920s and 1930s, but most readers in 1963 found it new and striking. They also often misunderstood it. Many people outside of the National Park Service took the report as a directive to preserve something static, as if a park could somehow freeze in place a vision of pre-Columbian America. Leopold, however, knew better than to portray nature as unchanging. Leopold and his committee understood the importance of fires, floods, and other natural processes.[32]

The report proposed restoring missing species, eliminating exotics, stopping artificial feeding, reducing road construction, eliminating inappropriate tourism facilities, and enhancing research capacity. The Leopold Report led Interior Secretary Stewart Udall to instruct the National Park Service to manage national parks for indigenous species while "preserving the total environment." In 1968, the service directed that the parks should be managed as ecological entities.

The Leopold Report noted that most parks were too small to contain all of the habitats required by resident species, and that past human manipulations or intrusions had so altered ecological processes that active intervention would be necessary to restore anything approaching a natural order. The report endorsed the idea that elk were overgrazing the northern range, and thus the herd had to be reduced through culling. Other forms of intervention might also be necessary: "Management will at times call for the use of the tractor, chain-saw, or flamethrower." Flamethrower? This was clearly not a group of men unwilling to manipulate nature. They suggested that in an ideal world, park managers would not need to interfere with the natural processes or wild populations in the parks, but they recognized that active management would sometimes be necessary.

At the same time, the Leopold Report emphasized naturalness—whatever that means—and set the stage for major changes in the way the National Park Service worked and thought. The report, along with a study by the National Academy of Sciences that appeared at the same time, had reinvigorated Charles C. Adams's vision of parks as places where natural laws might hold sway.[33] Leopold's committee recommended that the service "recognize the enormous complexity of ecological communities and the diversity of management procedures required to preserve them," and urged a far stronger role for science and scientists in managing the parks.[34]

The Park Service cited the Leopold Report's support for its elk policies and other kinds of vigorous management as an endorsement of its longstanding approach to the parks. Scientists and conservationists pointed to the report's emphasis on the role of science and its call for pristine wilderness. The report thus became a kind of scripture, a document to be parsed and interpreted. Leopold later commented that if the committee had known how carefully everyone would read its report, they would have spent more time writing it.[35]

The Leopold Report became official park policy soon after it was published. The public responded far more to its vision of primitive America than its acceptance of culling. Combined with the continuing outcry over the killing of elk in Yellowstone, the report led to Senate hearings, which prompted the Park Service to cease its efforts to reduce the herd. Instead, park managers would let Yellowstone take care of itself, an approach that in the late 1970s came to be called "natural regulation" or "natural process management." Few supporters of this idea believed it was a miracle cure for all the ills of the national parks, but saw it instead as an ideal toward which park managers should strive.[36]

A vigorous debate continues over Yellowstone's elk and natural regulation, but the furor seems rather misplaced once you see the elk as belonging not to the park but to all of Greater Yellowstone. The smaller the parks and the more intensively used the surrounding land, the less possible natural regulation becomes. Natural regulation doesn't work in a fishbowl. The idea of landscape- or ecoregional-scale conservation rests at least in part on the assumption or the hope that natural processes will remain intact and will continue to structure the environment. Arguments against natural regulation lose their force if you see the parks as part of the broader landscape and not as isolated museum pieces.

This should not come as a great surprise. Phil Sheridan knew it in 1882, and the Leopold committee knew it in 1963: "There is some deliberate tampering with natural processes within the parks which is made necessary by their relatively small size and their vulnerability to change induced from outside the park boundary."

HOW MANY BEARS FOR YELLOWSTONE?

That vulnerability has obvious implications for bears. The fate of the grizzly has stirred some of the fiercest debates in conservation, debates that often focus on scientific and technical details because the ideological and political forces that drive the behavior of federal agencies in the United States remain undeclared.

The Craighead brothers knew the grizzlies of Yellowstone better than anyone. They arrived at the park in 1959, and immediately began pioneering new methods in wildlife biology, particularly the use of radio transmitters to track animals. Thanks to the National Geographic Society documentaries, they became two of the most famous scientists in the country. An entire generation of conservation biologists can pinpoint one source of inspiration for their career to the day they saw Frank Craighead (or was it John?) being chased across the snow by a bear that woke up a bit early from the sedative they used while they attached a radio collar.

Just a few years after the Craigheads began their studies, the National Park Service decided to keep the bears out of the park's garbage dumps (park managers had ceased allowing people to watch the bears at the dumps in the 1940s). The Craigheads warned that closing the dumps abruptly would lower the stability, quality, and abundance of food for the grizzlies that had come to depend on them. They argued for a gradual closing. Without the predictability of the dumps, bears would be forced to travel further in search of food, and risk bringing them into unprotected areas and into more contact with humans.

Park biologists said closing the dumps was in keeping with the Leopold Report. They claimed that there would be little impact on the bears because the Craigheads had failed to account for bears that did not use dumps. That conclusion was based on tenuous and anecdotal data, since the Park Service, as was often the case, made a key decision with little scientific information of its own.[37]

After the Park Service closed the dumps, the Craigheads wanted to study how the bears dispersed. This would require tracking the bears by colored tags that the Craigheads would attach. Park officials said the tags, on animals the public rarely saw, were an unacceptable intrusion into the natural scene, and they effectively blocked the Craigheads' research and all other independent research programs until 1974.

The dumps remain closed, but the impact of that decision remains unclear even today, because bears live so long that it takes years to get an accurate reading on which way the population is headed. Understanding the factors that push a population one direction or another, however, reveals much about the future of the species, the role of the national parks and other protected areas, and the need to think and act at broad geographic scales.

＊ ＊ ＊

At least 127 bears were killed between 1969 and 1972, and more and more scientists became concerned.[38] Yellowstone's grizzlies spawned the first scientific attempts to evaluate and quantify the risk of extinction. In the mid-1970s, during his graduate studies at Duke University, Mark Shaffer took the Craigheads' dozen years of data and built a simulation model with them to explore the relationship between the size of the population and the likelihood that it would go extinct. Research on population biology and island biogeography had focused on the demography and genetics of extinction: the variations in the number of births and deaths, the ratio of the sexes, and the combinations of genes that shape populations. This work provided invaluable insights into the fate of small populations. Scientists like Robert MacArthur, E. O. Wilson, and Michael Soulé found that below a certain size, largely random variations in, say, mortality, which would be just blips in a large population, can push a small one down to zero.

Scientists call this "demographic stochasticity." Small populations also suffer more than large populations from another kind of variation, called genetic stochasticity. In a small population, individuals have few potential mates to choose from, with inbreeding the inevitable result. Harmful recessive genes that would have little impact on a normal-sized population suddenly pose a grave threat.

The work on the genetics and demographics of small populations was bench science, and it produced robust theories. These theories rarely touched on the problems of conservation in the field, since they focused on the dynamics of small populations rather than what caused them to be small in the first place. Mark Shaffer partly followed and partly diverted from this tradition. He never saw a grizzly bear while he wrote his dissertation, and he carried out a computer-based analysis of the Craigheads' demographic data. But he also did more. Shaffer stood atop the Craigheads' mountains of field data, with thousands of records of individual bears, their offspring, litter sizes, longevity, and so on, and took a broad view. In addition to genetic and demographic stochasticity, Shaffer identified two other kinds of effectively random events that can devastate a handful of animals in short order: environmental variation, such as drought or disease; and natural catastrophes, such as hurricanes, floods, and volcanoes.

All of these things, which Shaffer called "stochastic perturbations," introduce uncertainty into the future of populations. The future is always uncertain to one degree or another; Shaffer's point was that small populations of animals and plants face large uncertainties.

Not all the threats are random, of course. On the flip side of a typhoon wiping out the last population of a critically endangered bird are the predictable—"deterministic," in scientific terms—causes of extinction, which are usually related to human actions, like building too many dams or setting too many trap lines. These actions can set a species on a course toward extinction that can be changed only through great effort. The fate of the grizzly in the lower forty-eight states, and the bison and wolf, for that matter, ran as straight as the railroad tracks that brought the settlers who transformed the landscape of the Great Plains and the Rocky Mountains.

Some bears, wolves, and bison remain, but whether in sufficient numbers was the key question Shaffer and a few other ecologists had begun discussing by the late 1970s. The debate over reserve design focused on the question, how small is too small? For populations, the related question was, how few are too few? Two Australian ecologists, A. R. Main and M. Yadav, captured the crux of the issue in the term "minimum viable population," but their definition, contained in a now largely forgotten paper, rested on air: "the population likely to persist indefinitely."[39] Mark Shaffer tied the idea down by picking a number. The minimum viable population of grizzlies was the smallest bear population with a 95 percent probability of surviving one hundred years. It was arbitrary, but it was a start.

Unknown to Shaffer, at about the same time that he was contemplating the fate of Yellowstone's grizzlies, two other scientists, Michael Soulé and an Australian geneticist named Ian Franklin, were also trying to come up with more solid estimates of a minimum viable population, though neither used that exact term. Both Soulé and Franklin focused on the genetics of small populations, and working independently came to the conclusion that the rock-bottom population necessary to prevent inbreeding in the short term is 50. The number, however, refers not to a simple count of living individuals, but rather what is called the effective population, a figure derived mathematically that takes into account the number of offspring, the likelihood of being able to mate—among some species, for example, a few dominant males control all the females and the other males have no chance—and fluctuations in population size. In order to have an effective population of 50, you will need 150 to 200 individual animals.[40]

In the longer term, Franklin wrote, an effective population of 50 is much too small to avoid the harmful effects of inbreeding. Franklin had studied fruit flies (the genus *Drosophila*, the workhorse of laboratory ecology) and, based on this work, tentatively and cautiously suggested that an effective population of 500 was the minimum for long-term adaptability. Like Mark Shaffer, Franklin and Soulé sought to quantify an area that had been frustratingly vague, and they used the figures 50 and 500 as guideposts for conservation, fully aware of the ambiguity that remained. The hunger for simple answers, however, overwhelmed the details, and other scientists began referring to the "50/500 rule"—an early milestone, though a controversial one, in conservation biology. Though neither Franklin nor Soulé intended it, the almost fetishistic fascination with population numbers, sometimes to the exclusion of all other considerations, would burden many conservation efforts, including grizzly bear conservation in Yellowstone.

Franklin, Soulé, and Shaffer had proposed rough rules of thumb. Many wildlife managers, far more uncomfortable with uncertainty than ecologists, wanted rules, period. This was not just about obtuse bureaucrats, though that persistent species can always cause problems. In this case, even well-intentioned agency scientists felt at a loss. The National Forest Management Act of 1976, which governed the Forest Service, included a directive to manage fish and wildlife habitat "to maintain viable populations of existing native and desired non-native vertebrate species...." Congress passed the law before Franklin, Soulé, and Shaffer began to untangle the complex knot of genetics, demography, ecology, and disturbance that surrounds the idea of a minimum viable population, so federal land managers had little to guide them but their wits. The nice round numbers of the 50/500 rule became a simple bright line: above, all is well; below, write the species off as doomed and move on to something else. Officials in Costa Rica, for example, had to be convinced not to give up on their jaguars and harpy eagles just because they had fallen below the magic number.[41]

Mark Shaffer first published his ideas a year after the papers by Franklin and Soulé. Shaffer found that even relatively large populations face far greater risk than had previously been thought. Yellowstone's grizzlies were likely to last for a century, but the odds of extinction shot up soon after that, Shaffer said. A century, for a population of bears that has persisted since the end of the last ice age, amounts to no time at all.

※　※　※

Shaffer recognized that the concept of a minimum viable population had to be specific—this many grizzlies in Yellowstone, that many jaguars in Costa Rica—for it to have real utility for conservation. Soulé recognized the problem as well, and in 1986, he and an ecologist named Mike Gilpin introduced a method for carrying out just such an analysis, which they called population viability analysis, or PVA.[42] Now the focus shifted from a single number, the population, to the whole range of factors that Mark Shaffer had identified.

That was a huge improvement, and PVA became entrenched as a key idea in conservation science, with ever-more-sophisticated models and methods. As more and more scientists conducted PVAs, they also began to realize how much land many endangered species required to survive for more than just a few human generations. So even though PVAs concern particular species, they frequently lead directly to the need for conservation of enormous areas. The legal requirement to conduct a PVA of the northern spotted owl led to the Federal Ecosystem Management Assessment Team, perhaps the most significant event in the development of broad-scale thinking in conservation.

Still, the practice of PVA has not always lived up to the theoretical promise of the approach. A complete PVA requires years of data—data that do not exist for many endangered species. Even where the data exist, as with grizzlies in Yellowstone, the approach cannot answer every question. Where overhunting drives species down systematically, for example, the conservation challenge would be to stop the hunting, not worry about how some random process could lead to extinction. "The question that PVA was trying to get at was how small of a population can you have on average with the variability it experiences and not have it drift to extinction by chance," says Mark Shaffer. "That is a special case."[43]

"Anybody who has ever planted a garden understands natural variability," Shaffer says. "Some years are good for tomatoes but not strawberries, some years are good for nothing, and some years you can't give away what you are growing. For wildlife, if they are occupying a continent, it's unlikely that the whole continent is going to have a down year. But as you start to confine things to smaller and smaller ranges, smaller and smaller numbers, they become brittle, they become vulnerable to these things, and there is a way to quantify that. Because fundamentally, the surface of the earth is fixed, the human population is growing, there is more and more competition for land, and we are always at the end of the day answering the question, whether we want to or not, how much is enough? PVA was intended to try and become quantitative and defensible about answering that on behalf of wildlife."

In the industrial age, the greatest threats to species are posed not by random genetic reshuffling or unforeseeable environmental changes, but by the things we can predict or at least anticipate—usually the results of human intervention. For grizzly bears, that means climate change, loss of whitebark pine seeds, human population growth, and so on. Knowing this, says Mark Shaffer, the important question becomes, what are we going to do about it? "If the answer is, stop the habitat decline, well, where? How much? It may take a few steps, but you get to the point that you've got to say, 'here but not there, this much but not that much.' What do you base that on? I think you base it on PVA—PVA done well. Anything else is a guess."

BEAR POLITICS

A guess might have been better than the first grizzly bear recovery plan that the Fish and Wildlife Service produced in the early 1990s. At its core, the plan sought to establish viable populations in areas where bears existed at the time they were listed as endangered in 1975. The plan included Greater Yellowstone among the seven recovery areas in Montana, Idaho, Wyoming, and Washington. The plan was a disaster. "It confuses short-term stabilization with long-term recovery and will produce neither," Mark Shaffer wrote in a study of the plan for The Wilderness Society. Shaffer predicted that without changes in current management, when Yellowstone National Park celebrates its bicentennial in 2072, no grizzlies will remain in the park.[44]

Among other shortcomings, the recovery plan took Shaffer's work on PVA, based on data from the 1960s, and crafted management prescription from it, rather than reanalyzing current data and refining Shaffer's population model. The plan established numerical goals for each population—as few as fifty-seven bears for some areas—but did nothing to protect bear habitat. Over 25 percent of agency-defined occupied grizzly habitat was open to development. "Too little, too late," wrote Shaffer. The plan would create an "archipelago of isolated population remnants none of which is sufficiently large to be viable in its own right."[45]

In the short run, however, park managers began to see more bears, and they jumped to a logical but unfounded conclusion: improved management of the park led to a larger bear population. Most of the apparent increase, however, occurred after the fires of 1988 burned a good portion of the ecosystem, so bears may have simply become more visible, or may be in new territory because their old feeding grounds are in the process of growing back after the fires. Research by Dave Mattson and Craig Pease suggested the bear population increased after several good years for whitebark pine nuts, and decreased in the bad years. They found that the grizzly population in fact changed little between 1975 and 1995.[46] The belief, or perhaps hope, among Yellowstone's managers that they had the park under their control persisted nonetheless. That comfortable illusion would prove remarkably resilient in the face of repeated assaults.

Despite many years of data collection and population modeling, projecting the grizzly's future remains fraught with difficulties and inherently prone to error. Even with such an intensively studied animal, managing a small population of large animals will always be a hugely uncertain endeavor. Positive trends over the short term demand critical scrutiny and may well be unfounded. The combination of whitebark pine mortality and increasing human density should temper any optimism, as should the fact that the government makes nearly 40 percent of occupied grizzly bear habitat on federal land available for grazing.[47]

As the grizzlies rebounded from the heavy losses suffered after the closure of the dumps, states' rights activists, the Wise Use crowd, some hunters, and other opponents of the Endangered Species Act turned up the political pressure on the Park Service to declare victory and remove federal protection from the bear. Even some conservationists saw a need to demonstrate that species could be removed from the threatened and endangered lists. "The Clinton Interior Department was not a very good friend to grizzlies," says Steve Primm, a conservationist in Montana. "They were really looking for a success story there, and were willing to do it on the backs of Yellowstone grizzlies."

In December 1993, without warning, the Interagency Grizzly Bear Committee, made up of federal and state wildlife agencies in Washington, Idaho, Wyoming, Montana, and British Columbia, voted unanimously to remove the grizzly from the threatened species list. The committee, an institution unknown to just about everyone outside of the small community of bear researchers and conservation activists, could not unilaterally remove all legal protections from the bears. The vote was just the first step in a complex legal and administrative process that has still not played out, but it was remarkable nonetheless. The decision reflected some scientific leaps of faith, and the committee leapt without the advice of David Mattson, its own best scientist.[48]

If the committee was correct, then grizzlies had gone from threatened to recovered in under twenty years, a dramatic turnabout for a long-lived, slow-reproducing species, especially considering the 1988 fires, continued logging, blister rust, encroachment on important habitat, and other threats. Grizzlies may have been able to recover under these conditions, especially with good pine nut crops. Yet scientists still did not know how many bears actually remained in and around Yellowstone, and how many there needed to be before the species could be considered out of danger—several thousand are necessary by some estimates—and, most significantly, they did not know enough about the factors that conspire to drive those numbers down. The committee's decision thus seems like an act of faith, but of the political rather than spiritual variety: faith in the prevailing political ideology of the West, with its distrust of government and sanctification of private property.

Nothing is as sacred in modern American political culture as private property, but the lines between private and public land must blur if conservation across broad areas is to succeed. Political opponents constantly paint environmental regulations as sneak attacks on private property, and those portrayals, absurd as many are, create a considerable public stir. As legal scholar Eric Freyfogle and others demonstrate, however, ownership of land has never been an absolute license to use that land in whatever way the owner sees fit. Try putting a pig farm in your suburban backyard, and you will quickly learn the limits of your rights as an owner.

Conceptions of private property are also not static. Property-rights advocates will howl about the violation of American principles and betrayals of the Founding Fathers, but in fact the idea of property has changed before and will change again. Freyfogle and others increasingly see private property as a vital ecological resource that confers important communal benefits, and, as such, private property owners may no longer be entitled to complete autonomy. In short, says Freyfogle, "Property rights without responsibilities are virtual nonsense."[49]

Conceptions of private property change slowly, however, relative to the politics and bureaucratic maneuverings of grizzly bear conservation. The effort to remove the grizzly from the endangered species list and other management actions build on the comforting but largely unfounded assumption that we really know what we are doing. "The premise of management intervention having made the difference allows you to go forward with confidence with delisting, assuming that we have the system under control, so if subsequent changes need to be made we can make them," says Dave Mattson. "There is a lot of ideological appeal to that, there is a lot philosophical appeal, and it is also convenient to other agendas." The evidence Mattson has gathered does not support the conclusion that management actions rather than some unknown combination of ecological factors have determined the number of bears. Yet that conclusion is deeply embedded as a premise in the management plan, while park and forest managers downplay or ignore altogether the phenomena that have the best statistical support as determining bear populations, such as the availability of whitebark pine nuts.[50]

✦ ✦ ✦

Ideology often trumps science, so the push to delist the grizzly from the endangered species list continues despite all the unknowns. In early 2003, federal and state agencies in Greater Yellowstone developed a grizzly conservation strategy that sets the stage for delisting the bears, and spells out how the state and federal agencies will manage the bears once those legal safeguards have been removed.[51] The plan picks a population size—five hundred bears—that the various agencies will work to maintain, and then lists the population and habitat variables those agencies will monitor. If that monitoring shows that the bears are declining, supposedly the agencies will act.

That approach, says Dave Mattson, is wholly insufficient. "Whether it is five hundred or four hundred or six hundred bears doesn't really matter. What matters is why we have the bears we do, and what that means for the future." Federal bear managers have not figured this out. Instead of planning for the foreseeable future by defining what constitutes an adequate population of bears, says Mattson, the plan is to monitor, without specifying thresholds, how many bears are too many. Further clouding matters, bear managers in their monitoring of bear populations rely exclusively on counting the numbers of living and dead bears—notoriously uncertain measures of a small population of often reclusive animals spread out across an enormous landscape. The rather faint hope is that the monitoring will signal any changes in the system, and, an even fainter hope, that politicians will respond quickly enough to make a difference.

The alternative would be to create a model of what Yellowstone will look like in fifty or one hundred years, based on what we know about trends in climate and the key foods for the grizzlies, and then try to come up with estimates of how bears would fare. Mattson and some colleagues are attempting to do exactly that. "I realize this is a world of limited resources, but we are talking about Yellowstone grizzly bears, one of the best studied organisms on Earth, certainly a situation where we historically have had millions of dollars allocated. If we can't do it there, then where are we going to do it? At least set some sort of a benchmark for adequate appraisal and adequate analysis. Every policy you look at that governs the conduct of federal agencies says they must make provisions for future generations, which means conservation. And how do you do that but by looking at the future the best you can with what you've got, and we've got a lot for Yellowstone to inform our current decisions. If one has the understanding that it is food that has driven the demography as much as anything else, then logically one could project what the future holds for those foods, those drivers."

Mattson believes that traditional positivistic science falls short when confronted with the problems of grizzly bear conservation. Scientific positivists believe that better science is necessary and sufficient for better management. That faith in science has spawned a narrowly conceived form of scientific ecosystem management that continues to advocate value-free science, control by professional experts, and centralized decision-making with little input from citizens.[52]

The classic approach to science of hypothesis and deduction has been remarkably ineffective at posing questions and addressing problems arising from an intersection of the human social domain with complex ecological systems. First of all, we lack the money, time, and bears necessary to conduct replicated studies, and scientists cannot manipulate the behavior of humans at an appropriate scale simply for the convenience of research design, says Mattson. Second, there is a scale problem: since grizzlies exist at low densities in the Rockies, scientists collect data about them over a wide area, which means that the sample sizes from a specific area are rarely adequate for scientifically defensible inferences. Bear management, on the other hand, assesses proposed actions at the scale of a few square kilometers.

Bear managers ask researchers for definitive answers: How many roads can we put in? Can we expand this campground, or that one? But apart from broad generalities, scientists do not yet understand all the factors controlling grizzly bear mortality. So managers wait for answers that will not be forthcoming, and, lacking data that indicate harm, accommodate the compelling sociopolitical demands that favor the creation of wealth from natural resources.[53]

Even if science had perfect or near-perfect information, it would not necessarily change the behavior of the land management agencies. "The behavior of the agencies has to do with what motivates decision makers at high levels of organizations," says Mattson. "There is lots of evidence to suggest that it has more to do with power and wealth than enlightenment. It gets down to the ecology of information, what information matters within natural resource agencies. I would argue that scientific information does not matter all that much, it is more about budget and career opportunity, the next performance appraisal. That information matters a whole lot—the feedback loops are tighter, much tighter—while feedback from a managed system like the grizzly bear ecosystem is long delayed and hugely uncertain." If a senator gets frustrated that delisting is not moving fast enough, the consequences for agency staff are certain and immediate. The loss of grizzly bear habitat over the next century, in contrast, has no practical impact on the people making the decisions.

QUIET SUCCESS

The Fish and Wildlife Service recovery plan sought to merely stabilize existing grizzly populations. A far better approach, according to Mark Shaffer, would be to allow bears to return to a larger portion of the regional landscape than they currently occupy, and to re-establish links between populations. "By weaving back together the big remaining pieces of functional wilderness we can keep a viable native ecosystem in the Northern Rockies," he writes.[54] In essence, Shaffer says, the recovery plan thought small, when it needed to think big.

"Their recovery zones seem more like containment zones," Shaffer says. He points out that the recovery zones could be readily expanded to include additional good grizzly habitat, largely on public land. Bears may not be there now, but they may be if the population grows. Expanding the zones, however, has proven to be impossible. "I'm not going to fight anymore to expand the recovery boundaries of the Yellowstone ecosystem. It's like the twelfth charge at Fredericksburg," Shaffer says. Instead, the focus is on the health of the population that is there, and the existing habitat linkages. If they are growing as fast as the government biologists say they are, they will find their way to these other areas.

Grizzlies have already come down out of the Madison Range, along Yellowstone's northwestern edge, and crossed the Madison Valley into the Gravelly Range, a gentle stretch of big, grassy ridges that make ideal sheep and cattle country. The Madison Range lies within one of the recovery zones, and the Gravelly Range sits just outside it. Miners looking for gold and then ranchers looking for grass drove grizzlies and wolves out of the Gravellies by 1900, but bears started returning in the mid-1980s, fueled by good pine nut crops.

Steve Primm has been working here since the mid-1990s. "This has been a quiet success story," he says. "We realized in the mid-nineties that the Gravellies probably are occupied grizzly habitat, it's just that people aren't out there looking for them in these little roadless pockets, and we want that expansion to continue." Primm call the process "rolling out the coexistence carpet for bears" to be able to coexist with people and thrive. He is working with the Forest Service to implement regulations to keep bears out of trouble. Primm also has been trying to develop these coexistence measures, such as building poles for hikers and others to hang food from, in a participatory way with local people.[55]

"From the perspective of grizzly bear conservation, we have to work on private land," says Primm. "We have to be able to use a combination of easements, purchases, and just plain old cooperation in order to get it done. I don't see what our regulatory options are."

Only about half a dozen owner-operated ranches remain in the Madison Valley; wealthy absentee owners—software developers from the Bay Area or, says Primm, "the guy who makes all the leather stuff that you see in the Harley-Davidson catalog"—own the rest. The actor Steven Seagal owned one of the largest properties, Sun Ranch, until 1998. The new owners put an easement on more than a third of their eighteen thousand acres stipulating that the property will be managed as a ranch, and will not be subdivided, in perpetuity. The ranch is home to Conservation Beef, a program of The Nature Conservancy and Artemis Common Ground, a Helena, Montana–based organization that initiates and facilitates community-based conservation efforts. The Conservation Beef program pays a premium for grass-fed beef raised on ranches that commit to high-quality land stewardship.

Two other ranches in the Madison Valley raise Conservation Beef and all are members of the Madison Valley Ranchlands Group, an organization of ranchers who work with conservation interests and public-resource agencies to preserve family ranching and the open spaces on which it depends. As in Malpai, they are looking into grassbanking and ways to foster cooperative ranching on private land. The Madison Valley lies close enough to Bozeman that people commute to the city every day, meaning that this may be one place where the choice really is cows or condos.

Not everyone in the valley supports such endeavors. The state representative from the area claimed that the United Nations and The Wildlands Project had already designated the Madison Valley to be almost entirely core reserves or buffer zones, and that this will end all economic activity in the county. For Steve Primm, such hostility and misunderstanding raises a basic question: "If there are not significant gains to be made by doing all this detailed conservation planning and coming up with the perfect reserve design, then why do it? Why not start with a series of small-scale experiments?"

Primm's work embodies the potential of working with communities while keeping the bigger picture always in mind. "Some people think that if you are doing small-scale work, then you are running around willy-nilly, opportunistically working with local people wherever local people will work with you," he says. "You have to be strategic. I don't see much reason to work on the northeast corner of Greater Yellowstone on grizzly bear connectivity, because there is no place for them to go in that direction. It is much more strategic to work on the Madison Valley and the Gravelly Range, where you have some chance of reconnecting this population to somewhere else."

The most pressing need, says Primm, is not to spend endless hours and millions of dollars crafting the perfect reserve design, but to work with rural communities, guided by a broad-scale vision, to demonstrate to people what conservation will mean to them. "No one here wants to wreck everything and have the valley be wall-to-wall subdivisions," says Primm. "We want to have some economic use, as well as grizzlies and wolves traveling through here, living here periodically. We need to demonstrate to people that their values can still be protected and advanced at the same time that conservation's values are protected and advanced as well. An integration of values needs to take place, and you can't do that on a large scale, you have to have small-scale demonstrations of it."

❧ ❧ ❧

As in Malpai, the success of conservation in the Madison Valley and elsewhere in Greater Yellowstone will rest in large part on the ability of communities to work toward a common vision. Strong communities have the potential to create institutions, informal or otherwise, that have at their core an obligation to neighbors or to future generations, or to the well-being of people and the land. Most existing institutions serve not those values but rather power and wealth. Says Dave Mattson, "the reason why the practice of conservation is so, so difficult and complicated is because the values that it is serving are intrinsically disadvantaged in most institutions that society has created."

Greater Yellowstone provides a vivid illustration of the difficulties in challenging the institutions so dedicated to generating wealth and wielding power. But Greater Yellowstone also illustrates the changing social, political, and economic context that is gradually shifting the terms of the debate, and creating new possibilities for conservation across the entire vast ecosystem and beyond.

CHAPTER 9

GUARDING THE GOLDEN GOOSE

I have been impressed with the urgency of doing.
Knowing is not enough; we must apply.
Being willing is not enough; we must do.
LEONARDO DA VINCI

The Big Hole River, one of the few undammed rivers in the West, runs free for more than 150 miles, from its source high in the Bitterroot Range to its confluence with the Beaverhead and Ruby Rivers in southwestern Montana, just on the edge of the Greater Yellowstone ecosystem. The Big Hole watershed takes in over 1.8 million acres of semiarid high desert, granite canyons, and broad valleys, and the river itself boasts some of the country's best trout fishing. More important than the scenery or the recreation, however, is that the Big Hole illuminates one possible future for conservation in Greater Yellowstone.

The Big Hole watershed supports many notable species, including sage grouse, westslope cutthroat trout, lynx, and bighorn sheep. One species in particular, a small member of the salmon family called the fluvial (that is, river-living) Arctic grayling, has attracted the most attention and spurred some innovative thinking. A proposal to list the Big Hole grayling, the last self-sustaining, native population of the species in the lower forty-eight states, under the Endangered Species Act forced ranchers and agency regulators to work together. Their efforts capture the opportunities and the challenges posed by Greater Yellowstone's rapidly changing economy and its slowly evolving politics.

Fewer than two thousand people live in the Big Hole watershed. In a pattern repeated across the West, public land accounts for nearly two-thirds of the watershed, but private ranches dominate the valley bottom, where ranchers raise cattle and hay. These activities, plus logging and mining, have left deep scars: torn-up streams, overgrazed pastures, and invasive weeds, to name but three. Development pressures in the river valley, particularly second homes for people attracted by the world-class trout fishing, are increasing steadily.

Ranchers need water for their fields and cattle, but the grayling depends for its survival on healthy river flows: low river flows kill grayling by raising the water temperature or by stranding eggs or young fish, making it easier for predators to feed on fish concentrated in the remaining water. The deadly combination of hot, dry summers and water withdrawals regularly lower water levels so much that local pelicans have an easy time scooping up the grayling, and the Fish and Wildlife Service must use noisemakers to scare the birds off and keep them from devouring the grayling population. Grayling also become stranded in irrigation ditches and die when ranchers close the headgates before the fish can return to the river. In 1999, biologists counted thirty-five adult graylings per mile, down from ninety-seven per mile in 1997.

In the early 1990s, the Fish and Wildlife Service determined that the grayling belonged on the threatened species list, but that other species took priority. With the threat of a listing looming in the background, the state and federal governments, private landowners, and fishing outfitters formed the Big Hole Watershed Committee, which included ranchers, outfitters, conservationists, and land management agencies, to craft a series of voluntary steps. Under the voluntary plan, the ranchers who participated (about 90 percent of the water-rights holders in the basin) shut their irrigation ditches on July 4, and after that only used water for their cattle. The committee and the state drilled wells to provide an alternative source of stock water, which has the added benefit of allowing riparian vegetation to recover. The committee also developed a dry-year water management plan that triggers increasingly strict (but still voluntary) water use and fishing restrictions as water levels drop.

The voluntary measures have decreased the number of days with low flows, but the river still dries up regularly. This poses enough of a threat that state fisheries' biologists have been attempting to transplant grayling into four other rivers in Montana. None of these efforts has been successful yet, and in early 2003 conservationists filed suit again to list the grayling as an endangered species.

Conservation of the grayling may end up in court. In a less visible but perhaps even more important effort, the Big Hole Watershed Committee held community meetings to create a vision for the future of the Big Hole and develop guiding principles for future development. This process led to a land-use plan that all four counties in the basin adopted. The counties agreed to enforce the same standards across the watershed, including reviewing all development proposals within five hundred feet of the mean high-water mark of the Big Hole, mapping the one-hundred-year floodplain of the river, targeting new development around existing towns and roads and away from forests and floodplains, and working with willing sellers to support conservation easements as a land-use planning tool.

No other place in Montana has achieved that level of cooperation. "We had some interesting conversations at the beginning," says Jennifer Dwyer, director of the Big Hole Watershed Committee. "Some of the people who said 'This is communism!' and who yelled, at the end they said, 'You know, this zoning is a good idea.'"[1]

Dwyer and the Big Hole Watershed Committee would not have succeeded without the active involvement of the ranching community. The ranchers on the committee commanded the respect of their neighbors because of the deep roots they had there. "I had fourth-generation ranchers bringing the plan with me to the county commissioners," says Dwyer. "They had a little more collateral than I did." Even so, it took five years to reach this point.

✦ ✦ ✦

The experience in the Big Hole watershed illustrates the enduring challenges to maintaining a natural ecosystem that includes private landholdings.[2] The Sonoran Institute—the Tucson-based organization that worked on Las Cienegas National Conservation Area (see Chapter 5)—helps address these challenges in Greater Yellowstone as well by working with people to foster affordable, livable communities founded on shared visions of a future not constructed entirely around mining, ranching, or logging. "We are basically in the business of training rural residents how to protect landscapes they value, and they will value them for a whole variety of reasons. Wildlife is just one of them," says Ray Rasker, an economist with the Sonoran Institute's Northern Rockies Program, based in Bozeman.[3]

People treasure open land, whether they live in Greater Yellowstone, the Malpai Borderlands, the suburbs of Miami hard by the Everglades, or just about anywhere else. While preserving open space does not automatically equal biodiversity conservation, losing it certainly forecloses on conservation options. In Greater Yellowstone, subdivisions and development gobble up open land; Gallatin County, home to Bozeman, lost over 23 percent of its farmland in the last two decades. A report by the American Farmland Trust identified the areas around Bozeman as some of the most endangered agricultural land in the country.[4] Ranchers and residents of urbanizing communities see that it can be in their interests to preserve open land. Land Trusts have expanded in the region, and Gallatin County created an Open Lands Board to address the loss of agricultural land, wildlife habitats, and open space on private land.

As in the Big Hole Watershed, the success of the effort depended on the involvement of the ranching community. Ranchers made up half of the Open Lands Board, and the most influential rancher in the county served as chairman of the board. "We had all these PowerPoint presentations, and these facts and data, and we had to go present it all to the commissioners," says Ray Rasker. "[The chairman] just wore his biggest hat and his biggest belt buckle and he just looked the commissioner in the eye and said, 'Phil, you listen to me, we have known each other since we were yea-high to a grasshopper, and you should do this because it is good for agriculture.' The rest of us were working our butts off trying to come up with arguments and charts, and this guy just wore his hat and said, 'Do it.' And then we get beat up [by other environmentalists] because we're working with the ranchers. The reality is if you're not working with ranchers you are not at the table. If you don't have farmers and ranchers on your side you don't get anywhere, anywhere in the West," says Rasker.

An initiative called Heart of the Rockies is also working with a dozen or so land trusts across Greater Yellowstone to set conservation priorities in a systematic fashion by looking at where the vulnerable land is, developing a financial strategy for protecting it, building capacity for ecological management, and encouraging sound land-use planning. For the first time, land trusts in the region are setting priorities together. Heart of the Rockies combines money from several charitable foundations with state matching funds in Montana, Idaho, and Wyoming to enable public and private organizations—including national organizations like The Nature Conservancy, the Conservation Fund, and the Trust for Public Land, and regional land trusts such as the Teton Regional Land Trust, Gallatin Valley Land Trust, and the Jackson Hole Land Trust—to acquire private land or conservation easements from willing sellers and help local communities identify and protect natural resources.

These efforts occupy the foreground, while in the background, ranching traditions change slowly but inexorably with shifting economic and cultural realities across the rural West. People who play on rather than live off the land increasingly set new norms for the region, often to the dismay of farmers and ranchers. A Yellowstone lifestyle identity is beginning to develop, rooted in both the rural character of the region and what economists call its environmental amenities. As yet, however, young people growing up in the region have little exposure, through the public education system, to ideas and experiences about conservation writ large.

Debates, frequently heated ones, are the necessary and inevitable result of the simultaneous changes in both culture and conservation. The need to build broad-scale conservation efforts on scientific principles and give local communities a voice in their future demonstrates the impossibility of labeling one side in those debates good and the other bad. "Ranchers are like anybody else. There are some bad ones, there are some good ones," says Ray Rasker. "I can sit there and look at some ranchers that do really bad things and acknowledge it, but on the other hand I can look at some ecologists who are building their houses in the middle of riparian areas. They are just people."

THE GOLDEN GOOSE

The Big Hole watershed and Greater Yellowstone in general demonstrate the fundamental challenge for all big conservation: resolving conflicts among different landowners or managers with different values and objectives. Ideally, all the various players would work in harmony toward a single goal. At the very least they should not come to blows with one another. Yet while scientists and policymakers debate thorny questions about the extent to which logging, oil and gas development, livestock grazing, recreation, and so on impair conservation, an even broader and far more fundamental issue remains hidden: how many bears, wolves, or any other species one cares to name are we willing to sacrifice in the name of development? Only by reaching consensus about how to integrate humans and nature on all these lands, both public and private, can we craft an approach that addresses the whole of the Greater Yellowstone ecosystem.[5]

Remember Mark Shaffer's remark that worrying just about public land means defending the wrong perimeters? Greater Yellowstone provides the perfect example. Here the general western pattern of public land at higher elevations and private land in the valleys finds particularly dramatic expression, so conserving just public land leaves the rich bottomlands unprotected. Worse yet, the vast majority of ecological studies focus on the public land, so we don't even have a clear idea of what we would lose.

Many conservation organizations continue to focus on the battles over public land, but gradually the perspective appears to be shifting. One of the larger conservation organizations working in and around Yellowstone, the Greater Yellowstone Coalition, began in 1983 with a mission of public-land advocacy, specifically encouraging federal land managers to adopt an ecosystem management approach. The coalition gradually recognized that the condition of privately owned land also greatly affected the entire ecosystem. Rural private land makes up approximately 20 percent of the Greater Yellowstone ecosystem, generally the biologically rich valley bottoms, small streams, wetlands, and winter ranges.[6] The coalition made the decision to move into private land and take on such areas as bond issues and tax policy. According to Michael Scott, executive director of the coalition, the group now spends half of its project dollars on private land. The group has over thirteen thousand individual members, along with eighty conservation and outdoor organizations and 230 businesses.[7]

Dennis Glick has worked on conservation issues in the region for more than a decade, and he has witnessed the evolution. Glick worked with the Greater Yellowstone Coalition before joining the Sonoran Institute; he runs the organization's Northern Rockies Program from a small suite of offices on the third floor of a converted warehouse in Bozeman. An exclusive focus on one piece of the puzzle, say the public land, will no longer suffice, Glick says. "We can't avoid the complexity. We can't go back to wilderness areas protection alone; this isn't the 1970s."[8]

✦ ✦ ✦

Rapid population growth is putting pressure on both private and public land. During the 1980s, Greater Yellowstone expanded by 10 percent, adding population faster than the surrounding states of Idaho, Montana, and Wyoming, which during the same period grew by 6 percent, grew by 2 percent, and lost 2 percent respectively. Most rural counties in the United

States lost population in that period. Since the late 1960s, the Greater Yellowstone region has outperformed the United States in terms of job and income growth in every economic sector except mining.[9]

For years, the objective of many communities in Greater Yellowstone has been to promote growth. Now many of these same communities must try to control the same beast they had nurtured. People flock to the region, drawn by the intact wildlands, the trout streams, the grand landscape—its environmental amenities. Unfortunately, efforts to manage growth at the community and county level have largely failed because of state and local resistance to land-use planning.[10]

Organizations that promote smart growth have emerged at the state and local levels, but with the exception of Teton County, Wyoming, which has developed a comprehensive land-use plan limiting development of private land, local governments have been slow to enact planning and zoning ordinances.[11] In fact, just across the border, Teton County, Idaho, may be, in the words of conservation planner Craig Groves, "the poster child for terrible land-use planning.... Fifteen years ago I could ride the chairlift at Targhee Ski Area at the end of the day and see but a few lights on the valley floor. Now there are single lights of houses scattered everywhere in the most unthoughtful way for both people and nature."

"We have seen the future in the Greater Yellowstone ecosystem," says Glick. "This is an amenity-based economy now. Some people are still working in the extractive industries, but they are window dressing." Entrepreneurs and retirees are moving to the area, yet the conservation ethic remains undeveloped. As more and more people move in, settle wherever they want, and do much as they please, they threaten the very natural values that drew them to Greater Yellowstone in the first place. "We are plucking feathers from the golden goose," says Glick.

"The myth that is killing us is that we can have it all," he says. "We can't. But we can have what is really important—clean air, clean water, good schools, good jobs, and cultural diversity. You can go from seeing your son in a great sixth-grade play to seeing a grizzly bear feeding on an elk carcass that evening."

This perspective raises a fundamental question for any effort at broad-scale conservation: Who gets to decide what is really important? Not everyone wants to see a bear feeding on an elk carcass. Not everyone values things in the same way. Conservation science cannot provide the answer, but it can clearly define the consequences of the choices. Right now, in Greater Yellowstone, that question is not even open to debate, at least not among the institutions and individuals in power. We can have it all—that will be a tragic mistake.

The growth of Greater Yellowstone steams on regardless. Far from becoming more liberal as the population swells with new arrivals, the region is actually getting more and more conservative. "People have come here to get away from regulations, out-redneck the native rednecks," Glick says. With newcomers tending to support the conservative political agenda, the importance of local-level political organizing grows. The conservation community in the Rockies has expanded considerably in recent years, and is now well developed in Montana, though less so in Idaho and Wyoming.

While conservationists flourish in hotbeds like Bozeman, people in Greater Yellowstone and rural parts of the West often hold them in contempt. Even when the environmental position makes the most sense in terms of protecting both natural and economic values, many civil authorities fear the stigma of siding with the tree-huggers. For the people working in the federal agencies, advocating a broad approach to land management comes with clear costs: poor performance reviews, hostility from colleagues and neighbors, bad press, congressional hearings, and budget cuts . . . but uncertain rewards.

Despite all the problems, Greater Yellowstone remains a vital testing ground for broad-scale conservation, in large part because at the heart of the ecosystem lies Yellowstone National Park, still a symbol and an inspiration, a model for the creation of hundreds of national parks. "As goes Yellowstone, so go the parks of the world" may be a fair statement of the global interest in Yellowstone.[12] Greater Yellowstone has the intact habitat, economic foundation, committed conservationists, and community interest and support to make it possible. As Dennis Glick says, "If we can't do it here, we can't do it anywhere."

A VISION FOR YELLOWSTONE
Most conservation narratives rely for explanation on dichotomies between various groups of people: western ranchers vs. eastern environmentalists, urban elites vs. the rural working class, and so on. The differences between those groups may be neither as deep nor as insoluble as is often assumed.

The chasm that separates managers of adjacent national forests in Greater Yellowstone from each other and from the National Park Service, the Fish and Wildlife Service, and the Bureau of Land Management may actually be deeper and more significant. In the early 1980s, for example, managers recognized that the trumpeter swan *(Cygnus buccinator)* was in serious trouble in Greater Yellowstone, despite sixty years of study and management. Each agency managed the swans and habitats within its area, and each knew something of a piece of the puzzle. Only when managers began to look at the big picture did they realize that the crisis transcended political and bureaucratic boundaries.[13]

The federal agencies that manage land in and around Yellowstone have a firm grasp on their particular part of the elephant, or the swan as the case may be. They have far more trouble agreeing on the problems they face, and hence struggle to define common goals. Since the agencies hold nearly all the cards in Greater Yellowstone, this lack of a shared vision presents the biggest obstacle to broad-scale conservation in the region.[14]

Six national forests make up nearly three-quarters of Greater Yellowstone, so to a large degree the Forest Service will determine how, or whether, the agencies work together across the region. The agency, however, lacks technical skills to define, measure, monitor, and conserve species and their habitats, or to understand the effects of forest-management action on them, and has little motivation to build such skills. In fact, the motivation runs in the opposite direction, as the Forest Service remains firmly rooted, legally and culturally, in its history as a farmer of trees.[15]

For the most part, the Forest Service pays little heed when its activities may harm Yellowstone, or most any park. The service falls back on the traditional claim that its legal mandate requires approval for nearly any logging, grazing, and recreation. The Forest Service does not specify under what priorities it will apply diverse mandates, and its range of discretion appears limitless, permitting infinite evasion of any duty to recognize or establish priorities. Both the Forest Service and the Bureau of Land Management often simply disregard the effects their decisions have on adjacent public land—even land that falls within national parks.[16]

Fundamental differences of belief among administrators and constituency groups over how best to use public land, not scientific disputes, form the root obstacles to greater cooperation among the agencies.[17] The Forest Service and Bureau of Land Management remain dedicated to producing timber, grass, and minerals, while the National Park Service largely serves the visitors to the parks. Only the Fish and Wildlife Service has an explicit mission to protect species and ecosystems, and it also must serve hunters and anglers. The battle lines among the agencies blur, as small skirmishes with shifting alliances and tactics break out, with no grand and simple confrontation to provide closure. By pleasing the timber industry, the Forest Service sometimes makes everybody mad, including erstwhile friends, like hunters. The Island Park district of the Targhee National Forest, for example, once had the longest bull-elk hunt in the lower forty-eight states. Logging shredded the habitat and logging roads gave hunters ready access to once-remote hunting areas. The shooting party hit the elk population so hard that a hunting season that once lasted forty-five days has become a five-day war, and decimated outfitting and guiding businesses in the area.[18]

This little vignette reveals some of the complexity and uncertainty inherent in attempting to balance competing interests over land use. And these problems surface in one district within one national forest. Expand the scale to include five more forests, two national parks, cattle ranches, subdivisions, small towns, cities, airports, Indian reservations, and on and on, and the whole things seems overwhelming. So each of us simplifies the world, creating individual models, maps, or metaphors to help filter the deluge of information we face.[19]

These models help us but also hinder us. Since the way we see things determines what we see, individuals and groups have a hard time agreeing on even the problems we face. And if we cannot define the problems correctly, then finding appropriate solutions becomes just about impossible. The federal agencies responsible for most of the land in Greater Yellowstone may rarely escape their own traditions, values, and management processes, and no president has ever shown much leadership in wrangling the stubborn and independent agencies in the region. The absence of such leadership creates a vacuum, as no single entity has the authority to assess the impact of development within Greater Yellowstone. Even if a single entity had the authority, it would lack enough good information, or be unable to use the information it did have, or some combination of the two.

✦ ✦ ✦

Federal foresters know quite well the impact their actions have on the landscape around them, but the resistance to doing anything substantive about it runs deep in the agency's bones. In the early 1960s, for example, the Forest Service and the Park Service established the Greater Yellowstone Coordinating Committee as a forum for discussing coordination in the region. The agencies then undermined this positive step by neglecting to give the committee any decision-making power or authority. Coordination between the Forest Service and the Park Service remains largely voluntary and easily terminated. Not surprisingly, with so little muscle behind it, the coordination effort fell victim to the longstanding differences between the agencies.[20]

The inability or unwillingness of the Park Service and the Forest Service to work together would have been of little interest to most people outside the agencies had the issue been, say, Congaree National Park in South Carolina, the latest addition to the park system. After all, nothing defines large bureaucracies better than infighting and turf battles. But people pay close attention to what goes on in Yellowstone. Interest grew in the mid-1980s following both congressional hearings on resource management in Greater Yellowstone and a highly critical report from the Congressional Research Service that detailed, among other things, how the lack of coordination among the agencies imperiled Yellowstone's grizzlies.[21]

Spelling out the problems was simple, and depressing, enough. What came next was anything but simple, and reveals in a nutshell nearly all you need to know about the politics of big conservation in Yellowstone. In 1989, the Greater Yellowstone Coordinating Committee appointed four people from the Park Service and four from the Forest Service to craft an overarching mission statement and set of common goals for the region's future. The draft document—*Vision for the Future: A Framework for Coordination in the Greater Yellowstone Area*—proposed three broad goals: conserve the sense of naturalness and maintain ecosystem integrity by, for example, maintaining or improving air, water, soils, and biological diversity and protecting wilderness values; encourage biologically and economically sustainable economic opportunities; and improve coordination among the agencies.[22]

The draft *Vision*, released in August 1990, acknowledged that Greater Yellowstone extends far beyond the park and national forest boundaries, and even went so far as to use the word ecosystem—the label "Greater Yellowstone ecosystem" remained taboo, but the authors of the *Vision*, as it is called, whispered the concept, like Galileo before the cardinals: "No place in North America, perhaps no place on earth, is a more fitting site to pioneer ecosystem management. The Greater Yellowstone Area has the public and legislative support, the agency enthusiasm, and the unparalleled natural resources, to provide a world class model of such management. It is an opportunity the Forest Service and Park Service have wholeheartedly embraced."[23]

The agencies broke some new ground with the *Vision*, but struck a cautious rather than revolutionary tone. In Greater Yellowstone, they said, resource protection and resource use are not mutually exclusive. The region would continue to provide a diversity of livelihoods based on logging, ranching, and mining on federal land, but these activities would not disrupt ecological processes or intrude upon the natural landscape.[24]

Even with a cautious tone, the Park Service and the Forest Service knew that any mention of a broad-scale approach to land management in Greater Yellowstone would raise hackles both with the industries and within their own agencies. They took pains to be reassuring: "The *Vision* is not a regional plan. It is a statement of principles. It does not make specific land allocation decisions, and does not seek to change the separate missions of the national forests or the national parks. Management principles suggested in the *Vision* can be accomplished within the existing legal framework and without either agency going outside of its historic and legal mandates."

Opponents of any change in land management in Greater Yellowstone, mainly the extractive industries, nevertheless claimed that the *Vision* represented a giant land-grab, another federal lock-up. Outrage erupted despite repeated statements by the Greater Yellowstone Coordinating Committee that the *Vision* did not, would not, and could not change the legally established mandates of the National Park Service or the Forest Service. In seeking to coordinate without antagonizing their distinct constituencies, the agencies ignored the fact that managing the distinct values of those constituencies was part of the problem.[25]

The *Vision* implied the end of business-as-usual for the extractive industries—though not the end of their business altogether—and the potential beginning of more-benign development. Advocates of the *Vision* stressed the economic and ecological benefits that would result. Nearly all organized interests opposed it. Extractive industries feared their land use would be curtailed and participated in every venue to derail the process.[26]

The *Vision* became a battle cry for the Wise Use movement. People for the West! (note the exclamation mark they stole from Earth First!), a now-defunct group that received much of its funding from the mining industry, turned out seven hundred people to a hearing in Bozeman and had similar success at other hearings in the region. Public meetings in 1990 and 1991 drew thousands of participants. One newspaper described local reaction to the *Vision* as "nearly rabid"; at the meetings, children carried signs saying "save my daddy's job." Groups like the Mountain States Legal Foundation (one-time employer of two secretaries of the interior, James Watt and his protégée, Gayle Norton), said that the Park Service and the Forest Service had violated federal law and that they sought to ruin the western economy with "irresponsible and asinine" plans. Others accused the two agencies of "cultural genocide."[27]

The Wyoming, Montana, and Idaho congressional delegations condemned the *Vision*, and the governors of the three states demanded it be withdrawn or substantially revised. In Wyoming, the state legislature expressed unanimous outrage over the draft *Vision*, though only five representatives said they had actually read it.

On the other side, conservation groups supported the *Vision* but thought it was too general to be useful and that it did not go far enough in reining in damaging resource-management activities. Conservationists expressed little interest in the process and failed to support or improve the *Vision*, and were conspicuous in their absence from the debate.[28]

As a result of the furor, the Greater Yellowstone Coordinating Committee took over the drafting and created a short brochure renamed *A Framework for Coordination of National Parks and National Forests in the Greater Yellowstone Area*. The new version dropped most of the major points in the original. "These agencies spent three years developing a plan that calls for business as usual," said Ed Lewis, a former executive director of the Greater Yellowstone Coalition. Politicians and special interests took a seventy-four-page statement of principles and goals to guide comprehensive management for Greater Yellowstone and ground it down to ten pages of platitudes.[29]

While special interests hijacked the process in this case, the sorry spectacle provides some causes for optimism. The final framework, though gutted of many of its progressive recommendations, acknowledged that Yellowstone is larger than the park boundaries. The *Vision* document signaled a belated but welcome recognition that Greater Yellowstone represents an interconnected ecosystem that is being degraded because of management activities and conflicting mandates.[30]

THROUGH THE REARVIEW MIRROR

The *Vision* foundered in part on the fears, stirred by industry, that more conservation necessarily means fewer jobs. Ironically, no place demonstrates the absurdity of the "jobs vs. the environment" debate than Greater Yellowstone. Residents here simply do not need to choose between poverty and environmental degradation. Extractive industries have declined over the past three decades, and a more stable economy has emerged based on preserving the natural resources rather than exploiting them relentlessly.[31] In a 1996 study, Ray Rasker of the Sonoran Institute and Arlin Hackman of World Wildlife Fund Canada showed that employment and personal income levels in wilderness counties grew faster than resource-extraction counties. Though the study did not find a cause-and-effect relationship between wilderness protection and economic growth, it still offers a powerful counterargument to the claim, made repeatedly by the Wise Use movement and industry, that protecting wildland habitat throttles economic growth and puts loggers and ranchers on the bread lines.[32]

Protecting grizzlies, reintroducing wolves, reducing clear-cutting on public land, and other conservation efforts clearly have not made Greater Yellowstone a collection of ghost towns. In terms of growth, Greater Yellowstone does quite well, thank you. As of the 2000 census, more than 370,000 people lived in Greater Yellowstone, a 61 percent increase from 1970. The population of all but three of the twenty counties that make up Greater Yellowstone increased. The United States as a whole grew by 38 percent over the same three decades. Unemployment in Greater Yellowstone has been steadily declining; in 2001 unemployment stood at just 3.6 percent, lower than the surrounding states and the nation, though it fluctuates seasonally and can reach nearly 5 percent in the winter.[33]

Between 1997 and 2001, personal income and per capita personal income rose across Greater Yellowstone; personal income grew by 10 percent in Gallatin County, Montana, and by 12 percent in Teton County, Wyoming.[34] The cost of living has risen accordingly: nice old homes on the quiet, tree-lined streets of south Bozeman can sell for $350,000, and average home prices are on par with far more urban areas like Miami or Phoenix. Between 1980 and 1990, more than 5,000 people arrived in Flathead Valley, Montana, and 945 new homes were built. Between 1973 and 1992, more than 130,000 acres of private land were subdivided for residential development.[35]

Rapid growth brings its own distinct opportunities and problems for conservation. While the threat of industrial exploitation of Yellowstone is diminishing, even amenities-based economic growth could potentially destroy the region if it occurs in an environmentally unsound manner. Recreational use, for example, is expanding exponentially, and uncontrolled growth on private land is destroying ecologically important riparian areas and subdividing critical winter range and movement corridors throughout Greater Yellowstone.[36] Recent population growth has put pressure on the region's private land. As property values have risen, so has the pressure on private landowners to subdivide.

Some communities have already found their growth limitations. Lander, Wyoming, faces shortages of drinking water, little private land remains in West Yellowstone, and Jackson Hole ships its solid wastes to Pinedale, more than eighty miles away.[37] While some communities are electing officials on the basis of smart growth, county government remains the weak link, says Dennis Glick. Few people who move to Greater Yellowstone willingly take on the unglamorous, low-paying jobs with the counties, so those tasks remain in the hands of people tied, either emotionally or economically, to the traditional extractive industries.

Greater Yellowstone's growing economy now depends largely on service industries, a confusing category including both high-paying and low-paying jobs—stock brokers, insurance agents, realtors, doctors and nurses, freelance software designers, lawyers, hotel maids. "Everything from bankers to prostitutes," quipped *The Economist*. Nonlabor income, which includes investment earnings and payments from the government to individuals, such as Social Security and Medicare, makes up the other large segment of the region's economy. "In many rural communities of the West, the largest source of income is the mailbox," Rasker and Ben Alexander write in an analysis of Greater Yellowstone's economy.[38]

Services and nonlabor sources account for more than 75 percent of all personal income in Greater Yellowstone, and nearly all the growth since 1975. All the traditional industries of big open spaces now account for less than 10 percent of personal income in Greater Yellowstone, and they have stagnated. Some of these industries continue to thrive in other parts of the West.[39] The other 90 percent of income comes from myriad small businesses, from sheet metal fabrication to software design to pharmaceutical testing to home building. Extractive industries contributed just 1 percent of new personal income since 1975, and farming and ranching have been losing jobs since 1970.

Despite a good deal of shouting to the contrary, conservation contributes little to the overall decline of traditional western industries. That trend, many years in the making, reflects other factors: increasingly efficient production technology that require less labor and more capital, global competition, a slump in world markets for certain commodities, and production moving to low-cost areas outside the United States.

Still, even economists have a hard time with the fuzzy boundaries of the service sector, and "nonlabor income" sounds vaguely disreputable. Ranches and forests, on the other hand, are as tangible as can be. Ever since settlers spread west, they have earned their living off of those resources through hard work, so they play a defining role in how rural communities see themselves. This shared community vision resists change, says Thomas Power, professor of economics at the University of Montana in Missoula. "In that sense, conventional wisdom about the local economy is the view through the rearview mirror," he writes in *Lost Landscapes and Failed Economies,* the definitive work on the importance of environmental quality to local economies. "What could replace mining or ranching or timber in the Old West? What could replace steel and automobiles in Pittsburgh and Detroit?"[40]

The economic picture of Greater Yellowstone today does not resemble that of just a generation ago. Yet many people outside the region, endlessly enamored of their own vision of the western lifestyle, accept at face value what the extractive industries tell them about the overwhelming importance of those very industries. This nostalgia provides opponents of broad-scale conservation with a powerful weapon. A single group of economic interests has defined the economy as synonymous with its own commercial activity and has further defined local economic well-being as something that only these businesses primarily produce.[41]

"I blame a lot of it on geographers for producing those books we read when we were kids," says Ray Rasker. "For Florida they showed a picture of an orange, southern California had a movie reel, Kansas had a cornstalk, Montana had a cow's head." To test the validity of that idea, Rasker added up all the money from cattle, wheat, oil, and gas—all the farming, all the agriculture, and all the income from all those industries—and compared it to just retirement incomes in Greater Yellowstone. He found that retirement is now three times the size of agriculture. "Does that mean we are a retirement community? No, it just means in addition to those other industries we also have retirement, we have skilled manufacturing, and so on."

Seen through the rearview mirror, people living in Greater Yellowstone must exploit the land for all it is worth. For many people in the region, that view, while it defies reality, provides more comfort than trying to look down the road, for they see jobs changing sheets in neon motels in West Yellowstone or flipping burgers somewhere. Better the fraying nobility of life on the range than that, they think. That is a misperception almost as fundamental as the notion that Greater Yellowstone really depends on agriculture for its survival. No single large industry, not even tourism, predominates in the region today. Diversity is Greater Yellowstone's strength.

The backward-looking view of the economy has profound effects on politics. While the economy can change relatively rapidly, political priorities evolve slowly, especially where politics remains tied to the old but entrenched economic interests. The myth that resource extraction drives the western economy strengthens the influence of industry, along with what legal scholar Charles Wilkinson, professor of law at the University of Colorado at Boulder, calls the "lords of yesterday": timber, grazing, and mining laws still on the books from the nineteenth century.[42]

The political power of traditional industries, and the community attachment to the old way of life, can blind people to how profoundly things have changed. The standard economic model holds that distribution of natural resources determines where the jobs are, and then people must move to fill those jobs. Create jobs and wait for the job seekers to arrive at your door. So in Montana or Wyoming, if you stake a claim, open a saw-mill, or run cattle, they will come. As economists like Thomas Power and Ray Rasker point out, however, the opposite is closer to the truth.[43]

FOOTLOOSE IN GREATER YELLOWSTONE

More and more people can live anywhere, either because they draw on investment or retirement income or because they work in the so-called knowledge economy—consulting, software design, pharmaceutical test-ing, and so on—and have been freed from big urban markets by high-speed Internet connections and overnight delivery. In Greater Yellowstone, these "footloose entrepreneurs" demonstrate that migration often comes first, then jobs.[44]

In the new model for economic development in the West, a high qual-ity of life based in large part on the wild and scenic landscape draws people in, and then they stay. As Thomas Power puts it, people get two paychecks —the usual one from the job, plus a second payment from the flow of ser-vices from the social and natural environment. A generous payback from the natural amenities can more than offset the lower wages usually paid in small cities and rural areas. In many parts of the West, a high-quality en-vironment stimulates the economy.[45]

According to a 1993 study by Montana State University, the most im-portant reasons for locating a business in Greater Yellowstone have to do with cultural, social, and natural amenities—the single most important factor was scenery, followed by recreational opportunities and the charac-ter of the town. Factors such as availability of raw materials, labor, and capital ranked much lower.[46] In an amenity-based economy, chopping down or digging up the amenities for short-term gain makes as much sense as a farmer eating his seed corn. In Greater Yellowstone, recreation, not timber production, is by far the most important economic activity in the national forests, generating between 76 percent (Targhee National Forest) and 99 percent (Custer National Forest) of the direct jobs on the national forest land in the region.[47]

The recognition of the economic importance of environmental quality —a key comparative advantage for Greater Yellowstone—can help shift the most entrenched economic interests. In 1990, Crown Butte Mines, a subsidiary of Canadian mining giant Noranda Minerals Inc., proposed the New World Mine, a gold, silver, and copper mine beneath Mount Henderson, less than three miles from the border of Yellowstone National Park in Crown Butte, Montana; it would be nestled between the park the Absaroka-Beartooth Wilderness. According to the company, the mine would produce eighteen hundred tons of ore per day for ten to fifteen years. Facilities would include a work camp, a mill, and a 106-acre tailings impoundment for storage of 5.5 million tons of acid-generating tailings.[48]

Had Noranda proposed the New World Mine in 1970 rather than 1990, they would have faced opposition—this is Yellowstone, after all—but they may well have been able to start digging anyway. Times have changed. Local and national environmental organizations, the superintendent of Yellowstone, communities near the mine site, and people dependent on income from tourism mounted a fierce and well-organized campaign against the mine. Even the United Nations got into the act. In 1995, a delegation from the World Heritage Commission visited the park and placed Yellowstone on the list of world heritage sites "in danger."

The embarrassment for the United States of having its flagship park declared endangered, combined with national press coverage, played a key role in escalating the issue and may have been the event that turned the tide against the New World Mine. The Clinton administration negotiated a $65 million buyout of the mining leases. The agreement, Clinton said, "altogether proves that everyone can agree that Yellowstone is more precious than gold."

That may overstate the case—in Greater Yellowstone, everyone might not agree that the sun will rise in the morning—and current federal policies still encourage and subsidize extractive industries on federal land in the region.[49] In 1990, the Forest Service subsidized the local timber industry by selling timber for $12.6 million less than the cost of building roads, reforestation, and other development associated with timber extraction. In another subsidy, ranchers graze cattle on Forest Service land for about a quarter of the market rate.[50]

All the subsidies and all the political maneuvering amount to rearguard actions at this point. Without minimizing the need to redirect federal dollars to support positive economic trends and end below-cost timber sales, royalty-free mining claims, and incentives for land managers to engage in resource extraction, governments and communities in Greater

Yellowstone increasingly recognize that clear-cuts that denude mountain-sides, mines that pollute, and wells that dry up geysers may simply ruin the economy. Such development embodies the radical idea that not all economic growth is good. Sometimes growth produces not wealth, as dictated in the standard economics taught to undergraduates, but what the ecological economist Herman Daly (updating John Ruskin) calls "illth."[51]

The transition has already been made on some public land. In 1989, says Dennis Glick, the Greater Yellowstone Coalition was fighting to halt sixty timber sales in the region because of their environmental impact. Now about three are of genuine concern, he says.

If you want to understand the modern economy in the western states, you need slice it three ways, says Ray Rasker. First are the metropolitan areas and the counties within commuting distance, collectively called the commuter shed. The second type of area is rural and isolated, with no airport. Those areas face all sorts of economic hardships. Finally, there are rural, isolated areas that have airports. The structure of those counties is almost identical to the metropolitan ones. Gallatin County, home to Bozeman, is one of those largely rural areas that is structured very much like an urban county.

"Bozeman in a certain way is a bedroom community of Seattle. I mean quite literally," says Rasker. "Many people live here but do business outside of the region, and they depend on air travel. Most of the towns in Greater Yellowstone are within a two-hour drive of an airport." Some counties, those with a high percentage of preserved public land, a nearby airport with commercial service, and a relatively well-educated public, are on their way to becoming "new economy" centers, and some counties contiguous to these are becoming bedroom communities.

Yet not everyone has the skills and knowledge to make the transition to a new economy. Diversification skips by more remote towns, so they lose population and gradually sink into poverty. About 40 percent of the Greater Yellowstone's population growth occurred in its two most urban counties, while five counties produce about 70 percent of the region's personal income. The extent of local economic diversity also varies widely, with some communities still highly dependent upon extractive industries or tourism and hence not well-equipped to respond to change. The stereo-type of Greater Yellowstone as dependent on ranching and logging is untrue, but replacing it with another stereotype of a region riding the crest of the new economy to environmental salvation may be just as bad.

A second caveat in reading the economic tea leaves has to do with how well the data really characterize the Greater Yellowstone ecosystem as ecologists understand it. The most expansive definition of the ecosystem covers 26 million acres, but the twenty counties used to provide an economic measure of Greater Yellowstone cover 34 million acres. Those counties also do not function as a unit; the economy of Bozeman does not necessarily relate to the economy of Idaho Falls, Idaho, or Lander, Wyoming.[52]

✦ ✦ ✦

This is not a battle between dirty old industries and clean new ones; the challenges for conservation are changing, not disappearing altogether. The fact remains that logging, mining, and ranching will continue in some way and in some places in Greater Yellowstone. The trick will be finding the right places, and defining the right way, as conservationists and ranchers are trying to do in the Big Hole River watershed. The same goes for all the new people moving to the region. If they all build their houses on ten-acre plots along streams, then we will just swap old problems for new ones, and the decline of the logging and mining industries will be insignificant. On the other hand, if most people choose to live in town or nearby and live lightly, then the region can support quite a few new residents.[53] Finding places for the people and the various uses of the land will be impossible without a clear vision, the kind of vision informed by careful conservation planning.

The difficulties of working with local governments inhibit the implementation of new, creative tools for conserving private land. In addition to the traditional easements, there are different variations on zoning, the purchase of development rights, and tax relief for keeping land undeveloped, and there are limited-development options that try to address cases where ranchers are being forced to subdivide or face bankruptcy because ranching is not paying the bills. A limited-development option allows the rancher to benefit from the sale of some land, but puts the new homes where they will have the least impact on wildlife.

Zoning is usually a dirty word in the West; many people move west to escape restrictions on how they can use their land. One particularly ugly threat, however, has opened the door to talk of zoning in Greater Yellowstone: coalbed methane. Methane, or natural gas, usually occurs in conjunction with oil deposits, but it is also sometimes associated with coal seams. Getting the gas out of the coalbeds requires releasing water pressure by pumping out huge quantities of groundwater.

The destruction wrought by this type of large-scale industrial development can be considerable and include the disposal of millions of gallons of saline water, wells running dry, fragmentation of wildlife habitat, private property damage, underground fires, direct release of methane into the air, and potential aquifer contamination. Landowners and residents, along with the Greater Yellowstone Coalition and other conservation groups, such as American Wildlands, are working together to ensure that coalbed methane development does not turn into the unending headache for southwest Montana that it has become in places like Wyoming's Powder River Basin.

Gallatin County halted exploratory drilling near Bozeman Pass, and placed a moratorium on coalbed methane drilling. During a public hearing, a Gallatin County Commissioner admonished the company that had applied to drill several exploratory wells in the county: "It's not a mineral extraction state . . . where you can come in and do what you did one hundred years ago."

That a county commission in Montana would dare say such a thing speaks volumes about the changes underway in that state and across the West. The hideous nature of coalbed methane development may be the tipping point for communities to recognize that conservation does not threaten their way of life. Thoughtless economic exploitation of the land in the names of faceless corporations and their even more anonymous shareholders poses far greater threats. Rural communities and conservationists share far more than either group realizes, and as they figure out how to occupy common ground, they may become a potent force for hope.

After the final no there comes a yes
And on that yes the future world depends.
WALLACE STEVENS, The Well Dressed Man with a Beard

The human responsibility for the future of the wild places and wild creatures of the earth generally leads to despair as, like Pogo in the famous cartoon, we look over ravaged landscapes and realize we are our own worst enemy. The understandable but ultimately futile response has been defensive—to construct and defend the barricades around the fragments of nature that remain, in the hope that we can somehow stem the tide. Desperate acts can produce heroes and successes here and there, but not lasting and global solutions. For that we need something far more powerful and for too long a rarity for conservation: hope.

We can now see the outlines of hopeful conservation, of hope for a rich and varied future built on the unexpected fusion of community and science. The emerging new conservation draws strength from evolving concepts of conservation biology that reveal how each parcel, no matter how small, fits into a large whole, along with people and communities, like the ranchers in the Malpai region who value land as more than a purely economic resource. Such communities form deep bonds to special places —either places they live, or places they value simply for their wildness or their beauty. The bonds between people and land certainly do not form in every place, but they exist in more places and among more people than we imagine.

Romanticizing the idea of community poses as great a risk to conservation as ignoring communities altogether; the struggle to conserve Greater Yellowstone while exploiting its environmental amenities and the effort to restore the Everglades provide the object lessons. In Greater Yellowstone, the communities with the deepest roots in the region see their economic future tied to logging, ranching, and mining, while those industries continue to thwart conservation efforts wherever they can, despite all the evidence of their dwindling economic relevance. In what is left of rural

Florida, everything is for sale; social capital or emotional ties to the land simply do not exist, or crumble in the face of developers with bundles of money. Building a new conservation that respects the values of such communities, without necessarily sharing them, will not be easy, but it will be essential. We need to change our perspective; instead of painting people as the cause of every environmental problem, we must begin to see them as the solution.

Since the attachment to place often reflects deep social bonds as well, the new conservation needs to engage in the process of building social as well as natural capital. Conservationists and conservation organizations generally avoid that last step, and for good reason: no one knows exactly how to rebuild social capital once it has been depleted, and even if obvious methods existed, the task seem far outside the missions of conservation and science. So in the effort to save nature we often look either to the tools of science or to the emotional tug of a connection to a special place or a charismatic animal. Those two approaches seem distinct, and in fact many conservation organizations have institutionalized the differences, making emotional attachment the province of marketers and leaving science to the scientists. As a result, conservation remains incomplete and, in the end, unsuccessful. Science must inform and be informed by the connection of people to the land, while attachment to place cannot just be a marketing gimmick, but rather a different way of looking at the opportunities for conservation.

Emphasizing the role of communities reflects a sort of conservation populism, pitting the power of individuals and small communities against often-disconnected national governments and global corporations. A central challenge for the new conservation is to capitalize on the power of populism while at the same time expanding conservation planning and action to an ecologically meaningful scale. Traditional communities like the Amish have developed what some may see as an extreme solution to a similar problem of scale: they live at the pace of a horse-drawn wagon, and farm at the scale of a horse-drawn plow. While not advocating a universal return to such a lifestyle, that approach highlights the limits of human capacity for understanding and caring for land.

For the Amish, a community bounded by religious belief and the choice of particular technologies provides the appropriate scale for making decisions. For conservation, an ecoregion provides that defining scale and becomes the lens through which we can envision conservation success. Conservation action, however, will happen at finer scales than that. Ecoregional conservation provides the context for localism: Where should the open land be located? Where should we invest in conservation easements? Without the context, we have no rational way to make decisions.

Those decisions also have no weight unless people endorse them; we can no longer simply impose conservation on the unwilling. That means relying on democratic processes wherever possible, and through local democracy at that. In many countries, democracy does not exist now and may never exist. In those cases, conservation remains centralized, and the importance of science-based planning becomes even greater. Where individuals and communities have more say in their affairs, the challenge for the new conservation will be translating the idealized visions of science into workable approaches, without losing the conservation value in the process.

The new conservation applies the tools of science to turn the attachment to place into concrete plans for changing the way we use and conserve the land around us. Instead of assuming that protecting a special place means, by definition, not using it in any way, conservation science identifies what places must be set aside, but also what places people can continue to use, and how. This expands the universe of conservationists to include at least some farmers, ranchers, loggers, and miners—people for whom conservation generally remains the faceless foe of progress and humanity.

Conservation must be about where people live and work, and that means addressing people's values. Some of those values will further the cause of conservation; others will stand in opposition to it. But conservation does not operate solely on the high, hard ground of science, with clear answers to clear questions. Conservation takes place more often in the swampy lowlands, dealing with what policy scientists tellingly call "wicked" problems: those that defy easy definition, have better or worse solutions instead of right and wrong ones, and often have strong moral dimensions.[1]

Solving wicked problems, like replumbing the Everglades, has many technical elements but is not a process run by technicians. It is a social and political process, informed rather than directed by science. The decision to either use or not use any given piece of land fundamentally stems from a moral choice about who benefits from the decision. The processes behind conservation and development are still often quite different, but we can't have one group in society stand up for people and another stand up for nature, and then fight it out. Moral concerns do not end with either humans or nonhumans. We all must care for it all.

Conservation has often chosen to avoid wicked problems altogether by focusing on protected areas. Yet the focus of conservation simply cannot be limited to parks—the rock upon which modern conservation is built, but no longer its sum total. Even Yellowstone in all its glory will not suffice by itself. Without diminishing the ongoing importance of those areas, they clearly do not go far enough. We need a range of land uses, from complete protection to industrial use, and that means improving the use of land as well as the management of protected land. It is possible, as conservationist Aldo Leopold, farmer Wallace Berry, and scientist Michael Rosenzweig have all said in different ways and in different contexts, to use land well.

Choosing hope requires a fundamental shift in conservation and conservation science. While conservation biology originally and crucially focused on revealing the destructive impact of humans on the natural world, the public now suffers from crisis fatigue and has stopped listening. Conservation's obsession with loss—of species, of habitat, of wilderness—has created a backlash, reflected in the Pollyannaish belief that we need change nothing in our behavior or our values.

As scientists Kent Redford of the Wildlife Conservation Society and M. A. Sanjayan of The Nature Conservancy have observed, conservation science has, in contrast, taken on the role of Cassandra, the prophetess cursed to know the truth of her predictions, yet see them rejected. As Redford and Sanjayan say, we must retire Cassandra.[2]

An ecoregion-based approach provides a way out, a way to redefine conservation biology as an envisioning discipline, rather than a crisis discipline. Conservation as a whole needs to get away from constantly pointing out how bad things are and arguing that only fewer people and less consumption will save us. This is true if we assume that current patterns and products remain the same, but that is not necessarily a safe assumption. Architect and designer William McDonough, for example, makes a compelling case that we can turn human use of resources from something more or less destructive to nature into something that actually improves the world around us. Rather than trying to be less bad—destroying the earth more slowly, but destroying it nonetheless—McDonough advocates an approach to the design of buildings and materials and industrial processes that fits into the landscape and produces nutrients and energy.[3]

The same holds for conservation. "Be Less Bad" makes a poor slogan and rallying cry; we need a positive vision. The seeds for that vision have been sown through the myriad efforts to think big, to think beyond the boundaries of the national parks. The first shoots from those seeds provide the most compelling reasons for hope. Conservation science increasingly provides the tools to define what individuals and communities want from conservation—what is enough, what works, and what does not. With that knowledge in hand, conservation can once again fully engage in the debate over the landscape of our future.

I am fortunate to have a wonderful agent who is also a wonderful sister. Lisa Adams and her husband, David Miller, run the Garamond Agency in Newburyport, Massachusetts, and have been patient and persistent advocates for this book in all its many forms. Their creativity and good sense shaped the book in ways too numerous to count and I am deeply grateful. My brother, Jeff, also provided vital help with the research for this book, making it a true family effort.

Exuberant thanks to the people who read all or parts of the manuscript at various points in its development, with a special note to Craig Groves, who read the entire manuscript early on and helped steer it away from the shoals. Many thanks to Jean-Louis Ecochard, Rob Marshall, Steve McCormick, Guy McPherson, Kent Redford, Bob Unnasch, and Jora Young. Of course, any missteps remain entirely my own.

I have benefited greatly from the wisdom and experience of countless conservation scientists and practitioners, many of whom willingly gave me their time, hospitality, and friendship. This includes my current and former colleagues at The Nature Conservancy: Ann Bartuska, Jeff Baumgartner, Steve Cox, Mike Dennis, Jonathan Higgins, Peter Kareiva, Laura Landon, Brian Martin, Betsy Neely, Chris Pague, Brian Richter, M. A. Sanjayan, Dale Turner, Peter Warren, Bill Weeks, and John Wiens. The book's content and recommendations are mine and do not imply endorsement by the Conservancy's staff, senior managers, or board of governors.

At the Malpai Borderlands Group, a special thanks to Warner and Wendy Glenn for all their help and hospitality, and to Larry Allen, Scott Arena, Ron Bemis, Charles Curtin, Drum Hadley, Seth Hadley, Bill McDonald, Bill and Carole Miller, Nathan Sayre, and Greg Simons.

At the Sonoran Institute: Nina Chambers, Dennis Glick, Roseann Hanson, Luther Propst, and Ray Rasker.

At The Wildlands Project: Kathy Daly, Dave Foreman, Bob Howard, David Johns, Leann Klyza-Linck, and Michael Soulé.

At the Wildlife Conservation Society: Joel Berger, John Robinson, Amy Vedder, and Bill Weber.

At World Wildlife Fund: Sarah Christiansen, Eric Dinerstein, Bill

Eichbaum, Shannon Estenoz, Curt Freese, Colby Loucks, John Morrison, Taylor Ricketts, and Doreen Robinson.

I would also like to thank the following kind souls who helped me along the way: Paul Beier, Katrina Brandon, Carlos Carroll, Tim Clark, Deb Kmon Davidson, Carl Fitz, April Gromnicki, Matt Harwell, Deborah Jensen, Mark Kraus, Jeff Lerner, Bill Loftus, Tom Lovejoy, Dave Mattson, Reed Noss, John Ogden, Stuart Pimm, Steve Primm, Nick Salafsky, Michael Scott, Mark Shaffer, Fred Sklar, Matt Skroch, and David Wilcove, with the understanding that the names of others who contributed will occur to me after it is too late. Those I thank as well, with my apologies.

Finally, and most importantly, none of this work would have been possible or worthwhile without the support and understanding of my family: my wife, Susan, and my two children, Madeleine and Joseph, to whom this book is dedicated with all my love.

INTRODUCTION

1. T. F. H. Allen and T. W. Hoekstra, *Toward a Unified Ecology* (New York: Columbia University Press, 1992); R. V. O'Neill and A. W. King, "Homage to St. Michael: or, why are there so many books on scale?" in *Ecological Scale: Theory and Applications*, ed. D. L. Peterson and V. T. Parker (New York: Columbia University Press, 1998), 3–15.

2. P. Kareiva and M. Anderson, "Spatial aspects of species interactions: the wedding of models and experiments," in *Community Ecology*, ed. A. Hastings (New York: Springer-Verlag, 1989), 35–50.

3. H. Daly, *Beyond Growth: The Economics of Sustainable Development* (Boston: Beacon Press, 1996); N. Georgescu-Roegen, *The Entropy Law and the Economic Process* (Cambridge: Harvard University Press, 1971); K. E. Boulding, "A ballad of ecological awareness," in *The Careless Technology: Ecology and International Development*, ed. M. T. Farvar and J. P. Milton (New York: Doubleday, 1969).

4. R. B. Keiter, "Ecosystems and the law: toward an integrated approach," *Ecological Applications* 8 (1998): 332–341.

5. D. Botkin, *Discordant Harmonies: A New Ecology for the Twenty-first Century* (New York: Oxford University Press, 1990); S. T. A. Pickett and J. N. Thompson, "Patch dynamics and the design of nature reserves," *Biological Conservation* 13 (1978): 27–37; D. J. Simberloff et al., "Regional and continental restoration," in *Continental Conservation: Scientific Foundations of Regional Reserve Networks*, ed. M. E. Soulé and J. Terborgh (Washington, DC: Island Press, 1999), 65–98.

6. All quotes from Jora Young in this chapter are from an interview I conducted on May 14, 2003.

7. M. E. Soulé and J. Terborgh, preface to *Continental Conservation*, ix–xi; D. Ehrenfeld, *The Arrogance of Humanism* (New York: Oxford University Press, 1981).

8. W. Stegner, *Beyond the Hundredth Meridian* (New York: Penguin Books, 1992).

9. See C. R. Groves, *Drafting a Conservation Blueprint* (Washington, DC: Island Press, 2003), for the best introduction to the field.

10. K. Brandon, K. H. Redford, and S. E. Sanderson, eds., *Parks in Peril: People, Politics, and Protected Areas* (Washington, DC: Island Press, 1998).

11. S. C. Forrest et al., *Ocean of Grass: A Conservation Assessment for the Northern Great Plains* (report prepared for the Northern Plains Conservation Network and the Northern Great Plains ecoregion office of World Wildlife Fund, Bozeman, MT, 2004). For the Buffalo Commons, see D. E. Popper and F. J. Popper, "The Buffalo Commons: metaphor as method," *Geographical Review* 89 (1999): 491–510; F. Williams, "Plains sense," *High Country News*, 15 January 2001.

12. R. B. Keiter, *Keeping Faith with Nature: Ecosystems, Democracy, and America's Public Lands* (New Haven: Yale University Press, 2003); C. R. Sunnstein, "Beyond the Republican revival," *Yale Law Journal* 97 (1988): 1539–1590.

13. R. F. Noss, "The Wildlands Project: land conservation strategy," *Wild Earth* special issue (1992): 10–25.

14. E. T. Freyfogle, *The Land We Share* (Washington, DC: Island Press, 2003).

15. E. T. Freyfogle, "Bounded people, boundless land," in *Stewardship Across Boundaries*, ed. R. Knight and P. B. Landres (Washington, DC: Island Press, 1998), 15–38.

CHAPTER 1: A PARLIAMENT OF OWLS

1. D. Wilcove and D. Murphy, "The spotted owl controversy and conservation biology," *Conservation Biology* 5 (1991): 261–262.

2. See *Seattle Audubon Society v Lyons*, 871 F. Supp. 1291 (1994).

3. K. N. Johnson et al., "Forest ecosystem management assessment team assessments: case study," in *Bioregional Assessments: Science at the Crossroads of Management and Policy*, ed. K. N. Johnson et al. (Washington, DC: Island Press, 1999), 87–116.

4. *Seattle Audubon Society v Evans*, 771 F. Supp. 1081 (1991).

5. "The Forest Service's mandate—wildlife equal to logging under multiple-use law," *Seattle Post Intelligencer*, 8 July 1992; "Dwyer cracks down on Forest Service," *Seattle Post Intelligencer*, 25 July 1992.

6. C. Moseley, "The Applegate Partnership: innovation in crisis," in *Across the Great Divide*, ed. P. Brick, D. Snow, and S. van de Wetering (Washington, DC: Island Press, 2001), 102–111.

7. B. DeVoto, "The West against itself," *Harper's*, January 1947; reprinted in *The Western Paradox*, ed. D. Brinkley and P. N. Limerick (New Haven: Yale University Press, 2001), 45–73.

8. T. A. Lewis, "Cloaked in a wise disguise," in *Let the People Judge*, ed. J. D. Echeverria and R. B. Eby (Washington, DC: Island Press, 1995), 13–20.

9. David Quammen's *Song of the Dodo* (New York: Scribner, 1996) is by far the best popular discussion of biogeography, its founders, and its relevance to modern conservation.

10. T. E. Lovejoy et al., "Edge and other effects of isolation on Amazon forest fragments," in *Conservation Biology*, ed. M. E. Soulé (Sunderland, MA: Sinauer Associates, 1986), 257–285.

11. R. H. MacArthur and E. O. Wilson, "An equilibrium theory of insular zoogeography," *Evolution* 17 (1963): 373–387.

12. F. W. Preston, "The canonical distribution of commonness and rarity," parts 1 and 2, *Ecology* 43 (1962): 185–215, 410–432.

13. R. H. MacArthur and E. O. Wilson, *The Theory of Island Biogeography* (Princeton: Princeton University Press, 1967), 4.

14. A. L. Sullivan and M. L. Shaffer, "Biogeography of the megazoo," *Science* 189 (1975): 13–17.

15. M. E. Soulé and D. Simberloff, "What do genetics and ecology tell us about the design of nature reserves?" *Biological Conservation* 35 (1986): 19–40; M. J. Scott et al., "The issue of scale in selecting and designing biological reserves," in *Continental Conservation: Scientific Foundations of Regional Reserve Networks*, ed. M. E. Soulé and J. Terborgh (Washington, DC: Island Press, 1999), 19–37; R. F. Noss, "The Wildlands Project: land conservation strategy," *Wild Earth* special issue (1992): 10–25.

16. J. W. Thomas et al., *A Conservation Strategy for the Northern Spotted Owl: A Report of the Interagency Scientific Committee to Address the Conservation of the Northern Spotted Owl* (Portland, OR: U.S. Department of Agriculture Forest Service; U.S. Department of the

Interior Bureau of Land Management, Fish and Wildlife Service, and National Park Service, 1990).

17. Scott et al., "The issue of scale in selecting and designing biological reserves."

18. M. E. Soulé and B. A. Wilcox, eds., *Conservation Biology: An Evolutionary-Ecological Perspective* (Sunderland, MA: Sinauer Associates, 1980).

19. J. A. Wiens, "Scientific responsibility and responsible ecology," *Conservation Ecology* 1 (1997): 16. Available at http://www.consecol.org/vol1/iss1/art16.

20. W. D. Newmark, "A land-bridge island perspective on mammalian extinctions in western North American parks," *Nature* 325 (1987): 430–432; W. D. Newmark, "Extinction of mammal populations in western North American parks," *Conservation Biology* 9 (1995): 512–526; Noss, "The Wildlands Project."

21. J. W. Thomas et al., *Viability Assessments and Management Considerations for Species Associated with Late-Successional and Old-Growth Forests of the Pacific Northwest* (Washington, DC: U.S. Department of Agriculture Forest Service, 1993).

22. *Seattle Audubon Society v. Lyons,* 871 F. Supp. 1291 (1994).

23. Ibid.

24. See L. Caldwell, "The ecosytem as a criterion for public land policy," *Natural Resources Journal* 10 (1970): 203–221; F. Craighead, *Track of the Grizzly* (San Francisco: Sierra Club Books, 1979); J. K. Agee and D. R. Johnson, *Ecosystem Management for Parks and Wilderness* (Seattle: University of Washington Press, 1988); M. E. Jensen et al., "Ecosystem management: a landscape ecology perspective," *Water Resources Bulletin* 32 (1996): 203–216. Agee and Johnson was the first book-length treatment of the subject.

25. S. L. Yaffee et al., *Ecosystem Management in the United States* (Washington, DC: Island Press, 1996).

26. S. L. Yaffee, "Three faces of ecosystem management," *Conservation Biology* 13 (1999): 713–725.

27. T. W. Clark and A. W. Harvey, "The Greater Yellowstone ecosystem policy arena," *Society and Natural Resources* 3 (1990): 281–284; Yaffee, "Three faces of ecosystem management."

28. R. F. Noss et al., "Core areas: where nature reigns," in *Continental Conservation,* 99–128.

29. B. G. Golley, *A History of the Ecosystem Concept in Ecology* (New Haven: Yale University Press, 1993); R. B. McIntosh, *The Background of Ecology: Concept and Theory* (Cambridge: Cambridge University Press, 1985).

30. G. K. Meffe et al., *Ecosystem Management: Adaptive, Community-Based Conservation* (Washington, DC: Island Press, 2002).

31. Craighead, *Track of the Grizzly;* R. F. Noss et al., *A Biological Conservation Assessment for the Greater Yellowstone Ecosystem: Report to the Greater Yellowstone Coalition,* July 2001.

32. R. B. Keiter, "Taking account of the ecosystem on the public domain: law and ecology in the Greater Yellowstone region," *University of Colorado Law Review* 60 (1989): 923–1007.

33. T. W. Clark et al., "Policy and programs for ecosystem management in the Greater Yellowstone ecosystem: an analysis," *Conservation Biology* 5 (1991): 412–422.

34. T. H. Ricketts et al., *Terrestrial Ecoregions of North America* (Washington, DC: Island Press, 1999).

CHAPTER 2: DO BIG THINGS RUN THE WORLD?

1. J. B. C. Jackson et al., "Historical overfishing and the recent collapse of coastal ecosystems," *Science* 293 (2001): 629–638.

2. M. E. Soulé and J. Terborgh, "Conserving nature at regional and continental scales—a scientific program for North America," *BioScience* 49 (1999): 809–817.

3. N. G. Hairston, F. E. Smith, and L. B. Slobodkin, "Community structure, population control, and competition," *The American Naturalist* 94 (1960): 421–425.

4. R. T. Paine, "Food web complexity and species diversity," *The American Naturalist* 100 (1966): 65–75.

5. See S. Carpenter, *The Trophic Cascade in Lakes* (Cambridge: Cambridge University Press, 1993); J. A. Estes, N. S. Smith, and J. F. Palmisano, "Sea otter predation and community organization in the western Aleutian Islands, Alaska," *Ecology* 59 (1978): 822–833.

6. K. R. Crooks and M. E. Soulé, "Mesopredator release and avifaunal extinction in a fragmented system," *Nature* 400 (1999): 563–566; M. E. Soulé et al., "Reconstructed dynamics of rapid extinctions of chaparral-requiring birds in urban habitat islands," *Conservation Biology* 2 (1988); R. L. Beschta, "Cottonwoods, elk, and wolves in the Lamar Valley of Yellowstone National Park," *Ecological Applications* 13 (2003): 1295–1309.

7. M. E. Soulé and R. F. Noss, "Rewilding and biodiversity: complementary goals for continental conservation," *Wild Earth* 8 (1998): 18–28.

8. J. Terborgh et al., "Ecological meltdown in predator-free forest fragments," *Science* 294 (2001): 1923–1926.

9. M. E. Power et al., "Challenges in the quest for keystones," *BioScience* 46 (1996): 609–620; N. B. Kotliar, "Application of the new keystone species concept to prairie dogs: How well does it work?" *Conservation Biology* 14 (2000): 1715–1721.

10. Kotliar, "Application of the new keystone species concept to prairie dogs"; Soulé and Noss, "Rewilding and biodiversity"; M. E. Soulé et al., "Ecological effectiveness: conservation goals for interactive species," *Conservation Biology* 17 (2003): 1238–1250.

11. See http://www.fosonline.org.

12. D. Quammen, *Monster of God* (New York: W. W. Norton, 2003).

13. M. E. Soulé and J. Terborgh, preface to *Continental Conservation: Scientific Foundations of Regional Reserve Networks*, ed. M. E. Soulé and J. Terborgh (Washington, DC: Island Press, 1999).

14. Soulé and Noss, "Rewilding and biodiversity"; Soulé and Terborgh, "Conserving nature at regional and continental scales."

15. Soulé and Terborgh, "Conserving nature at regional and continental scales."

16. Ibid.

17. Soulé and Terborgh, preface to *Continental Conservation*, citing noted ecologist Paul Ehrlich.

18. S. Zakin, *Coyotes and Town Dogs* (New York: Viking, 1993).

19. D. Foreman, "Earth First!" *The Progressive,* October 1981, 39–42.

20. Quoted in R. F. Noss, "In defense of Earth First!" *Environmental Ethics* 5 (1983): 191–192.

21. R. F. Noss, "A regional landscape approach to maintain diversity," *BioScience* 33 (1983): 700–706.

22. M. Udvardy, *Classification of the Biogeographical Provinces,* IUCN Occasional Paper, no. 18 (Morges, Switzerland: International Union of Conservation of Nature and Natural Resources, 1975); J. J. Parson, "On 'bioregionalism' and 'watershed consciousness,'" *The Professional Geographer* 37 (1985): 1–6. In his autobiography, Dasmann writes, "For reasons now obscure to me, I did not put my name on the final product and so missed out on any fame that might have adhered to it. Udvardy was certainly willing to have me as coauthor or senior author, but I declined. Does it matter? No." (Raymond F. Dasmann, *Called by the Wild* [Berkeley: University of California Press, 2002].)

23. Soulé and Terborgh, preface to *Continental Conservation.*

24. *Seeing Things Whole: The Essential John Wesley Powell,* ed. W. deBuys (Washington, DC: Island Press, 2001); D. Kemmis, *This Sovereign Land* (Washington, DC: Island Press, 2001).

25. W. Stegner, *Beyond the Hundredth Meridian: John Wesley Powell and the Second Opening of the West* (New York: Penguin Books, 1992).

26. Zakin, *Coyotes and Town Dogs.*

27. All quotes from Michael Soulé in this chapter are from an interview I conducted on March 10, 2003.

28. Quoted in D. Quammen, "Only connect," *Outside,* December 1993, 29–35.

29. Ibid.

30. H. Locke, "A balanced approach to sharing North America," *Wild Earth* 10 (2000): 7–10. See also http://www.y2y.org.

31. D. Foreman, "The Wildlands Project and the rewilding of North America," *Denver University Law Review* 76 (1999): 535–553; R. F. Noss, "The Wildlands Project: land conservation strategy," *Wild Earth* special issue (1992): 10–25.

32. D. Foreman et al., "The Wildlands Project mission statement," *Wild Earth* special issue (1992): 3–4.

33. E. O. Wilson, "A personal brief for The Wildlands Project," *Wild Earth* 10 (2000): 1–2.

34. All quotes from Reed Noss in this chapter are from an interview I conducted on May 12, 2003.

35. M. E. Soulé, "An unflinching vision," *Wild Earth* 9 (1999): 39–46.

36. R. B. Keiter, *Keeping Faith with Nature: Ecosystems, Democracy, and America's Public Lands* (New Haven: Yale University Press, 2003), 323.

CHAPTER 3: SAVE SOME OF EVERYTHING

1. I am indebted to Mark Shaffer and Bruce Stein for the notions of "save some of everything" and "save enough to last," and to Kent Redford for the notion of "puma-ness."

2. E. Dinerstein, *Tigerland* (Washington, DC: Island Press, in press).

3. M. L. Rosenzweig, *Win-Win Ecology: How the Earth's Species Can Survive in the Midst of Human Enterprise* (New York: Oxford University Press, 2003).

4. R. F. Noss and A. Y. Cooperrider, *Saving Nature's Legacy* (Washington, DC: Island Press, 1994); R. F. Noss, "The Wildlands Project: land conservation strategy," *Wild Earth* special issue (1992): 10–25.

5. R. F. Noss et al., "Core areas: where nature reigns," in *Continental Conservation: Scientific Foundations of Regional Reserve Networks,* ed. M. E. Soulé and J. Terborgh (Washington, DC: Island Press, 1999), 99–128.

6. J. Steinbeck, *Travels with Charley: In Search of America* (1962; reprint, New York: Penguin Books, 1997), 123.

7. J. M. Scott et al., "Nature reserves: Do they capture the full ranges of America's biological diversity?" *Ecological Applications* 11 (2001): 999–1007; J. M. Scott, R. J. F. Abbitt, and C. R. Groves, "What are we protecting? The United States conservation portfolio," *Conservation Biology in Practice* 2 (2001): 18–19; Noss et al., "Core areas."

8. A. Runte, *National Parks: The American Experience* (Lincoln: University of Nebraska Press, 1987).

9. D. Foreman, "The Wildlands Project and the rewilding of North America," *Denver University Law Review* 76 (1999): 535–553.

10. J. M. Scott, "A representative biological reserve system for the United States," *Society for Conservation Biology Newsletter* 6, no. 2 (May 1999). In 1890, Ferdinand von Mueller, a German pharmacist who became one of Australia's greatest botanists, called for a representative system of biological reserves.

11. G. M. Wright, J. S. Dixon, and B. H. Thompson, *Fauna of the National Parks of the United States* (Washington, DC: GPO, 1933); A. Leopold, *Game Management* (New York: Charles Scribner's Sons, 1933); V. E. Shelford, *Naturalist's Guide to the Americas* (Baltimore: The Williams and Wilkins Company, 1926); V. E. Shelford, "The preservation of natural biotic communities," *Ecology* 14 (1933): 240–245.

12. C. R. Groves, *Drafting a Conservation Blueprint* (Washington, DC: Island Press, 2003).

13. See http://www.natureserve.org.

14. All quotes from David Wilcove in this chapter are from an interview I conducted on September 24, 2003.

15. The first good test was carried out in Australia in 2002. The results suggest that the coarse filter works reasonably well for mammals, birds, and trees, but not so well for invertebrates and reptiles. See R. E. Mac Nally et al., "How well do ecosystem-based planning units represent different components of biodiversity?" *Ecological Applications* 12 (2002): 900–912.

16. R. E. Jenkins, "Information methods: why the Heritage programs work," *Nature Conservancy News* (1985): 21–23; R. E. Jenkins, "Natural Heritage data center network: managing information for managing biodiversity," in *Biodiversity in Managed Landscapes,* ed. R. C. Szaro and D. Johnston (New York: Oxford University Press, 1996), 176–192; B. A. Stein and F. W. Davis, "Discovering life in America," in *Precious Heritage: The Status of Biodiversity in the United States,* ed. B. A. Stein, L. S. Kutner, and J. S. Adams (New York: Oxford University Press, 2000), 19–53.

17. Scott, *A representative biological reserve system for the United States;* J. M. Scott et al., "Gap analysis: a geographic approach to protection of biological diversity," *Wildlife Monographs* 123 (1993): 1–41; S. Vickerman, "Using gap analysis data for statewide biodiversity planning: case studies of applied gap analysis for planning of land use and biological resources," in *Gap Analysis: A Landscape Approach to Biodiversity Planning,* ed. J. M. Scott, T. Tear, and F. W. Davis (Bethesda, MD: American Society for Photogrammetry and Remote Sensing, 1996), 195–207; Scott, Tear, and Davis, *Gap Analysis: A Landscape Approach;* R. F. Noss, "From plant communities to landscapes in conservation inventories: a look at The Nature Conservancy (USA)," *Biological Conservation* 3 (1987): 11–37.

18. M. L. Shaffer, "The promise of gap analysis for understanding biodiversity," in *Gap Analysis: A Landscape Approach*, 3–5.

19. R. F. Noss, "Ecosystems as conservation targets," *Trends in Ecology and Evolution* 11 (1996): 351; Scott et al., "Gap analysis: a geographic approach."

20. Scott et al., "Gap analysis: a geographic approach"; C. R. Margules and R. L. Pressey, "Systematic conservation planning," *Nature* 405 (2000): 243–253.

21. L. Mumford, "Regions—to live in," *Survey Graphic* 54 (1925): 151–152.

22. B. A. Minteer, "Regional planning as pragmatic conservation," in *Reconstructing Conservation: Finding Common Ground*, ed. B. A. Minteer and R. E. Manning (Washington, DC: Island Press, 2003), 93–114.

23. C. R. Margules and M. B. Usher, "Criteria used in assessing wildlife conservation potential: a review," *Biological Conservation* 21 (1981): 79–109; M. B. Usher, "Wildlife conservation evaluation: attributes, criteria, and values," in *Wildlife Conservation Evaluation*, ed. M. B. Usher (London: Chapman and Hall, 1986); Margules and Pressey, "Systematic conservation planning."

24. Groves, *Drafting a Conservation Blueprint*; R. L. Pressey and D. M. Olson, "A framework for conservation planning," manuscript, 2002; R. M. Cowling and R. L. Pressey, "Rapid plant diversification: planning for an evolutionary future," *Proceedings of the National Academy of Sciences* 98 (2001): 5452–5457.

25. Pressey and Olson, "A framework for conservation planning."

26. Pressey and Olson, "A framework for conservation planning"; Margules and Pressey, "Systematic conservation planning."

27. Cowling and Pressey, "Rapid plant diversification."

28. W. Jackson, "Nature as measure," *Wild Earth* 8 (1998): 48–50. See also http://www.landinstitute.org.

29. H. Locke, "A balanced approach to sharing North America," *Wild Earth* 10 (2000): 7–10.

30. M. E. Soulé and R. F. Noss, "Rewilding and biodiversity: complementary goals for continental conservation," *Wild Earth* 8 (1998): 18–28; Soulé and Terborgh, preface to *Continental Conservation*.

31. See, for example, C. Caufield, *In the Rainforest* (Chicago: University of Chicago Press, 1984); S. Hecht and A. Cockburn, *The Fate of the Forest* (New York: HarperCollins, 1990); N. Myers, *The Primary Source* (New York: W. W. Norton, 1992); A. Revkin, *The Burning Season* (Boston: Houghton Mifflin, 1990).

32. E. O. Wilson, ed., *Biodiversity* (Washington, DC: National Academy Press, 1988).

33. N. Myers, "Threatened biotas: 'hot spots' in tropical forests," *The Environmentalist* 8 (1988): 187–208; N. Myers et al., "Biodiversity hotspots for conservation priorities," *Nature* 403 (2000): 853–858; Wilson, *Biodiversity*.

34. K. H. Redford et al., "There is more to biodiversity than the tropical rainforests," *Conservation Biology* 4 (1990): 328–330.

35. V. Krever et al., *Conserving Russia's Biological Diversity: An Analytical Framework and Initial Investment Portfolio* (Washington, DC: World Wildlife Fund, 1994).

36. E. Dinerstein et al., *A Conservation Assessment of the Terrestrial Ecoregions of Latin America and the Caribbean* (Washington, DC: The World Bank, 1995).

37. D. M. Olson and E. Dinerstein, "Ecoregion-based conservation planning: identify-

ing priority sites and activities within ecoregions," manuscript, World Wildlife Fund, 1994. A. Leopold, *A Sand County Almanac and Sketches Here and There* (New York: Oxford University Press, 1949); D. M. Olson and E. Dinerstein, "The Global 200: a representation approach to conserving the earth's most biologically valuable ecoregions," *Conservation Biology* 12 (1998): 502–515.

38. All quotes from Steve McCormick in this chapter are from an interview I conducted on March 18, 2003.

39. R. E. Jenkins, Jr., "The bioreserve concept," *The Nature Conservancy,* Arlington, VA, May 1991.

40. All quotes from Brian Richter in this chapter are from an interview I conducted on June 4, 2003.

41. W. Stegner, "Wilderness letter," originally written to the Outdoor Recreation Resources Review Commission in 1960, republished in *Marking the Sparrow's Fall: Wallace Stegner's American West,* ed. P. Stegner (New York: Henry Holt, 1998).

CHAPTER 4: CONSERVATION IN EXURBIA: FLORIDA AND CALIFORNIA

1. R. F. Noss and L. D. Harris, "Nodes, networks, and MUMs: preserving diversity at all scales," *Environmental Management* 10 (1986): 299–209.

2. M. E. Soulé, "An unflinching vision," *Wild Earth* 9 (1999): 39–46.

3. M. E. Soulé, "Is connectivity necessary?" (paper presented at "Missing Linkages: Restoring Connectivity to the California Landscape," a conference held at the San Diego Zoo, San Diego, CA, 2 November 2000); R. F. Noss, "The Wildlands Project: land conservation strategy," *Wild Earth* special issue (1992): 10–25.

4. R. H. MacArthur and E. O. Wilson, *The Theory of Island Biogeography* (Princeton: Princeton University Press, 1967).

5. T. Merrill and D. J. Mattson, "Defining grizzly bear habitat in the Yellowstone to Yukon," in *A Sense of Place: Issues, Attitudes, and Resources in the Yellowstone to Yukon Region* (Alberta, Canada: Yellowstone to Yukon Conservation Initiative, 1998), 103–111.

6. A. Dobson et al., "Corridors: reconnecting fragmented landscapes," in *Continental Conservation: Scientific Foundations of Regional Reserve Networks,* ed. M. E. Soulé and J. Terborgh (Washington, DC: Island Press, 1999): 129–170.

7. M. E. Soulé and J. Terborgh, preface to *Continental Conservation.*

8. B. Miller et al., "Using focal species in the design of nature reserve networks," *Wild Earth* 8 (1998): 81–92.

9. Dobson et al., "Corridors."

10. Ibid.

11. P. Beier and R. F. Noss, "Documenting the conservation value of corridors" (paper presented at "Missing Linkages: Restoring Connectivity to the California Landscape," a conference held at the San Diego Zoo, San Diego, CA, 2 November 2000).

12. Dobson et al., "Corridors."

13. R. T. T. Forman and M. Godron, "Patches and structural components for landscape ecology," *BioScience* 31 (1981): 733–740.

14. Dobson et al., "Corridors."

15. All quotes from Paul Beier in this chapter are from an interview I conducted on November 26, 2003.

16. R. Hunter, *South Coast Regional Report: California Wildlands Project Vision for Wild California* (Davis, CA: California Wilderness Coalition, 1999).

17. P. Beier et al., "South Coast missing linkages: restoring connectivity to wildlands in the largest metropolitan area in the United States," in *Connectivity and Conservation,* ed. K. R. Crooks and M. A. Sanjayan (New York: Oxford University Press, in press).

18. P. Beier, "Rewilding southern California—documenting the demise of fatalism and the rise of hope," submitted to *Wild Earth* (in press).

19. See, e.g., I. M. Mansergh and D. J. Scotts, "Habitat continuity and social organization of the mountain pygmy-possum restored by tunnel," *Journal of Wildlife Management* 53 (1989): 701–707.

20. P. Beier, "Dispersal of juvenile cougars in fragmented habitat," *Journal of Wildlife Management* 59 (1995): 228–237; P. Beier, "Metapopulation modeling, tenacious tracking, and cougar conservation," in *Metapopulations and Wildlife Management,* ed. D. R. McCullough (Washington, DC: Island Press, 1996), 293–323.

21. The sponsors of the conference were the California Wilderness Coalition, The Nature Conservancy, the Biological Resource Division of the United States Geological Survey, the Center for Reproduction of Endangered Species, and California State Parks.

22. M. A. Sanjayan, "Wildlife corridors: lifelines for nature," *The Nature Conservancy of California Newsletter,* spring 2001, available at http://www.tnccalifornia.org/news/newsletters/newsletter_spring_2001.asp#6; K. Penrod, R. Hunter, and M. Marrifield, *Missing Linkages: Restoring Connectivity to the California Landscape* (Davis, CA: California Wilderness Coalition, 2000), available at http://scwildlands.org/pdf/ml_conf/Sec1.pdf.

23. P. Beier, presentation to South Coast Missing Linkages Workshop, Frazier Park, CA, 30 September 2002. Available at http://scwildlands.org/missinglinks/reports/Report_SanGab_Castaic/SanGab_Castaic_APPENDIX_B_WORKSHOPMINUTES.PDF.

24. I. Hanski, "Single-species spatial dynamics may contribute to long-term rarity and commonness," *Ecology* 66 (1985): 335–343; I. Hanski, "Single-species metapopulation dynamics—concepts, models, and observations," *Biological Journal of the Linnean Society* 42 (1991): 17–38; I. Hanski, "A practical model of metropolitan dynamics," *Journal of Animal Ecology* 63 (1994): 151–162; D. D. Murphy, K. E. Freaks, and S. B. Weiss, "An environment-metapopulation approach to population viability analysis for a threatened invertebrate," *Conservation Biology* 4 (1990): 41–51; S. Harrison, D. D. Murphy, and P. R. Ehrlich, "Distribution of the bay checkerspot butterfly, *Euphydras editha bayensis* —evidence for a metapopulation model," *American Naturalist* 132 (1988): 360–382.

25. I. Hanski and M. Gilpin, "Metapopulation dynamics—brief history and conceptual domain," *Biological Journal of the Linnean Society* 42 (1991): 3–16; G. C. Meffe and C. R. Carroll, *Principles of Conservation Biology* (Sunderland, MA: Sinauer Associates, 1994); P. H. Singleton, W. L. Gaines, and J. F. Lehmkuhl, *Landscape Permeability for Large Carnivores in Washington: A Geographic Information System Weighted-Distance and Least-Cost Corridor Assessment,* U.S. Department of Agriculture Forest Service and Pacific Northwest Research Station research paper, PNW- RP-549, December 2002.

26. There are exceptions, of course. Finnish ecologist Ilka Hanski has demonstrated over

the course of two decades that a particular butterfly, the Granville fritillary, fits the strict definition.

27. Noss, "The Wildlands Project."

28. All quotes from John Wiens in this chapter are from an interview I conducted on January 31, 2003.

29. T. H. Ricketts et al., "Countryside biogeography of moths in a fragmented landscape: biodiversity in native and agricultural landscapes," *Conservation Biology* 15 (2001): 378–388.

30. All quotes from Kent Redford in this chapter are from interviews I conducted on October 2, 2002, and July 30, 2003.

31. R. J. Hobbs, D. A. Saunders, and G. W. Arnold, "Integrated landscape ecology: a western Australian perspective," *Biological Conservation* 64 (1993): 231–238.

32. R. B. Keiter, *Keeping Faith with Nature: Ecosystems, Democracy, and America's Public Lands* (New Haven: Yale University Press, 2003), 317.

33. All quotes from Michael Soulé in this chapter, unless otherwise noted, are from an interview I conducted on March 10, 2003.

34. All quotes from Reed Noss in this chapter, unless otherwise noted, are from interviews I conducted on November 25, 2002, and July 30, 2003.

35. Hobbs, Saunders, and Arnold, "Integrated landscape ecology," 231–238.

36. M. L. Rosenzweig, *Win-Win Ecology: How the Earth's Species Can Survive in the Midst of Human Enterprise* (New York: Oxford University Press, 2003).

37. Ibid, 7.

38. T. H. Ricketts, data, Stanford University.

39. J. R. Miller and R. J. Hobbs, "Conservation where people live and work," *Conservation Biology* 16 (2002): 330–337.

40. Quoted in C. Meine, *Aldo Leopold: His Life and Work* (Madison: University of Wisconsin Press, 1988), 310.

CHAPTER 5: APPOINTMENT IN SONORA

1. C. J. Bahre, *A Legacy of Change: Historic Human Impact on Vegetation in the Arizona Borderlands* (Tucson: University of Arizona Press, 1991).

2. C. R. Groves, "Future Directions for Ecoregional Planning in The Nature Conservancy," The Nature Conservancy, Arlington, VA, 2001.

3. K. H. Redford et al., "Mapping the conservation landscape," *Conservation Biology* 17 (2003): 116–131.

4. C. R. Groves, *Drafting a Conservation Blueprint* (Washington, DC: Island Press, 2003); R. L. Pressey and D. M. Olson, "A framework for conservation planning," manuscript, 2002; C. R. Margules and R. L. Pressey, "Systematic conservation planning," *Nature* 405 (2000): 243–253.

5. J. R. Prendergast et al., "Rare species, the coincidence of diversity hotspots, and conservation strategies," *Nature* 365 (1993): 335–337; S. L. Pimm and J. H. Lawton, "Planning for biodiversity," *Science* 279 (1998): 2068–2069; R. E. Mac Nally and E. Fleishman, "Using 'indicator' species to model species richness: model development and predictions," *Ecological Applications* 12 (2001): 79–92.

6. Margules and Pressey, "Systematic conservation planning."

7. J. M. Scott et al., "The issue of scale in selecting and designing biological reserves," in *Continental Conservation: Scientific Foundations of Regional Reserve Networks,* ed. M. E. Soulé and J. Terborgh (Washington, DC: Island Press, 1999), 19–37.

8. B. Miller et al., "Using focal species in the design of nature reserve networks," *Wild Earth* 8 (1998): 81–92; S. J. Andelman and W. F. Fagan, "Umbrellas and flagships: efficient conservation surrogates or expensive mistakes?" *Proceedings of the National Academy of Sciences* 97 (2000): 5954–5959; Scott et al., "The issue of scale in selecting and designing biological reserves."

9. E. W. Sanderson et al., "A conceptual model for conservation planning based on landscape species requirements," *Landscape and Urban Planning* 58 (2002): 41–56.

10. Margules and Pressey, "Systematic conservation planning"; Sanderson et al., "A conceptual model for conservation planning."

11. All quotes from Amy Vedder in this chapter are from an interview I conducted on July 30, 2003.

12. D. Foreman et al., "The Sky Islands Network," *Wild Earth* 10 (2000): 11–16.

13. J. M. Hoekstra et al., "A comprehensive review of Endangered Species Act recovery plans," *Ecological Applications* 12 (2002): 630–640; E. Harvey et al., "Recovery plan revisions: progress or due process?" *Ecological Applications* 12 (2002): 682–689; J. M. Hoekstra, W. F. Fagan, and J. E. Bradley, "A critical role for critical habitat in the recovery planning process? Not yet," *Ecological Applications* 12 (2002): 701–707.

14. Groves, *Drafting a Conservation Blueprint;* T. H. Tear et al., "Recovery plans and the Endangered Species Act: Are criticisms supported by data?" *Conservation Biology* 9 (1995): 182–195.

15. Groves, *Drafting a Conservation Blueprint.*

16. Margules and Pressey, "Systematic conservation planning."

17. R. L. Pressey, "Conservation planning—a young science playing in the big league," *Society for Conservation Biology Newsletter,* 4 November 2001.

18. R. M. Cowling et al., "From representation to persistence: requirements for a sustainable system of conservation areas in the species-rich Mediterranean desert climate of southern Africa," *Diversity and Distributions* 5 (1999): 51–71. Recent work by the Australians and South Africans focuses on minimizing the extent to which habitat loss that occurs while the system of conservation areas is developing compromises the original representation goals; they call this process retention. See also E. Meir, S. Andelman, and H. P. Possingham, "Does conservation planning matter in a dynamic and uncertain world?" *Ecology Letter* 7 (2004): 615–622.

19. Redford et al., "Mapping the conservation landscape."

20. All quotes from Bill Eichbaum in this chapter are from an interview I conducted on December 23, 2003.

21. All quotes from Michael Soulé in this chapter are from an interview I conducted on March 10, 2003.

22. Pima County, *Preliminary Sonoran Desert Conservation Plan* (September 2000), 3.

23. All quotes from Rob Marshall in this chapter are from an interview I conducted on December 16, 2003.

24. All quotes from Roseann Hanson in this chapter are from an interview I conducted on January 21, 2003.

25. R. Hanson, "Cienega Creek watershed: a case study in community stewardship, southeast Arizona," the Sonoran Institute *Vision*, January 2003.
26. Ibid.

CHAPTER 6: THE NATIVE HOME OF HOPE

1. All quotes from Warner Glenn in this chapter are from interviews I conducted on January 22 and January 23, 2003.
2. See http://www.uwyo.edu/enr/ienr/malpai.html.
3. All quotes from Mike Dennis in this chapter are from an interview I conducted on January 10, 2003.
4. All quotes from Guy McPherson in this chapter are from an interview I conducted on January 22, 2003.
5. A. Leopold, *A Sand County Almanac and Sketches Here and There* (New York: Oxford University Press, 1949).
6. D. Hadley, "The origin and future of the grassbank," in *A Hundred Years of Horse Tracks: The Story of the Gray Ranch*, by G. Hilliard (Silver City, NM: High-Lonesome Books, 1996): 156–163.
7. N. F. Sayre, "The cattle boom in southern Arizona: towards a critical political ecology," *Journal of the Southwest* 41 (1999): 239–271.
8. Hilliard, *A Hundred Years of Horse Tracks*, 41.
9. Ibid.
10. A. A. Erwin, *The Southwest of John Horton Slaughter* (Spokane, WA: Arthur A. Clark Company, 1997).
11. T. E. Sheridan, *Arizona: A History* (Tucson: University of Arizona Press, 1995).
12. T. E. Sheridan, "Cows, condos, and the contested commons: the political ecology of ranching on the Arizona-Sonora borderlands," *Human Organization* 60 (2001): 141–152.
13. D. A. Griffiths, quoted in Sayre, "The cattle boom in southern Arizona."
14. R. W. Cooke and R. W. Reeves, *Arroyos and Environmental Change in the American South-West* (Oxford: Oxford University Press, 1976).
15. J. W. Powell, *Report on the Lands of the Arid Region of the United States, with a More Detailed Account of the Lands of Utah*, 45th Cong., 2nd sess., 1879, H. Doc. 73. For an excellent overview of Powell's work and thought, see W. deBuys, *Seeing Things Whole: The Essential John Wesley Powell* (Washington, DC: Island Press, 2001).
16. W. Glenn, *Eyes of Fire* (El Paso, TX: Printing Corner Press, 1996).
17. V. Klinkenborg, "Crossing borders," *Audubon*, September/October 1995, 36–47.
18. All quotes from Bill McDonald in this chapter are from an interview I conducted on January 23, 2003.
19. W. McDonald and R. J. Bemis, "Community involvement and sustainability: the Malpai Borderlands effort," in *Nature and Human Society: The Quest for a Sustainable World*, ed. P. H. Raven and T. Williams (Washington, DC: National Academy Press, 1999).
20. Quoted on PBS's *NewsHour with Jim Lehrer*, 13 February 1996. See http://www.pbs.org/newshour/bb/environment/range_2-13.html.
21. G. J. Gottfired et al., "Research support for land management in the southwestern bor-

derlands," in *Land Stewardship in the Twenty-first Century: The Contributions of Watershed Management*, ed. P. F. Ffolliott et al. (Fort Collins, CO: U.S. Department of Agriculture Forest Service conference proceedings, RMRS-P-13, March 2000), 330–334.

22. D. Remley, *Bell Ranch: Cattle Ranching in the Southwest, 1824–1947* (Albuquerque: University of New Mexico Press, 1993).

23. W. Stegner, "Land, America's history teacher," in *Marking the Sparrow's Fall: Wallace Stegner's American West*, ed. P. Stegner (New York: Henry Holt, 1998).

24. Quoted in Hadley, "The origin and future of the grassbank."

25. All quotes from Bill Weeks in this chapter are from an interview I conducted on January 16, 2003.

26. All quotes from Charles Curtin in this chapter are from an interview I conducted on January 15, 2003.

27. J. H. Brown, T. J. Vallone, and C. G. Curtin, "Reorganization of an arid ecosystem in response to recent climate change," *Proceedings of the National Academy of Science* 94 (1997): 9729–9733.

28. Ibid.

29. C. G. Curtin and J. H. Brown, "Climate and herbivory in structuring the vegetation of the Malpai Borderlands," in *Changing Plant Life of La Frontera: Observations on Vegetation in the United States/Mexico Borderlands*, ed. G. L. Webster and C. J. Bahre (Albuquerque: University of New Mexico, 2001), 84–94.

30. All quotes from Wendy Glenn in this chapter are from interviews I conducted on January 22 and January 23, 2003.

31. Hilliard, *A Hundred Years of Horse Tracks*, 15.

32. Ibid.

33. B. Selcraig, "The continuing saga of New Mexico's Gray Ranch," *High Country News*, 22 February 1993.

34. D. Hadley, preface to Hilliard, *A Hundred Years of Horse Tracks*, 1.

35. See http://www.lta.org.

36. Quoted in Hadley, "The origin and future of the grassbank."

37. J. Page, "Ranchers form a 'radical center' to protect wide-open spaces," *Smithsonian*, June 1997, 52–61.

38. T. L. Burgess, "Desert grasslands, mixed shrub savanna, shrub steppe, or semidesert scrub? The dilemma of coexisting growth forms," in *The Desert Grassland*, ed. M. P. McClaran and T. R. Van Devender (Tucson: University of Arizona Press, 1995), 31–67.

39. M. P. McClaran, "Desert Grasslands and Grasses," in *The Desert Grassland*, 1–30.

40. Bahre, *A Legacy of Change.*

41. J. E. Mitchell, *Rangeland Resource Trends in the United States* (Washington, DC: U.S. Department of Agriculture Forest Service, 2000); T. L. Fleischner, "Ecological costs of livestock grazing in Western North America," *Conservation Biology* 8 (1993): 629–644.

42. G. R. McPherson and J. F. Weltzin, *Disturbance and Climate Change in United States/Mexico Borderland Communities: A State-of-the-Knowledge Review* (Fort Collins, CO: U.S. Department of Agriculture Forest Service, Rocky Mountain Research Station general technical report, RMRS-GRT-50, April 2000).

43. D. Worster, *The Wealth of Nature* (Oxford: Oxford University Press, 1993).

44. And not terribly original, either; the phrase "cow free" first appeared in 1893: "Cow Free in '93."

45. McPherson and Weltzin, *Disturbance and Climate Change.*
46. A. J. Belsky, A. Matzke, and S. Uselman, "Survey of livestock influences on stream and riparian ecosystems in the western United States," *Journal of Soil and Water Conservation* 54 (1999): 419–431.
47. Sonoran Institute, *Economic Profile System,* 2004. Available at http://www.sonoran.org/eps.
48. G. Wuerthner, "Subdivisions versus agriculture," *Conservation Biology* 8 (1994) 905–908.
49. B. McDonald, "Anticipating future landscape conditions: a case study," in *Land Stewardship in the Twenty-first Century.*

CHAPTER 7: SAVE ENOUGH TO LAST: FLORIDA AND THE EVERGLADES

1. M. L. Shaffer and B. A. Stein, "Safeguarding our precious heritage," in *Precious Heritage: The Status of Biodiversity in the United States,* ed. B. Stein, L. S. Kutner, and J. S. Adams (New York: Oxford University Press, 2000), 301–321. Craig Groves adds that protected areas should also be "restorative," and calls the whole package the "4R Framework." (C. R. Groves, *Drafting a Conservation Blueprint* [Washington, DC: Island Press, 2003].)
2. All quotes from Jora Young in this chapter are from an interview I conducted on May 14, 2003.
3. J. A. Cox et al., *Closing the Gaps in Florida's Wildlife Habitat Conservation System* (Tallahassee, FL: Florida Game and Fresh Water Fish Commission, 1994); R. S. Kautz and J. A. Cox, "Strategic habitats for biodiversity conservation in Florida," *Conservation Biology* 15 (2001): 55–77; Shaffer and Stein, "Safeguarding our precious heritage."
4. Kautz and Cox, "Strategic habitats."
5. F. J. Mazzotti and L. A. Brandt, "Ecology of the American alligator in a seasonally fluctuating environment," in *Everglades: The Ecosystem and Its Restoration,* ed. S. Davis and J. C. Ogden (Delray Beach, FL: St. Lucie Press, 1994), 485–505.
6. S. S. Light and J. W. Dineen, "Water control in the Everglades: a historical perspective," in *Everglades: The Ecosystem and Its Restoration,* 47–84.
7. S. M. Davis et al., "Landscape dimension, composition, and function in a changing Everglades ecosystem," in *Everglades: The Ecosystem and Its Restoration,* 419–458.
8. P. S. White, "Synthesis: vegetation pattern and process in the Everglades ecosystem," in *Everglades: The Ecosystem and Its Restoration,* 445–480.
9. Davis et al., "Landscape dimension."
10. See http://www.nps.gov/ever/eco/conserve.htm.
11. M. A. Harwell, "Ecosystem management of South Florida," *Bioscience* 47 (1997): 499–512.
12. J. C. Ogden, "A comparison of wading bird nesting colony dynamics (1931–46 and 1974–89) as an indication of ecosystem conditions in the southern Everglades," in *Everglades: The Ecosystem and Its Restoration,* 533–570.
13. F. H. Sklar et al., "The design of ecological landscape models for Everglades restoration," *Ecological Economics* 37 (2001): 379–401.
14. E. Maltby and P. J. Dugan, "Wetland ecosystem protection, management, and restoration: an international perspective," in *Everglades: The Ecosystem and Its Restoration,* 741–756.

15. Quoted in M. Grunwald, "An environmental reversal of fortune," *Washington Post*, 26 June 2002.

16. All quotes from Shannon Estenoz in this chapter are from an interview I conducted on May 12, 2003.

17. *Water Resources Development Act of 2000*, Public Law 106-541, 106th Cong., 2d sess. (24 January 2000).

18. M. Kraus, in an interview I conducted on May 13, 2003.

19. M. A. Harwell, "Science and environmental decision-making in South Florida," *Ecological Applications* 8 (1998): 580–590.

20. All quotes from John Ogden in this chapter are from an interview I conducted on May 15, 2003.

21. S. M. Davis and J. C. Ogden, "Toward ecosystem restoration," in *Everglades: The Ecosystem and Its Restoration*, 769–796.

22. Science Sub-Group of the South Florida Management and Coordination Working Group, *Federal Objectives for the South Florida Restoration*, 15 November 1993. See http://www.sfrestore.org/sct/docs/subgrouprpt/index.htm.

23. Davis et al., "Landscape dimension."

24. C. S. Holling and G. K. Meffe, "Command and control and the pathology of natural resource management," *Conservation Biology* 10 (1996): 328–337.

25. R. Walker and W. Solecki, "South Florida: the reality of change and the prospects for sustainability," *Ecological Economics* 37 (2001): 333–337.

26. M. A. Harwell, "Ecosystem management of South Florida."

27. G. P. Nabhan, "Lost gourds and spent soils on the shores of Okeechobee," in *The Book of the Everglades*, ed. S. Cerulean (Minneapolis, MN: Milkweed Editions, 2002), 32–54; G. H. Snyder and J. M. Davidson, "Everglades agriculture: past, present, and future," in *Everglades: The Ecosystem and Its Restoration*, 85–115.

28. Light and Dineen, "Water control in the Everglades."

29. W. D. Solecki, "The role of global-to-local linkages in land use/land cover change in South Florida," *Ecological Economics* 37 (2001): 339–356.

30. Ibid.

31. Light and Dineen, "Water control in the Everglades."

32. David Guggenheim, then co-chairman of the Everglades Coalition, quoted in M. Enserink, "Ecological restoration—plan to quench the Everglades' thirst," *Science* 285 (1999): 180–180; M. Kraus, in an interview I conducted on May 13, 2003.

33. Snyder and Davidson, "Everglades agriculture."

34. M. A. Harwell, "Ecosystem management of South Florida."

35. Quoted in P. Elmer-Dewitt, "Facing a deadline to save the Everglades," *Time*, 21 June 1993.

36. L. H. Gunderson, S. S. Light, and C. S. Holling, "Lessons from the Everglades," *Bioscience* (1995): S66–S73.

37. *U.S. v South Florida Water Management District*, 847 F. Supp. 1567 (S.D. Fla 1992).

38. M. A. Harwell, "Science and environmental decision-making in South Florida."

39. M. Grunwald, "Between rock and a hard place," *Washington Post*, 24 June 2002.

CHAPTER 8: BLIND MEN AND ELEPHANTS

1. D. J. Mattson, K. C. Kendall, and D. P. Reinhart, "Whitebark pine, grizzly bears, and red squirrels," in *Whitebark Pine Communities: Ecology and Restoration,* ed. D. F. Tomback, S. F. Arno, and R. E. Keane (Washington, DC: Island Press, 2001), 121–136.

2. T. W. Clark and S. C. Minta, *Greater Yellowstone's Future: Prospects for Ecosystem Science, Management, and Policy* (Moose, WY: Homestead Publishing, 1994).

3. Greater Yellowstone Coalition, *The Greater Yellowstone Ecosystem.* See http://www.greateryellowstone.org/gyc/home_gye.html.

4. J. E. Anderson, "A conceptual framework for evaluating and quantifying naturalness," *Conservation Biology* 5 (1991): 347–352.

5. R. B. Keiter, "An introduction to the ecosystem management debate," in *The Greater Yellowstone Ecosystem: Redefining America's Wilderness Heritage,* ed. R. B. Keiter and M. S. Boyce (New Haven: Yale University Press, 1991), 3–18.

6. Clark and Minta, *Greater Yellowstone's Future.*

7. J. D. Varley, "Research in Yellowstone," *Bioscience* 43 (1993): 131–132.

8. Clark and Minta, *Greater Yellowstone's Future;* Congressional Research Service report cited in T. McNamee, *The Return of the Wolf to Yellowstone* (New York: Henry Holt, 1997).

9. J. Berger, "Greater Yellowstone's native ungulates: myths and realities," *Conservation Biology* 5 (1991): 353–363.

10. S. A. Primm and T. W. Clark, "The Greater Yellowstone policy debate: What is the policy problem?" *Policy Sciences* 29 (1996): 137–166.

11. C. S. Holling, "The resilience of terrestrial ecosystems: local surprise and global change," in *Sustainable Development of the Biosphere,* ed. W. C. Clark and R. E. Munn (Cambridge: Cambridge University Press, 1986).

12. "Is there any point to which you would wish to draw my attention?"
    "To the curious incident of the dog in the night-time."
    "The dog did nothing in the night-time."
    "That was the curious incident," remarked Sherlock Holmes. (It's from the short story "Silver Blaze.")

13. U.S. Department of the Interior, *A Brief History of the National Park Service* (1940). Available at http://www.cr.nps.gov/history/online_books/kieley/index.htm.

14. A. L. Haines, *The Yellowstone Story: A History of Our First National Park* (Washington, DC: U.S. Department of the Interior National Park Service, 1974). Available at http://www.cr.nps.gov/history/online_books/haines1/index.htm.

15. P. Schullery, *Searching for Yellowstone: Ecology and Wonder in the Last Wilderness* (Boston: Houghton Mifflin, 1997).

16. J. L. Sax, *Mountains Without Handrails* (Ann Arbor: University of Michigan Press, 1980).

17. Schullery, *Searching for Yellowstone.*

18. Schullery, *Searching for Yellowstone;* McNamee, *The Return of the Wolf to Yellowstone.*

19. G. B. Grinnell, "Game in the Great West," *Forest and Stream,* 8 July 1890.

20. J. A. Pritchard, *Preserving Yellowstone's Natural Conditions: Science and the Perception of Nature* (Lincoln: University of Nebraska Press, 1999).

21. D. W. Smith, W. G. Brewster, and E. E. Bangs, "Wolves in the Greater Yellow-

stone ecosystem: restoration of a top carnivore in a complex management environment," in *Carnivores in Ecosystems: The Yellowstone Experience,* ed. T. A. Clark et al. (New Haven: Yale University Press, 1999), 103–126; McNamee, *The Return of the Wolf to Yellowstone.*

22. R. McIntyre, *War Against the Wolf: America's Campaign to Exterminate the Wolf* (Stillwater, MN: Voyageur Press, 1995).

23. Schullery, *Searching for Yellowstone.*

24. Pritchard, *Preserving Yellowstone's Natural Conditions.*

25. C. C. Adams, "The conservation of predatory mammals," *Journal of Mammalogy* 6 (1925): 83–96; See also D. Worster, *Nature's Economy: A History of Ecological Ideas* (Cambridge: Cambridge University Press, 1994).

26. G. M. Wright, J. S. Dixon, and B. H. Thompson, *Fauna of the National Parks of the United States* (Washington, DC: GPO, 1933).

27. Ibid.

28. R. B. Keiter, "Preserving nature in the national parks: law, policy, and science in a dynamic environment," *Denver University Law Review* 74 (1997): 649–695.

29. M. B. Coughenour and F. J. Singer, "The concept of overgrazing and its application to Yellowstone's northern range," in *The Greater Yellowstone Ecosystem,* 209–230.

30. R. W. Sellars, *Preserving Nature in the National Parks* (New Haven: Yale University Press, 1997).

31. A. S. Leopold et al., "Wildlife management in the national parks," *Transactions of the North American Wildlife and Natural Resources Conference* 28 (1963): 28–45. Available at http://www.cr.nps.gov/history/online_books/leopold/leopold.htm.

32. C. L. Shafer, "The northern Yellowstone elk debate: policy, hypothesis, and implications," *Natural Areas Journal* 20 (2000): 342–359.

33. Pritchard, *Preserving Yellowstone's Natural Conditions.*

34. Sellars, *Preserving Nature in the National Parks.*

35. Scullery, *Searching for Yellowstone.*

36. D. E. Huff and J. D. Varley, "Natural regulation in Yellowstone National Park's northern range," *Ecological Applications* 9 (1999): 17–29; Shafer, "The northern Yellowstone elk debate."

37. Sellars, *Preserving Nature in the National Parks.*

38. D. J. Mattson and J. J. Craighead, "The Yellowstone grizzly bear recovery program: uncertain information, uncertain policy," in *Endangered Species Recovery: Finding the Lessons, Improving the Process,* ed. T. Clark, R. P. Reading, and A. L. Clarke (Washington, DC: Island Press, 1994), 101–129; Sellars, *Preserving Nature in the National Parks.*

39. A. R. Main and M. Yadav, "Conservation of macropods in reserves in western Australia," *Biological Conservation* 3 (1971): 123–133.

40. I. R. Franklin, "Evolutionary change in small populations," *Conservation Biology: An Evolutionary-Ecological Perspective,* ed. M. E. Soulé and B. A. Wilcox (Sunderland, MA: Sinauer Associates, 1980), 135–149; G. Caughley, "Directions in conservation biology," *Journal of Animal Ecology* 63 (1994): 215–244.

41. D. Quammen, *The Song of the Dodo* (New York: Scribner, 1996).

42. M. E. Gilpin and M. E. Soulé, "Minimum viable population: processes of species extinction," in *Conservation Biology: The Science of Scarcity and Diversity,* ed. M. E. Soulé and B. A. Wilcox (Sunderland, MA: Sinauer Associates, 1986), 19–34.

43. All quotes from Mark Shaffer in this chapter are from interviews I conducted on November 12, 2002, and October 2, 2003.

44. M. L. Shaffer, *Keeping the Grizzly Bear in the American West: A Strategy for Real Recovery* (Washington, DC: The Wilderness Society, 1992); Primm and Clark, "The Greater Yellowstone policy debate."

45. Shaffer, *Keeping the Grizzly Bear in the American West.*

46. C. M. Pease and D. J. Mattson, "Demography of the Yellowstone Grizzly Bears," *Ecology* 90 (1999): 957–975.

47. R. B. Keiter, "An introduction to the ecosystem management debate," in *The Greater Yellowstone Ecosystem;* D. J. Mattson and M. W. Reid, "Conservation of the Yellowstone grizzly bear," *Conservation Biology* 5 (1991): 364–372.

48. T. Wilkinson, *Science Under Siege: The Politicians' War in Nature and Truth* (Boulder, CO: Johnson Books, 1998).

49. E. T. Freyfogle, *The Land We Share* (Washington, DC: Island Press, 2003).

50. All quotes from Dave Mattson in this chapter are from interviews I conducted on September 28, 2002, and September 24, 2003.

51. Interagency Conservation Strategy Team, *Final Conservation Strategy for the Grizzly Bear in the Yellowstone Ecosystem,* March 2003.

52. R. E. Grumbine, *Ghost Bears* (Washington, DC: Island Press, 1992).

53. D. J. Mattson et al., "Science and management of Rocky Mountain grizzly bears," *Conservation Biology* 10 (1996): 1013–1025.

54. Shaffer, *Keeping the Grizzly Bear in the American West.*

55. All quotes from Steve Primm in this chapter are from an interview I conducted on October 17, 2003.

CHAPTER 9: GUARDING THE GOLDEN GOOSE

1. All quotes from Jennifer Dwyer in this chapter are from an interview I conducted on January 16, 2004.

2. D. Glick and B. Alexander, "Development by default, not design: Yellowstone National Park and the Greater Yellowstone ecosystem," in *National Parks and Rural Development,* ed. G. M. Field (Washington, DC: Island Press, 2000), 181–205.

3. All quotes from Ray Rasker in this chapter are from an interview I conducted on December 10, 2002.

4. See http://www.farmland.org/farmingontheedge/index.htm.

5. T. W. Clark and A. W. Harvey, "The Greater Yellowstone ecosystem policy arena," *Society and Natural Resources* 3 (1990): 281–284.

6. *Greater Yellowstone Coalition Annual Plan, 2002;* Glick and Alexander, "Development by default, not design."

7. See http://www.greateryellowstone.org.

8. All quotes from Dennis Glick in this chapter are from an interview I conducted on October 17, 2002.

9. R. Rasker and A. Hackman, "Economic development and the conservation of large carnivores," *Conservation Biology* 10 (1996): 991–1002.

10. D. Glick, D. Neary, and R. Rasker, "Conservation in Greater Yellowstone, case study 15" (paper presented at the Liz Claiborne and Art Ortenberg Foundation Community Based Conservation Workshop, October 1993).

11. *Greater Yellowstone Coalition Strategic Plan, 2002–2006;* R. B. Keiter, "An introduction to the ecosystem management debate," in *The Greater Yellowstone Ecosystem: Redefining America's Wilderness Heritage,* ed. R. B. Keiter and M. S. Boyce (New Haven: Yale University Press, 1991), 3–18.

12. Glick, Neary, and Rasker, "Conservation in Greater Yellowstone."

13. R. S. Gale, "Learning from the past, preparing for the future," *Greater Yellowstone Report* 4 (1987): 12–14.

14. T. W. Clark et al., "Policy and programs for ecosystem management in the Greater Yellowstone ecosystem: an analysis," *Conservation Biology* 5 (1991): 412–422.

15. Ibid.

16. The 1916 law that created the National Park Service provides a substantial legal basis for protecting the parks from threats from adjacent land, particularly those from other public land. See W. J. Lockhart, "'Faithful execution' of the laws governing Greater Yellowstone: Whose law? Whose priorities?" in *The Greater Yellowstone Ecosystem: Redefining America's Wilderness Heritage.*

17. J. D. Varley, "Research in Yellowstone," *Bioscience* 43 (1993): 131–132.

18. S. A. Primm and T. W. Clark, "The Greater Yellowstone policy debate: What is the policy problem?" *Policy Sciences* 29 (1996): 137–166.

19. T. W. Clark, "Interdisciplinary problem-solving: next steps in the Greater Yellowstone ecosystem," *Policy Sciences* 32 (1999): 393–414.

20. T. W. Clark et al., "Policy and programs for ecosystem management in the Greater Yellowstone ecosystem"; P. Lichtman and T. W. Clark, "Rethinking the 'vision' exercise in the Greater Yellowstone ecosystem," *Society and Natural Resources* 7 (1994): 459–478.

21. Lichtman and Clark, "Rethinking the 'vision' exercise"; Keiter, "An introduction to the ecosystem management debate."

22. "Vision for the future: a framework for coordination in the greater Yellowstone area (draft)," August 1990.

23. "Vision for the future"; T. W. Clark and S. C. Minta, *Greater Yellowstone's Future: Prospects for Ecosystem Science, Management, and Policy* (Moose, WY: Homestead Publishing, 1994).

24. "Vision for the future."

25. Lichtman and Clark, "Rethinking the 'vision' exercise."

26. Glick and Alexander, "Development by default, not design."

27. B. Goldstein, "The struggle over ecosystem management at Yellowstone," *BioScience* 42 (1992): 183–187; Primm and Clark, "The Greater Yellowstone policy debate."

28. Clark, et al. "Policy and programs for ecosystem management in the Greater Yellowstone ecosystem"; Lichtman and Clark, "Rethinking the 'vision' exercise."

29. *Billings Gazette,* 12 September 1991; Primm and Clark, "The Greater Yellowstone policy debate."

30. Glick and Alexander, "Development by default, not design."

31. T. M. Power, "Ecosystem preservation and the economy in the Greater Yellowstone ecosystem," *Conservation Biology* 5 (1991): 395–404.

32. Rasker and Hackman, "Economic development and the conservation of large carnivores."

33. R. Rasker and B. Alexander, *Getting Ahead in Greater Yellowstone: Making the Most of*

Our Competitive Advantage (Bozeman, MT: Sonoran Institute; Yellowstone Business Partnership, 2003).

34. Bureau of Economic Analysis, *Regional Economic Accounts* (2003). See http://www.bea .gov.

35. Rasker and Hackman, "Economic development and the conservation of large carnivores."

36. Primm and Clark, "The Greater Yellowstone policy debate."

37. Rasker and Hackman, "Economic development and the conservation of large carnivores."

38. Rasker and Alexander, *Getting Ahead in Greater Yellowstone.*

39. Ibid.

40. T. M. Power, *Lost Landscapes and Failed Economies* (Washington, DC: Island Press, 1996), 9.

41. Primm and Clark, "The Greater Yellowstone policy debate."

42. Glick, Neary, and Rasker, "Conservation in Greater Yellowstone."

43. T. M. Power, *Lost Landscapes and Failed Economies;* Rasker and Alexander, *Getting Ahead in Greater Yellowstone.*

44. Glick and Alexander, "Development by default, not design"; T. M. Power, "Ecosystem preservation and the economy in the Greater Yellowstone ecosystem," *Conservation Biology* 5 (1991): 395–404; Rasker and Hackman, "Economic development and the conservation of large carnivores."

45. R. Rasker and D. Glick, "Footloose entrepreneurs: pioneers of the new West?" *Illahee Journal for the Northwest Environment* 10 (1994): 34–43; Glick and Alexander, "Development by default, not design"; Rasker and Hackman, "Economic development and the conservation of large carnivores."

46. Glick, Neary, and Rasker, "Conservation in Greater Yellowstone."

47. Primm and Clark, "The Greater Yellowstone policy debate."

48. P. Dykstra, "Defining the mother lode: Yellowstone National Park v. the New World Mine," *Ecology Law Quarterly* 24 (1997): 299; M. Humphries, "New World Gold Mine and Yellowstone National Park," Congressional Research Service report, 96-669 ENR, 27 August 1996; M. Humphries, "New World Gold Mine near Yellowstone: a project abandoned." Congressional Research Service report, 96-693 ENR, 27 August 27 1996.

49. Primm and Clark, "The Greater Yellowstone policy debate."

50. The rate of $1.81 per Animal Unit Month (one cow and one calf, the standard unit of measure for federal grazing regulations), while the market rate is closer to $4.60 to $9.20 per AUM.

51. H. E. Daly and J. B. Cobb, Jr., *For the Common Good: Redirecting the Economy toward Community, the Environment, and a Sustainable Future* (Boston: Beacon Press, 1989).

52. Clark and Minta, *Greater Yellowstone's Future.*

53. R. Rasker and B. Alexander, "The changing economy of Yellowstone to Yukon: good news for wild lands," *Wild Earth* 10 (2000): 99–103.

CONCLUSION

1. H. W. J. Rittel and M. M. Webber, "Dilemmas in a general theory of planning," *Policy Sciences* 4 (1973): 155–169; D. Schön, *The Reflective Practitioner: How Professionals Think in Action* (New York: Basic Books, 1983).

2. K. Redford and M. A. Sanjayan, "Retiring Cassandra." *Conservation Biology* 17 (2003): 1473–1474.

3. W. McDonough and M. Braungart, *Cradle to Cradle: Remaking the Way We Make Things* (San Francisco: North Point Press, 2002).

Adams, Charles C., 186–87
agriculture: impact on western ecoregion, 139; irrigation issues, 37, 159, 208; land loss, 210; polluted runoff from, 147, 162–63; and subsidence, 160–61; sugar industry, 142, 157, 158–61; sustainable, 58, 129. *See also* ranchers/ranching
Alaska, Kenai Peninsula erosion example, 23–26
Aleutian Islands, 24–25
Alexander, Ben, 222
American commons, 134
Animas Foundation, 129–30
Appalachian Trail, 45
Applebaum, Stuart, 148
Applegate Partnership, 7
aquifers in Florida, 165–66
Arizona: Central Arizona Project, 37; habitat fragmentation/loss, 89–90; Malpai Ranch, 116–17; Sonoran Desert plan, 88–89, 101–7. *See also* desert southwest
Army Corps of Engineers, 148, 152, 157–60, 163, 165, 168–69
Artemis Common Ground, 204–5

Babbitt, Bruce, 105, 117
Bailey, Robert, 21
Beier, Paul, 76–78
Berg, Peter, 35
Berry, Wendell, xxiii
Big Hole watershed at Yellowstone, 207–9
biodiversity: conservation of Florida's, 142; definition, 59; of Orange County, California, 76–77; stewardship protection of, 123, 172, 210; targeting method for protection of, 92
biogeography, 10–12, 15, 28, 61, 72–73, 94–95
biological hierarchy, 21, 62–63

bioregionalism, 36–37, 43
bioreserves, 65
bison, xx
"blinking out/on" population processes, 81–82
BLM (Bureau of Land Management), 98, 103–4, 105–6, 119, 215–16
Bozeman, Montana, 180, 210, 221, 226
Brener, Pablo, 127
A Brief History of the National Park Service, 181
broad-scale conservation: community and social capital roles in, xvi–xviii, 107, 205–6, 230; and connectivity, 10–11, 31, 74–76; fundamental principles, 142, 163; goal setting in, 96–97; representation as foundation for, 97; rewilding, 30–31, 38–45; science as base for planning, 38, 99, 148, 165, 177, 211; Sonoran Desert plan, 90–91, 96, 97–98; The Wildlands Project, 38–45, 86–87, 100. *See also* conservation planning; Everglades; Greater Yellowstone ecosystem; ranchers/ranching
Broward, Napoleon Bonaparte, 157
Brower, David, 38
Brown, Jim, 124, 125
Buffalo Commons, xx–xxi
buffer zones, 51, 205
Bureau of Land Management (BLM), 98, 103–4, 105–6, 119, 215–16
Bush, George H. W., 6, 16
Bush, George W., 141
Bush, Jeb, 159

cactus ferruginous pygmy-owl, 101
California, puma example, 76–81
California Critical Areas Program, 64
Caribbean area, WWF efforts in, 62–64
Caribou-Targhee National Forest, 179

carnivores. *See* predators

carrying capacity of grazing land, 134

Cathedral Pines preserve, xi–xii

Center for Biological Diversity, 89

Central and South Florida Project for Flood Control (C&SF Project), 158–59, 162

Central Arizona Project, 37

CERP (Comprehensive Everglades Restoration Plan), 165

Chiles, Lawton, 164

Cienega Corridor Conservation Council, 106

Cienega Creek, Arizona, 88–89

clear-cutting of timber, 5, 10, 179

climate: desert southwest, 113–15, 123–26, 161; and grazing issues, 124–26; and linkages, 73, 83

Clinton, Bill, 16, 17, 141

Coal Canyon, California, 79–81

coarse-filter/fine-filter approach, 53–54, 55, 91

Coe, Ernest, 146

Committee on Preservation of Natural Areas for Ecological Study, 51

Committee on Preservation of Natural Conditions for Ecological Study, 187

communal land management, 131

community-driven conservation, 103–7, 119–21, 204–5

community (human): collective/shared vision, 104–6, 120–21, 205–6, 208–9, 222; consensus processes, 43; new conservation role of, xviii–xx, xxii, 122, 230; rural issues, 8, 9; and social capital, xvi–xviii, xxiii

Comprehensive Everglades Restoration Plan (CERP), 165

Connecticut, xi–xii

connectivity. *See* linkages

Conservancy. *See* The Nature Conservancy

Conservation Beef program, 204–5

conservation biology: and balance of nature, xi–xii; community's role in, xvi–xvii; emergence of, 13–14, 51–52; as new perspective, xii–xviii; opponents of, 74–75; overview, ix–x; and scientific vs. emotional choices, xv–xvi, xxii, 14, 213–14; scientists as advocates for, 14–15, 32; spotted owl programs as new paradigm, 3–7

Conservation Biology: An Evolutionary-Ecological Perspective (Soulé and Wilson), 13

Conservation by Design, 67

conservation committee (The Nature Conservancy), 65–67

Conservation Data Centers, 53, 65

conservation easements, 129–30, 131, 171, 204, 211

conservation planning: ecoregional, 63–68, 90–91; ethics of, 58, 206, 231–32; goal setting in, 95–97, 119, 153–54, 215–17; human factors in, 35–36, 56, 58, 99–100, 230–33; overview, xviii–xx; and scale for conservation, 46, 64–65; science as basis for, 38, 99, 148, 165, 177, 211; systematic, 56–58; targets for, 91–95; uncertainties in, 98–99. *See also* broad-scale conservation; methodologies, conservation; scale for conservation

Cooke, Jay, 182–83

corridors: California example, 78–81; Cienega, 106; dispersal vs. habitable, 74, 78–79; economic cost of, 75; migration-dispersal, 31, 73, 82. *See also* linkages

"cows or condos" controversy, 138–39

Craighead, Frank and John, 177–78, 192–93

Critical Areas Program, 64–65

CS&F Project (Central and South Florida Project for Flood Control), 158–59, 162

Csuti, Blair, 47

cultural resources, 102, 103, 137, 205
Curtin, Charles, 122–23, 125
Custard Apple Muck, 157

Dasmann, Ray, 35
Defense, Department of, 90, 98
democracy, need to revitalize, xx, xxii
demographic stochasticity, 194
Dennis, Mike, 110
desertification, 115, 123–24, 125
desert southwest: climate, 113–15, 123–26, 161; grazing history, 132–35; historic profile, 113–15, 132. *See also* ranchers/ranching
Designing a Geography of Hope: Guidelines for Ecoregion-Based Conservation in The Nature Conservancy, 68
deterministic extinction, 194
DeVoto, Bernard, 8
Diamond A Ranch (Gray Ranch), 127–31
Dinerstein, Eric, 47, 60–62, 63, 66
dispersal of populations, 76–81, 82
distribution mapping, 55
Dixon, Joseph S., 187
Donaldson, Mac and John, 103–4
Douglas, Marjory Stoneman, 146
Drafting a Conservation Blueprint (Groves), 92
drought catastrophes, 114–15, 123, 161
Dugelby, Barbara, 37–38
Dwyer, Jennifer, 209
Dwyer, William L., 4, 6–7, 16, 17

EAA (Everglades Agricultural Area), 158, 160–61
Earth Day, 71
Earth First!, 33–35, 37–38
ecological inertia, 135
Ecological Society of North America, 50–51
Ecologists' Union, 51. *See also* The Nature Conservancy
ecology of information, 203

economic issues: amenity-based economy, 213, 224; corridor system costs, 75; "cows or condos" controversy, 138; federal support of sugar industry, 158; Florida conservation costs, 144, 164; free market impact on ecology, xxiii; grazing fees, 117, 225; income level, influence of, xix; local interests vs. federal land management, 43; planning and economic expansion, 101; socioeconomic growth and environmentalism, 9, 220–28; in spotted owl conservation, 6; tax burden on landowners, 130; timber market fluctuations, 16–17; tourism and ecosystem, 148. *See also* industrial culture; ranchers/ranching
ecoregional planning, 63–68, 90–91
ecoregions: as fundamental conservation unit, 63, 67, 231; Kenai Peninsula example, 23–26; overview, xxi, 21–22; in rewilding, 31. *See also* linkages; scale for conservation
ecosystem decay, 9–11, 15
ecosystems: defining, 19–22; directional self-regulation in, 26–29; dynamics of, 124–25; keystone species in, 28–29; management overview, 18–20. *See also* natural communities
edge effect, 34–35, 75
Ehrenfeld, David, xv
Eichbaum, Bill, 99–100
elk, 27–28, 183–84, 186, 188–89, 190–92, 216
Empire-Cienega Resource Management Area, 103–4
employment issues at Yellowstone, 220–24. *See also* economic issues
Endangered Species Act: Big Hole grayling conservation, 207; Forest Service interpretation of, 16; and God Squad, 6; implementation issues, 89–90; influence on reserve selection, 53;

and Sonoran Desert planning, 102; and spotted owl conservation, 4, 17

environmental quality and socioeconomic growth, 220–28

equilibrium theory, 10

erosion, 23–26, 115

Estenoz, Shannon, 151, 152, 159–60, 164, 168, 169

Estes, Jim, 24, 26–27

estuary balance, 160

ethical issues: and conservation planning, 58, 206, 231–32; Earth First!'s tactics, 34; and land ownership, xxiii, 200; Leopold's land ethic, 112; and Progressive conservationism, 186

Everglades: biogeography, 154–56; as biological reserve, 50; drainage of, 157–60; Everglades National Park, 146; and fate of EAA, 161; implementation strategies, 168–70; importance of understanding ecosystem, 151–54; overview, 141–43, 145–51; restoration efforts, 162–68; statewide plans, 143–45; stewardship possibilities, 170–72; transformation history, 156–60; and WWF, 100

The Everglades: River of Grass (Douglas), 146

Everglades Agricultural Area (EAA), 158, 160–61

Everglades Forever Act, 163

Everglades National Park, 146

extinction, dynamics of, 10, 81, 194

extractive industries. *See* resource extraction industries

extremist movements, 32–33, 37

Fauna of the National Parks of the United States (Wright, Thompson, and Dixon), 187

Federal Ecosystem Management Assessment Team (FEMAT), 5, 17, 197

federal government: Bureau of Land Management, 98, 103–4, 105–6, 119, 215–16; Defense Department role, 90, 98; Interior Department role, 181. *See also* Fish and Wildlife Service (FWS); Forest Service; National Park Service; public land use

"50/500 rule" for viable populations, 195

fine-filter/coarse-filter approach, 53–54, 55, 91

fires/fire management, 118–19, 135, 159

Fish and Wildlife Service (FWS): distribution mapping efforts, 55; grayling conservation, 208; grizzly bear recovery plan, 198–99; industry influence on, 89; and inter-agency conflict, 215–16; interpretation of federal law, 6; pygmy owl conservation, 101; spotted owl conservation, 4–5, 16

fishing industry, 25, 152, 207–8

flagship species, 93–94

flood/rain issues, 115, 124–25. *See also* Everglades

Florida Audubon Society, 72

Florida Game and Freshwater Fish Commission, 143

Florida Natural Areas Inventory, 72

Florida's regional reserve network plan, 35, 72. *See also* Everglades

fluvial Arctic grayling, 207–9

Foreman, Dave, 32–34, 37–40

forest products industry, 72. *See also* timber industry

Forest Service: and fire management in desert southwest, 118; in Greater Yellowstone ecosystem, 178, 215, 218–19; and inter-agency conflict, 179, 215–16, 217; interpretation of federal law, 6, 16; and Malpai Borderlands Group, 119; and spotted owl vs. timber industry, 4–5, 6–7, 16–17

Forest Summit of 1993, 17

The Fragmented Forest (Harris), 34

fragmented landscapes. *See* habitat fragmentation/loss

*A Framework for Coordination of National
    Parks and National Forests in the Greater
    Yellowstone Area,* 219
Franklin, Ian, 195
Freshwater, Diana Barnes, 103
Freyfogle, Eric, xxiii, 200
fur industry, 24
FWS (Fish and Wildlife Service). *See*
    Fish and Wildlife Service (FWS)

game management, 184, 186, 188–92
Game Management (Leopold), 188
Gang of Four, 6
gap analysis, 55–56
Gatewood, Steve, 143
genetic stochasticity, 194
Gila Wilderness, 50
Gilpin, Mike, 196
Glen Canyon Dam, 32
Glenn, Warner, 108–10, 116–17, 120
Glenn, Wendy, 116, 120
Glick, Dennis, 212, 213, 214, 221
goal setting, 95–97, 119, 153–54, 215–17
God Squad, 6
Governor's Commission on a Sustainable
    South Florida, 164
Graham, Bob, 162
Graham, Curley Bill, 127
Grand Canyon of the Yellowstone (Moran),
    182
grassbanking, 131–32, 205
grasslands, desert southwest, 109–10,
    113–14, 123–26, 132–35
Gravelly Range, 204
Gray, Michael, 127
grayling, fluvial Arctic, 207–9
Gray Ranch (Diamond A), 127–31
grazing issues: arguments on, 137–39; and
    climate, 124–26; effect on streambeds,
    127, 135; federal fees, 117, 225; grizzly
    bear habitat, 199; history of desert
    southwest, 132–35; overgrazing, 114–
    15, 188–89, 190–91; radical center
    approach, 112–13; rest/rotation strategy,

103; scientific justifications, ambiguity
    of, 125–26, 135–36
Greater Okefenokee ecosystem, 72
Greater Yellowstone Coalition, 212
Greater Yellowstone Coordinating
    Committee, 217–19
Greater Yellowstone ecosystem: advocacy
    for, 184; Big Hole watershed programs,
    207–9; broad-scale conservation
    opportunities, 180–81; fragmented
    management in, 215–20; grizzly bears
    in, 177–78, 203–6; land-use planning
    in, 209–14; overview, 178–80; socioeco-
    nomic growth effects, 220–28. *See also*
    Yellowstone National Park
greenways movement, 76
Grinnell, George Bird, 184
grizzly bears, 175–76, 177–78, 192–94,
    198–206
Gromnicki, Allison, 164–65
Groves, Craig, 57, 90, 91, 213
Guri, Lago, 28

habitat fragmentation/loss: Arizona
    example, 89–90; and connectivity, 38,
    73–74, 78–79; and edge effect, 34–35; in
    island biogeography, 10; of Okefenokee
    Swamp, 71–72
Hackman, Arlin, 220
Hadley, Drummond "Drum," 126–27,
    129–31
Hadley, Puddie, 129
Hadley, Seth, 126, 129
Hanson, Roseann, 102, 103, 104–5, 106, 107
Harris, Larry, 34, 35, 72, 142
Hawaii, gap analysis example, 54–55
Hayden, Ferdinand V., 182
Hearst, George, 127
Heart of the Rockies, 210–11
Hedges, Cornelius, 181
herbivores: elk, 27–28, 183–84, 186, 188–89,
    190–92, 216; historic domination of
    American West by, 30–31
Hoover dike, 157

Hornaday, William Temple, 184
hotspots, ecological, 59–60
Hough, Emerson, 184
human factors: in bioreserves, 65; and
    categorizing of conservation efforts,
    83–84; in conservation planning,
    35–36, 56, 58, 99–100, 230–33; and
    deterministic extinction, 194; in
    ecosystem management, 19–22; and
    landscape species, 94–95, 143; and pos-
    itivistic science, 202; and reconciliation
    ecology, 85–86; and restoration ecol-
    ogy, 85, 190; suburbanization threat to
    habitat, 138–39, 161, 171; urbanization,
    138–39, 158, 210. See also community;
    economic issues; Everglades; linkages
hunting, 183–85, 188–89, 197, 216
hydroelectric facilities, 28
hydrology of Everglades, 149, 153–55,
    164, 165

IMADES (Mexican state agency), 91
immigration (non-human), dynamics
    of, 10
industrial culture: fishing industry, 25, 152,
    207–8; and Greater Yellowstone, 179,
    218–19, 221–25; and local socioeco-
    nomic identity, 223–24; mining indus-
    try, 167, 213, 219, 224–25, 228; sugar
    industry, 142, 157, 158–61; and "wasted"
    resources, 49–50. See also resource
    extraction industries
Interagency Grizzly Bear Committee,
    199–200
Interagency Scientific Committee, 5
interconnectivity. See linkages
Interior, Department of, 181
invasive plants, 149–50
Ironwood Forest National Monument,
    102
irrigation, 37, 159, 208. See also Everglades
island biogeography, 10–12, 15, 28, 72–73,
    94–95

Jackson, Wes, 58
Jackson, William Henry, 182
jaguars, 108–9
Jenkins, Robert, Jr., 52–53, 65

Keiter, Robert, 43
kelp forests, 25
keystone species, 28–29, 93–94, 124
killer whales. See orcas
King Canyon National Park, 50
Kissimmee River/Canal, 157, 162, 163–64,
    170
Klinkenborg, Verlyn, 116
Kolbe, Jim, 105
Kraus, Mark, 156

landscape dynamics, 82–83
landscape species, 94–95, 143
land trusts, 129, 180, 210–11
land-use planning, 36, 42, 84, 86, 104–5,
    208–14. See also conservation planning;
    maps as conservation tools
Las Cienegas National Conservation
    Area, 88, 105
Latin America, WWF's efforts in, 62–64
Leopold, Aldo, xxiii, 86, 112, 188–89
Leopold, Aldo Starker, 189–90
Leopold Report, 190–92
Lewis, Ed, 219
limestone quarrying in Everglades,
    167
linear habitats, 76. See also corridors
linkages: Earth First! philosophy, 33;
    Florida proposal, 32, 72; as habitats,
    74–75; megalinkages, 44; in metapopu-
    lation theory, 80–82; Missing Linkages
    conference, 80; in Northern Rockies,
    203–4; overview, 10–11, 72–76; and
    rewilding, 31; Sonoran missing link,
    105–6; in The Wildlands Project,
    38–45. See also corridors
Loftus, Bill, 151, 155
logging industry. See timber industry

Lost Landscapes and Failed Economies (Power), 222

Lovejoy, Tom, 10–11

MacArthur, Robert, 10–11

MacKaye, Benton, 56

Madison Valley Ranchlands Group, 205

Main, A. R., 195

Maine North Woods National Park, 44

Malpai region, 116–21, 126, 130

maps as conservation tools: in ecoregional concept development, 66–67, 83; in Florida, 35–36, 72, 143; and gap analysis, 55; for Latin America/Caribbean study, 62–63; linkages, 74, 80; propagandized maps, 41; in reserve design, 43; in Sonoran Desert ecoregion, 91

marine ecosystems, 23–26

Marshall, Rob, 89–90, 102

Masai, management techniques of, 131

Mattson, Dave, 146, 200–202, 206

Maze (plateau), 118

McCormick, Steve, 64–65, 66–68

McDonald, Bill, 109–13, 117, 120, 139

McDonald, Mary, 120

McDonough, William, 232–33

McPherson, Guy, 111, 123, 125–26, 135, 136–37

megalinkages, 44

Mencken, H. L., 135

metapopulation theory, 81–82

methane, coalbed, 228

methodologies, conservation: active management, 191; adversarial, 7–9, 32–33; coarse-filter/fine-filter, 53–54, 55, 91; decentralized, 41–44; ecoregional, 62–68; landscape-species, 94–95; mid-level critical, 64–65; natural regulation, 181–82; opportunism, 48–49, 51–52; preventive, 47; radical center, 110–13, 116, 139; representational, 46, 48, 52; rewilding, 30–31, 38–45; systems-based approach, 122. *See also* linkages

Mexico and Sonoran Desert plan, 90–91

Miller, Bill, Jr., 120

Miller, Bill, Sr., 119

minimum viable population, 195, 196

mining industry, 167, 213, 219, 224–25, 228

Missing Linkages conference, 80

Montana, 180, 210, 221, 226

Moran, Thomas, 182

Mount McKinley, 50

Muir, John, 111, 185

Mumford, Lewis, 56

mussels in predation study, 27

Myers, Norman, 59–60

Naess, Arne, 38

national conservation area (NCA), 105

National Forest Management Act, 6, 16, 196

National Landscape Conservation System, 105

National Park Service: early ecological enthusiasm, 187–88; and grizzly conservation, 192–93; and interagency conflict, 215–17; Leopold Report, 189–92; management strategies, 187–92; and spotted owl conservation, 5; and *Vision for the Future*, 217–20

natural communities: categorizing of, 52; as coarse filters, 53, 91; in desert southwest, 132; and process conservation, 57–58; representation concept for, 46, 48, 55, 57, 97, 142; as subset of ecoregions, 63; targeting of, 64, 92. *See also* ecoregions

natural conditions, restoring/preserving, 73, 186–87, 191

natural disasters: in balance of nature, xi–xii; effect on small populations, 194; hurricanes, 157–58; and scale for viability, 29, 142, 145

Natural Heritage Network, 52–53, 64–65

Naturalist's Guide to the Americas (Shelford), 51

natural regulation approach, 191–92
The Nature Conservancy: Everglades
    restoration role of, 170, 171; formation
    and early strategies of, 51–54; and the
    Gray Ranch, 128–31; in Malpai group,
    117, 119; new conservation perspective
    role of, xiv; public resistance to, 72;
    shift toward broad-scale planning,
    62–68; Sonoran Desert planning,
    90–91, 96, 98
nature reserves: core principles for, 12;
    and ecosystem decay, 15; and island
    biogeography, 10–12, 15, 28, 72–73,
    94–95; networking in, 35; Russian
    zapovedniks, 60–61; scale in, x–xii,
    12, 48–49; scope of habitats in, 49, 51;
    site selection for, 49–50, 52–58, 97–98.
    See also conservation planning;
    linkages
NatureServe, 53
NCA (national conservation area), 105
"neighboring" practice among ranchers,
    119–20
networks, ecoregional. See linkages
new conservation perspective: community
    role in, xviii–xx, xxii, 122, 230; future
    of, 229–33; historical development
    of, 56; population dynamics in, 11;
    science's role in, 29; spotted owl con-
    troversy as paradigm for, 3–7; and
    Yellowstone National Park, xxi–xxii.
    See also conservation biology
Newmark, William, 15
New Mexico Cattle Growers Association,
    128
Northern Pacific railroad, 183
Northwest Forest Plan (Option 9), 17–18
Noss, Reed: and ecoregional networks,
    34–35; and Florida regional reserve
    plan, 35, 72, 142; on land-use planning,
    84–85; and rewilding, 30, 40, 44

oceanic ecosystems, 23–26
Ogden, John, 149, 153, 165, 166

Okeechobee, Lake, 154, 161
Okefenokee Swamp, 71–72
Olmstead, Frederick Law, 76
Olson, David, 60–61, 63
Open Lands Board, 210
Option 9 (Northwest Forest Plan), 17–18
Orange County, California: pumas in,
    76–81
orcas, 24–25
Osceola National Forest, 72
otters, 24–25
overgrazing. See grazing issues

Pacific Northwest: economic shifts in,
    16–17; and Gang of Four, 6; predation
    study in, 27; spotted owl in, 4
Paine, Robert, 27
Park Avenue of the Rockies, 180
Park Service. See National Park Service
pattern representation, 46, 48, 55, 57–58,
    97, 142
People for the West!, 219
permeability, landscape, 84
phosphorous pollution, 147, 162–63
Pima County, Arizona, 101–7
Pimm, Stuart, 150
pine nuts, 175–76
Pinhook Swamp, 72
political issues: conflict among agencies,
    217–20; Greater Yellowstone dynamic,
    179, 223–24; historical boundaries vs.
    bioregionalism, 36–37; land use in
    spotted owl conservation, 6; presiden-
    tial campaigns, 16–17, 141. See also
    industrial culture
pollution, 147, 162–63
Popper, Frank and Deborah, xx–xxi
population dynamics (human): and cli-
    mate, 124; ecosystem decay, 9–11, 15;
    island biogeography, 10–12, 15, 28,
    72–73; and managed hunting, 184–85;
    metapopulations, 81–82; population
    viability analysis (PVA), 196–98; repre-
    sentation concept, 46, 48, 55, 57, 97,

142; and scale in new conservation, 11; of small populations, 194–96; spatial, 82

population growth (wildlife) in Greater Yellowstone, 212–13, 226

Powell, John Wesley, xvi–xvii, 36–37, 115

Power, Thomas, 222

predators: jaguars, 108–9; orcas, 24–25; poisoning of, 184; pumas, 76–81; and rewilding approach, 30–31; in top-down regulation, 26–30; wolves, 27–28, 184–86, 204; in Yellowstone, 185–88

Pressey, Bob, 56, 97

Preston, Frank, 11

Primm, Steve, 199, 204, 205–6

private land: eastern and western profile, 44; in Greater Yellowstone ecosystem, 178, 204–6, 209–12; and land trusts, 129, 180, 210–11; and property rights, xxiii, 200; and scope of habitat, 49; value vs. public land, 49. See also ranchers/ranching

process preservation, 58, 95, 122

public land use: community-based management plans, 104–5; federal vs. local control, 8–9, 162–63; and service goals of administrators, 215–17. See also federal government; grazing issues; timber industry

pumas and corridor concept, 76–81

PVA (population viability analysis), 196–98

Quammen, David, 10

radical center approach, 110–13, 116, 139

rainforests, 59–62

ranchers/ranching: cultural heritage of, 103; Diamond A Ranch (Gray Ranch), 127–31; ecological management strategies, 103–4, 123, 127; in Everglades, 169–70; in Greater Yellowstone ecosystem, 204–5, 207–9, 210–11; limited-development options for, 227; Malpai

Ranch, 116–17; radical center approach, 110–13; in San Bernardino, 114–16; stereotypes of, 111, 113, 121; and stewardship of wilderness areas, 109–10, 123, 127, 139–40, 170–72, 205; traditional view of, 122–23. See also grazing issues

Rasker, Ray, 209, 211, 220, 222

reconciliation ecology, 85–86

Redford, Kent, 35–36, 60, 62, 67–68, 83

red squirrels, 175–76

redundancy ecosystem, 142

Redwood National Park, 50

Regional Planning Association of America, 56

representation concept, 46, 48, 55, 57, 97, 142

reservation ecology, 85

reserves. See nature reserves

resource extraction industries: and fears of new conservation program, 218–19, 224–25; and Greater Yellowstone, 179, 213, 220, 222–26, 228; mining industry, 167, 213, 219, 224–25, 228; and tyranny of local control, 43. See also timber industry

restoration ecology, 85, 190

rewilding, 30–31, 38–45

Richter, Brian, 66–67

Rosenzweig, Michael, 47, 85–86

Runte, Alfred, 50

rural communities: economic future of, 9; and resource control, 8; role in new conservation, xviii–xx, xxii; shared vision in, 209. See also ranchers/ranching

Russian nature reserves (zapovedniks), 60–61

Sagebrush Rebellion, 8–9, 111

San Bernardino National Wildlife Refuge, 114–16

Santa Ana Mountains, 80

Save Our Everglades program, 162

sawgrass, 147, 154, 162
Sawhill, John, 66
scale for conservation: bioregional maps,
    36; and connectivity, 10–11, 31, 74–76;
    and conservation planning, 46, 64–65;
    and ecosystems, 15, 122; emerging
    understanding of, xx–xxi, 230–31;
    and island biogeography, 10–11; and
    National Park Service, 187–88, 190–92;
    in reserves, x–xii, 12, 48–50, 194–95;
    spotted owl programs as new paradigm
    for, 3–7; and top-down regulation, 29;
    and traditional view of ranchers, 122–
    23. See also broad-scale conservation;
    ecoregions
Schullery, Paul, 183–84, 185
science: ambiguous justifications of,
    125–26, 135–36; and community, 102,
    107, 122, 230; vs. emotional choices,
    xv–xvi, xxii, 14, 213–14; as enemy of
    ecology, 37; in Everglades restoration,
    153, 164–65; planning role of, 38, 99,
    148, 165, 177, 191, 211; vs. politics, 6;
    positivistic, 202; scientists as advocates,
    14–15, 32; and tyranny of rainforest,
    59–62. See also conservation biology
Scott, Michael (Greater Yellowstone
    Coalition), 47, 212
Scott, Mike (Fish and Wildlife Service),
    55
seals and sea lions, 24–25
Seattle Post Intelligencer, 7
sea urchins, 25
Shaffer, Mark, xix, 12, 58, 193–94, 197–98,
    203–4
Shelford, Victor, 51, 187
Sheridan, Philip, 184
Shipley, Jack, 7
"shoot, shovel, and shut up" principle, 108,
    117
Simberloff, Daniel, 74
simulation modeling, 193
sinks, habitat, 74, 82
Sky Island Alliance, 106

Slaughter, John Horton, 114, 115–16
social capital: of community, xvi–xviii,
    xxiii; of individuals, xxiii; and sense of
    place, 205–6, 230; and shared vision,
    107, 120
Sonoita Valley Planning Partnership, 104
Sonoran Desert Conservation Plan, 101–7
Sonoran Desert National Monument, 102
Sonoran Desert plan, 90–91, 96, 97–98
Sonoran Institute, 90–91, 104–5, 106, 209
Soulé, Michael: on bottom-up regulation,
    26–27; on certainty in ecology, 75; on
    conservation planning, 100; and emer-
    gence of conservation biology, 13–14;
    on linkages, 72; on permeability, 84;
    and population dynamics, 195; and
    PVA, 196; rewilding, 29–32; and The
    Wildlands Project, 38–44
South Coast Wildlands, 79–80
Southern Rockies Ecosystem Project, 100
southwestern willow flycatcher, 89–90
spatial dynamics, 82
spotted owls, 3–7, 18–19
Springer, Alan, 24
squirrels. See red squirrels
starfish, as predators, 27
state control of public land. See public
    land use
Stegner, Wallace, xvi, 67–68
Steinbeck, John, 49
stewardship, 109–10, 123, 127, 139–40,
    170–72, 205
strategic radicalism, 33
subsidence, 160–61
suburbanization, threat of, 138–39, 161, 171
sugar industry, 142, 157, 158–61
Sullivan, Arthur L., 12
surrogates for target species, 91–95
systematic conservation planning, 56–58
systems-based approach, 122

Tansley, Arthur, 19
targets/targeting, species, 91–95
10 percent rule, 26

Terborgh, John, 28, 30
Texas John Slaughter (TV series), 115
The Economist, 221
The Theory of Island Biogeography
    (MacArthur and Wilson), 11
Thomas, Jack Ward, 5, 6, 16–17
Thomas Committee/Report, 5–6, 12
Thompkins, Doug, 38–39
Thompson, B. H., 187
Tigerland (Dinerstein), 47
timber industry: clear-cutting effects, 5,
    10, 179; in Greater Yellowstone, 180,
    225; and Main North Woods National
    Park, 44; as service goal of Forest Ser-
    vice, 216; and spotted owl conserva-
    tion, 4, 5–7, 16–17
Track of the Grizzly (Craighead), 178
Travels with Charley (Steinbeck), 49
trophic cascade, 24–25

umbrella species, 93–94
underpass, wildlife, 80–81. *See also*
    corridors
urbanization, 138–39, 158, 210

Vedder, Amy, 94–95
*Vision for the Future: A Framework for
    Coordination in the Greater Yellowstone
    Area*, 217–20
Vision (newsletter), 103
voluntary action, 208

Washburn-Langford-Doane expedition,
    181–82
water issues: drought catastrophes, 114–15,
    123, 161; in Everglades, 147, 162–63,
    165–66; importance of management,
    170–71, 208
WCS (Wildlife Conservation Society),
    36, 94–95
weather and climate. *See* climate
Webb, Jim, 162

Weber, Bill, 94–95
Weeks, Bill, 121, 122
Welfare Ranching, 139
wetlands restoration. *See* Everglades
whaling, 24–25
whitebark pine trees, 175–76
Wiens, John, 82–83
Wilcove, David, 53–54
Wilcox, Bruce, 13
Wild Earth, 40–41
The Wilderness Society, 33
The Wildlands Project, 38–45, 86–87, 100
Wildlife Conservation Society (WCS),
    36, 94–95
wildlife management, 183–84, 188–92.
    See also herbivores; predators
Wildlife Management in the National Parks
    (Leopold, A. S.), 190–92
Wilkinson, Charles, 223
Wilson, E. O., 10–11, 41, 59
Win-Win Ecology (Rosenzweig), 85
Wise Use movement, 9, 219
wolves, 27–28, 184–86, 204
woolgrowers associations, 112
World Heritage Commission, 225
World Wildlife Fund (WWF), 62–64,
    98–100
Worster, Donald, 134
Wright, George M., 187–88

Yadav, M., 195
Yellowstone National Park: creation of,
    181–83; employment issues at, 220–24;
    grizzly bears in, 175–76, 192–94; man-
    agement of, 183–84, 188–92; and new
    conservation, xxi–xxii; overview, 177;
    predators in, 185–86; size of, 20. *See
    also* Greater Yellowstone ecosystem
Young, Jora, xiv, 142, 169–70, 171–72

zapovedniks, 60–61
zoning in new west, 227–28